THE VERB 'BE' AND ITS SYNONYMS

(5)

FOUNDATIONS OF LANGUAGE

SUPPLEMENTARY SERIES

VOLUME 14

THE VERB 'BE' AND
ITS SYNONYMS

PHILOSOPHICAL AND GRAMMATICAL STUDIES

(5)

URDU / TURKISH / BENGALI / AMHARIC
INDONESIAN / TELUGU / ESTONIAN

Edited by

JOHN W. M. VERHAAR

D. REIDEL PUBLISHING COMPANY / DORDRECHT-HOLLAND

Library of Congress Catalog Card Number 79–159659

ISBN 90 277 0217 9

Printed in The Netherlands by D. Reidel, Dordrecht

EDITORIAL PREFACE

The present volume is the fifth of a series of studies analysing the verb 'to be' and/or synonyms in a number of languages. It is expected that these studies will provide some of the necessary foundational material for research in logic, the theory of knowledge, and ontology; and possibly in other philosophical disciplines. The concluding volume of the series will attempt to assess the linguistic and philosophical impact of all the contributions.

Except for the concluding volume, the present volume is the last in the series which collects contributions by more than one author. I have availed myself of this opportunity to reprint here, with the authors' permission, two papers on 'to be' which appeared earlier in *Foundations of Language*: "'Being' and 'Having' in Estonian", by Ilse Lehiste, and "'Being' in Linguistics and Philosophy: a Preliminary Inquiry", by A. C. Graham. These two papers appear at the end of the volume; all other papers appear in the order in which they reached the editor's desk.

Two more volumes are to precede the concluding volume: a study of 'to be' in Ancient Greek, by Charles H. Kahn; and a study on 'to be' in biblical Hebrew and biblical Greek, by James Barr.

JOHN W. M. VERHAAR

TABLE OF CONTENTS

RUQAIYA HASAN

THE VERB 'BE' IN URDU*†

1.0. The aim of this paper is to provide a description of the semantics of the Urdu verb *honaa* (to be). Although my examples will be taken from the educated variety of Lakhnavi Urdu, the statements made here are expected to be applicable to all the social varieties of the language as spoken by the native speakers of the language in Uttar Pradesh (India). The conventions employed for the transcription of Urdu sentences in Roman script are borrowed from Harter *et al.* (1960) with the following modifications:

(i) the letter *G* is used instead of γ to represent the voiced velar fricative, exemplified by the initial sound in the name of the famous Urdu poet Gaalib;

(ii) the symbol *o* is used, instead of *oo*, to represent that pure vowel in Urdu which is nearest to the cardinal vowel number seven (Abercrombie, 1967, p. 154); the vowel in *lo!* (take!) exemplifies the sound;

(iii) the symbol *e* is used to represent that pure vowel in Urdu which is nearest to the second cardinal vowel (Abercrombie, *ibid.*), exemplified by the vowel in *bel* (one of the forms of the verb *beelnaa*, which means 'to roll out', used mainly with reference to *dough*);

(iv) the complex *sh* is used, instead of ʃ, to represent the voiceless palato-alveolar fricative, exemplified by the initial sound in *shaam* (evening).

1.1. Examples are first presented in Roman script; they are followed by a word rank literal translation in English, where the sequence of the translated version is determined by the original. Structural markers such as *nee*, which have no word equivalent in English, reappear verbatim in the word rank translation. If an Urdu word has more than one word rank translation equivalent, only one of these appears in the translation. The decision in these cases is based upon the suitability of the item to represent an example of the type which is under focus. The word rank translation is followed by the clause rank translation.

1.2. The description presented here is based on the systemic model of gram-

* I am deeply grateful to Michael Halliday who discussed various aspects of the syntax of Urdu with me. Although specific reference to his work is not provided here except in special cases, this article presupposes the technique of grammatical description as expounded in his 'Notes on Transitivity and Theme in English' (Parts 1–3). The responsibility for the statements made in this article is, however, my own.
† Received January 19, 1969 – Ed.

mar. In particular, this article makes extended reference to Halliday's 'Notes on Transitivity and Theme in English' (Parts 1, 2, and 3) and presupposes the technique of grammatical description as expounded there, naturally without taking over all the details of the systemic networks, since these were set up with specific reference to English. Each clause is viewed here as realizing certain systemic options; each of these systemic options can be related directly to the semantics of the clause. The implication is that if two given clauses realize the same set of systemic options then their semantic description cannot vary except by virtue of the lexical choices. The term 'feature' is used interchangeably with 'systemic option'.

2.0. The verb *honaa* is a multivalent item; that is, it may have different functions. Thus grammatically it may function as an auxiliary or it may function as the lexical verb, signifying the process of the clause. Both these functions of the verb are recognised by traditional Urdu grammars, which assign the item simultaneously to two different sub-classes of verb. Thus it is a member of the class of verbs labelled *feel-ee-imdaadi* (auxiliary) along with such items as *saknaa* (can, be able to) and *cuknaa* (to finish, e.g. in *jab woh khaanaa khaa cukaa*=when he food ate finished=when he finished eating the food); at the same time, *honaa* is listed as a member of the class of verbs labelled *feel-ee-asl* (real verb, i.e. lexical verb) along with items such as *sonaa* (to sleep), *jaanaa* (to go), *paanaa* (to find), etc.

The translation equivalents of the lexical verb *honaa* are as follows: *to be, to exist, to have, to own, to become,* and *to happen.* Examples of each are provided below:

(1)   laRki xuubsurat hai.
        girl beautiful is
        the girl is beautiful.

(2)   kariim sadar hai.
        Kariim president is
        Kariim is the president.

(3)   xudaa hai
        God exists
        God exists.

(4)   kariim kee do bahneẽ haĩ.
        Kariim of two sisters has
        Kariim has two sisters.

(5)   rafta rafta kariim tandrust huaa.
        gradually Kariim healthy became
        gradually Kariim became healthy.

(6)   Kariim sadar huaa.
        Kariim president became
        Kariim became president.

(7)   kal shaam shahar meẽ balwaa huaa.
        last evening city in riot happened
        Last evening a riot took place in the city.

2.1. Grammatical and lexical multivalence is not unique to the verb *honaa*. Items such as *jaanaa* (to go) and *rahnaa* (to live, to stay) can function either as auxiliary or as lexical verb as is evident from the following pairs:

(8) (a)   woh kal shaam landan gayaa.
        he last evening London went
        He went to London last evening.

    (b)   meeraa santraa kaun khaa gayaa?
        my orange who ate went
        who ate up my orange?

(9) (a)   woh yahaã sirf caar din rahaa.
        he here only four days lived
        he stayed here only for four days.

    (b)   bacca saari raat rotaa rahaa.
        child whole night cries lived
        the child kept crying the whole night.

As examples of lexical multivalence elsewhere one may cite items such as *phuulnaa* (to swell, to blossom), *rakhnaa* (to own, to put), *samajhnaa* (to understand, to think, to consider). It is of course true that where two or more formal items have the same graphological or phonological realization, there may exist some historical relationship between the formal items, but this is by no means always necessary. Thus it cannot be maintained that at some stage in the history of Urdu the verb *honaa* was univalent (i.e. had only one function) and that the various meanings are historically derived from this original one. Even if two formal items are historically related it cannot be argued that their synchronic description at a given stage will be identical. Indeed the very fact that they are perceived as two distinct formal items suggests that the description of one is going to be different from that of the other in some respect. In the following sections an attempt has been made to show in what respects the different senses of *honaa* differ from one another and in what respects they are alike; at the same time the relationship of clauses (1)–(7) to other clause types has been explored with a view to determining the place of these *honaa*-clauses in the transitivity system network.

3.0. In traditional Urdu grammars clauses (1)–(2) and (5)–(6) would be described as *jumlaa xabariyaa* (clause with news); the verb *honaa* in all four would be regarded as belonging to the category *naaqis* (defective). Thus Maulvi Abdul Haq in his *Qawaaid-ee-Urdu* (Grammar of Urdu) makes the following comments:

feel (verb) is that from which appears (i.e. is signified, R.H.)[1] the existence or performance of anything ....

    With regard to meaning verbs can be subdivided into three categories:
      i. laazim[2]
      ii. mutaaddi
      iii. naaqis.

feel laazim is that through which the doing of some action may be signified, but its (the verb's, R.H.) effect may be limited to the actor of the action i.e. *faael*[3] (subject) and no more. Example: *ahmad aayaa* (Ahmad came).

    feel mutaaddi is that whose effect reaches the *mafuul*[4] (object or complement) via the *faael*; (*mafuul* is that on which the action takes place). Example: *ahmad nee xat likhaa* (Ahmad wrote a letter). Here *likhaa* is *feel*, *ahmad* its *faael* and *xat* (on which the *feel* of *likhnaa* takes place) is its *mafuul*.

    feel naaqis is that which does not affect anything/anyone but signifies an effect. Example: *ahmad biimaar hai* (Ahmad is ill). In this clause the *feel* signifies not an action but existence; *ahmad* which is *faael* here is not an actor but an effect-bearer (patient) of the *feel* and *biimaar* provides *xabar* (news) regarding his state (*Qawaaid-ee-Urdu*, p. 119).

In addition to (1)–(2) and (5)–(6), clauses such as *woh baRaa beewaquuf niklaa* (he big idiot turned-out = he turned out a big idiot) and *maĩ nee us ko beewaquuf samjhaa* (I nee he to idiot considered = I considered him an idiot) would also be regarded as *jumlaa xabariyaa*, with the implication that the verbs in these clauses belong to the category *naaqis*. Three of the implications of such an analysis could be stated as follows: (i) *feel naaqis* is considered to be in contrast with *laazim* and *mutaaddi*; according to this analysis no Urdu clause may be labelled simultaneously as *xabariyaa* and *mutaaddiyaa*

---

[1] Wherever in a translated text a bracket has my initials, this implies that such a bracket did not exist in the original text and has been introduced by me in order to make the import as clear as possible.

[2] *laazim* can be literally translated as 'obligatory, compulsory'; its nearest terminological translation in English would be 'intransitive', though the two are not identical. *mutaaddi* literally means 'that which goes beyond, extends, is infectious'; its nearest terminological equivalent in English is 'transitive'. *Naaqis* may be literally translated as 'defective'; to my knowledge there is no traditional term in English which could be considered its equivalent, unless we postulated that it is nearest the copula in its meaning. Halliday's (1968) term 'relational' would however be better.

[3] *faael* is often translated as subject; like subject, it is used sometimes to mean 'grammatical subject' (see the discussion of *naaqis* verb in the passage quoted from Haq in Section 3.0) and sometimes it is used as if it were determined entirely by its transitivity function of 'actor' (as is evident from Haq's definition of the item in the para). See the discussion of the term *mubteedaa* in Section 3.4; and note also the implications of recognizing a structural label such as *qaaem-muqaam-ee-faael* (officiating subject) discussed in Section 4.1.

[4] *mafuul* may be translated as 'object' or sometimes as 'complement'. Again attention must be drawn to the terms *mubteedaa* and *xabar*.

or *xabariyaa* and *laazmiyaa*. However, since *maĩ nee us ko beewaquuf samjhaa* is a *jumlaa xabariyaa*, the validity of such a position may be questioned. (ii) If the latter clause is regarded as a *jumlaa xabariyaa*, it follows that the transitivity functions associated with the subject of the *xabariyaa* clauses vary, since clearly *maĩ* in the latter clause and *laRki* in (1) do not have the same functions. (iii) The verb class *naaqis* contains, besides *honaa*, other verbs such as *paanaa* (to find), *mannaa* (to regard, to acknowledge), *samajhnaa* (to consider, to think, to regard), *lagnaa* (to seem), *qaraar deenaa* (to acknowledge), and so on.

One might ask, then, whether all these verbs have the same syntactic function so that what is said about one will also hold true of the others or whether there are any grounds for further distinctions.

3.1. I shall assume that as for English, so for Urdu, it is not valid to contrast *feel naaqis* with *laazim/mutaaddi* (Halliday, 1967b; 1968), and will simply concentrate on the characteristics of clauses labelled *jumlaa xabariyaa*. As is clear, *feel naaqis* and *jumlaa xabariyaa* may be seen as mutually defining labels; whatever clause can be labelled *xabariyaa* must in its predicator have a lexical verb of the *naaqis* class; whatever verb can be labelled *naaqis* must occur only in the predicator of a *xabariyaa* clause. If we take some lexically multivalent items such as *maannaa*, *paanaa* and *samajhnaa* which may function either as a *naaqis* verb or as a non-*naaqis* one, it will be possible to throw some light on the defining characteristic of the *xabariyaa* clause; consider:

(10) (a) maĩ nee us ki baat sahi maani.
       I nee he of talk correct considered
       I considered his comments correct.

    (b) maĩ nee us ki baat maani.
       I nee he of talk accepted
       I agreed with his comments.

(11) (a) maĩ nee laRki ko xuubsurat paayaa.
       I nee girl to beautiful found
       I found the girl beautiful.

    (b) maĩ nee laRki ko kamree mẽe paayaa.
       I nee girl to room in found
       I found the girl in the room.

(12) (a) maĩ nee un kaa sawaal beejaa samjhaa.
       I nee he of question inappropriate thought
       I thought his question inappropriate.

    (b) maĩ nee un kaa sawaal samjhaa.
       I nee he of question understood
       I understood his question.

The member (a) of each of these pairs would be regarded as a *xabariyaa*, whereas member (b) would be regarded as non-*xabariyaa*. It would appear then that the characteristic of the *naaqis* verb is that it signifies a relational process: more specifically the relation it establishes can be only of intensional type (Halliday, 1967, pp. 62–63; Lyons, 1968, p. 454); thus the two 'things' intensionally related must form an integral part of the clause where the verb is *naaqis*. It is not the case that in members (b) the process does not relate the participants to each other, but here the relation is extensional (Halliday, 1967; Lyons, 1968, p. 454). I shall now refer to the clauses of type (a) as 'relational'. The verb *honaa* in one of its senses is then like the other verbs used in this clause type in that it can be used for the realization of an intensional relation. It does not need to be pointed out that the lexically multivalent verbs when used in a relational clause have a different meaning from that which they have when used in extensional clauses.

3.2. In Urdu at least two types of relational clauses can be recognized; these are exemplified by (1) and (2). In (1) *laRki xuubsurat hai* the two related 'things' are *laRki* and *xuubsurat*; such clauses may be called 'attributive' in that the intensional relationship exists between an attribuand *laRki* and an attribute *xuubsurat*. In (2) *kariim sadar hai* the two related things are *kariim* and *sadar*; such clauses may be called 'equative' in that the relationship exists between an identity[5] *sadar* and an identified *kariim* which are

---

[5] The terms for the participants and circumstance in the equative clause here differ from those used by Halliday (1968). In the clause *John is the leader* (*ibid.*, 190–93), *John* would be regarded as having the transitivity function of 'identified', which is in keeping with my treatment of *kariim* in *kariim sadar hai* (Kariim is the president); however Halliday's label for *the leader* is 'identifier' whereas I would use the label 'identity' for *the president*, thus leaving the term 'identifier' to be used as a label for a function corresponding to 'attributor' in the attributive clause. In a clause such as *us nee kariim ko sadar banaayaa* (He made Kariim president) *he* would have the function of actor and identifier, *kariim* that of affected and identified while I would regard *president* as having the function of 'circumstance' of the type 'identity'. The Urdu equative and attributive clauses show a great degree of similarity, as if the 'identity' were a particular kind of 'attribute' and vice versa. Thus both identity and attribute may be thematic, e.g. in *sadar kariim hai* (it is Kariim who is the president) and *xuubsurat laRki hai* (it is the girl who is beautiful); in both these cases the tonic must be carried by the identified and the attribuand. The nominal group functioning as 'identified' or 'attribuand' may be 'definite' or 'indefinite', e.g. in *ek laRkaa kahĩ taalibilm thaa* (a boy was a student somewhere) and *kahtee haĩ kee ek laRki baRi xuubsurat thi* (it is said that a girl was very beautiful); the tonic is carried here by *laRkaa* (identified) and *laRki* (attribuand), and *eek*, the non-specific deictic, is reduced. When we have an item which may function as adjective or as a noun, e.g. *biimaar* and the other element in the clause is realized by an indefinite nominal group, the tonic alone determines the transitivity functions in the clause. *biimaar koii musaafir hai* is an ambiguous clause (ill some traveller is); if *biimaar* carries the tonic then the clause is to be interpreted as *the ill man is some traveller*; if *musaafir* carries the tonic, the clause would be interpreted as *it is some traveller who is ill*. Because of these close similarities between the equative and the attributive, I have not discussed them separately in great detail.

equated. *xuubsurat* and *sadar* may be regarded as 'circumstance' of participant whereas *laRki* and *kariim* may be regarded as the participants of a process.
It is necessary for all relational clauses to have one element in their structure
which realizes the circumstance and another which realizes the participant to
whom the circumstance is ascribed.

3.3. It is not the case that circumstance can be selected only in relational
clauses. Thus it is possible to say:

(13)   darzi nee kurtaa choTaa siyaa.
         tailor nee jumper small sewed
         the tailor sewed the jumper small (i.e. sewed it so, that it was
         small).
(14)   laRki nee kapRee gandee paaee.
         girl nee clothes dirty found
         the girl found the clothes dirty.
(15)   maĩ nee caar rupyaa jurmaanaa diyaa.
         I nee four rupees fine gave
         I paid four rupees as fine.

In these clauses, the attribute-attribuand relationship may be said to exist
between *choTaa* and *kurtaa* in (13) and *gandee* and *kapRee* in (14); the
identity-identified relationship may be said to exist between *jurmaanaa* and
caar rupyaa in (15). These clauses are not regarded as relational on the ground
that the circumstance is not a 'necessary' part of the clause in the sense that
if it is removed from these clauses the clauses still remain grammatical and
the relationship of the process to the remaining items does not change;
moreover the participants stand in the same relation to each other in which
they stand when the circumstance is present in the clause. Thus consider:

(13a)   darzi nee kurtaa siyaa.
         tailor nee jumper sewed
         the tailor sewed the jumper.
(14a)   laRki nee kapRee paaee.
         girl nee clothes found
         the girl found the clothes.
(15a)   maĩ nee caar rupyaa diyaa.
         I nee four rupees gave
         I paid four rupees.

If we compare the pairs here with the pairs (10)–(12), it will be clear that
circumstance is an obligatory element in a relational clause, so that if
circumstance is removed the clause may no longer be regarded as relational;
further the meaning of the process-signifying item undergoes a change and

often (if the verb is not multivalent or if some other restrictions on the selection of the verb exist) the resultant clause would be regarded as ungrammatical; thus consider *naqqaad nee un kahaaniyõ ko muxrib-ee-ixlaaq maanaa* (critic nee those stories to immoral regarded = the critic regarded those stories as immoral) and **naqqaad nee un kahaaniyõ ko maanaa* (the critic regarded those stories). Thus although circumstance may be selected in non-relational clauses and it may be related to one of the participants in the clause, this relationship is not crucial to the clause in the same way as it is to the relational clause; this is because the process of the non-relational clause is not itself relational in the intensional sense. The fact that there are multivalent lexical verbs and that circumstance may be selected in non-relational clauses accounts for the ambiguity of certain clauses in the language. Consider (14), which may be decoded as a relational clause or as a non-relational one; as a relational clause it will be decoded as *laRki nee paayaa ke kapRee gandee thee* (girl nee found that clothes dirty were = the girl found that the clothes were dirty) while as a non-relational clause it may be decoded as *laRki nee kapRee paaee aur kapRee gandee thee* (girl nee clothes found and clothes dirty were = the girl found the clothes and the clothes were dirty).

3.4. The systemic option of relational vs. non-relational is applicable to all major clauses in Urdu; that is, any given major clause will either have the feature relational or non-relational. So far in the discussion of the relational clauses only those elements have been considered which are intensionally related. In clauses such as (10a) *maĩ nee us ki baat sahi maani*, there is yet another participant to be considered, namely *maĩ*. The function of *maĩ* in this clause is that of 'attributor'; where the relational clause is equative, the function of the corresponding participant may be labelled 'identifier' e.g. in *maĩ nee kariim ko sadar samjhaa* (I nee Kariim to president thought = I thought Kariim president, i.e. took him to be president), *maĩ* would have the function of identifier.

Traditional Urdu grammars recognize the fact that *kurtaa* in (13a) has a different transitivity function from that of, say, *laRki* in (11a). They also assign the attribute and the identity a transitivity function in the clause, and do not regard *xuubsurat honaa* or *sadar honaa* as compound verbs with the items *xuubsurat* and *sadar* as part of the verbal group. (However, see footnotes 10 and 33.) Thus in a clause such as *ahmad biimaar hai* (see the quotation from Abdul Haq, cited above, Section 3.0) the verb is *hai* and not *biimaar hai*. The grammars agreed unanimously in labelling 'circumstance' as *xabar* (report, news); thus the term *xabar* is less delicate than the labels 'attribute' and 'identity', and should be considered as an adequate translation equivalent of 'circumstance' but not of the other two as such. Opinion was divided as to the best suited label for the participant which has here been labelled 'attribuand' in the attributive, and 'identified' in the equative clause. A summary of the arguments could be presented in the words of Maulvi Fateh Mohammad Khaan (1945):

In Arabic there are two kinds of nominal clauses.[6] First, that in which there is absolutely no verb and such a clause must consist of at least two nominals e.g. in *zaidun qaaeemun* (Zaid standing=Zaid is standing); second, that in which there is a verb but it is *naaqis* e.g. in *kaana zaidun qaaeemun* (was Zaid standing=Zaid was standing). In clause type one, they call the *musnad ileha*[7] (topic) *mubteedaa*[8] (initiating item) and *musnad*[9] (comment) *xabar*, while in clause type two they call the *musnad ileha*, *ism* (noun) and *musnad*, *xabar*. But neither Persian nor Urdu has clause type one; that is to say, a clause may not be made up of two nominals only. In Persian not only should there be a *musnad ileha* and a *musnad* but also another word, namely *hast* or *ast*, whether it is overt or covert... Similarly in Urdu *hai* is obligatory,[10] whether (it occurs, R.H.) overtly or covertly...

As you see from these examples, where in Arabic only two words were sufficient, there in Urdu and Persian three are required. Most grammarians of Persian and Urdu, following the grammars of Arabic, have labelled the *musnad ileha*, *mubteedaa* and the *musnad*, *xabar* and have regarded *ast/hast* and *hai* as *harfee-rabt*[11] (connecting word), but so far as we

---

[6] I understand from Dr. Arafat (Department of Arabic, School of Oriental and African Studies, London) that in Arabic *jumlaa ismiah* (nominal clause) is used to designate all clauses which have no verb in them. If therefore *kaana zaidun qaaeemun* is regarded as a nominal clause, the underlying assumption would be that *kaana* does not function as verb. This causes some confusion with reference to some of the statements made by Fateh Mohammad Khaan.

[7] *musnad ileha* may be literally translated as 'that to which something is related'; it seems to correspond fairly closely with both 'topic' and 'grammatical subject'. Note that *musnad ileha* need not be the initial item of the clause; in *darwaazaa zaid nee kholaa* (door Zaid nee opened=it was Zaid who opened the door) not *darwaazaa* but *Zaid* would be labelled *musnad ileha*. I have used the term 'topic' for *musnad ileha* in the translation in order to keep it distinct from *faael* (subject).

[8] *mubteedaa* literally means 'that which constitutes the beginning'. Its use in Urdu grammars has been discussed in some detail in Section 3.4.

[9] *musnad* can be translated as 'that which relates to something'. If one is thinking in terms of the distinction between topic and comment, *musnad* may be translated as 'comment'. In those grammars where a stage in grammatical analysis involves a binary segmentation of the clause, that segment which in such grammars is labelled 'predicate' is closest in its meaning to the term *musnad*. The segment thus labelled, therefore, usually contains the verbal group constituent of the clause and will also contain the permissible participants and circumstances, etc. In Urdu grammars a confusion arises when *musnad ileha* is equated with *faael* and *musnad* with *mafuul*, so that the verbal group is seen as having the function of joining the two to each other, as is implicit in this passage from Fateh Mohammad Khaan.

[10] The dots indicate that some items from the original text have not been translated. The two omissions here are of examples from Persian and Urdu poetry to show what the author means by 'overt' and 'covert'. It is, however, not necessary to appeal to the poetic variety of language for the exemplification of 'covert' selection. (The significance of the emphasis Fateh Mohammad Khaan places on covert selection is discussed in some detail in the Appendix.)

[11] *harfee-rabt* literally means 'word-of-connection'. The class thus labelled contains words which may most readily be associated with preposition, post-position and conjunction in English, but structure markers such as *nee*, *ko*, *kee liyee* etc. are also referred to by this label.

are concerned these are not connecting words; they are verbs ... (Vol. 2, pp. 21–22.)

Those who consider *hai* as a connector, regard *mahmuud* as *mubteedaa* and *aalim* as *xabar* in a clause such as *mahmuud aalim hai* (Mahmuud learned is = Mahmuud is learned), but we would ask why in *mahmuud aalim thaa* (Mahmuud learned was = Mahmuud was learned) they do not consider *mahmuud mubteedaa* and *aalim xabar*. If we consider *hai* as a connector, we wonder what reasons could be provided for a distinction between *hai* and *thaa* ... (*ibid.*, p. 27.)

If *hai* is a connector why is *thaa* not a connector? No one describes *thaa* as a connector and yet there is no difference between *hai* and *thaa* except that through *hai* is signified present tense and through *thaa* past tense. (*ibid.*, p. 27.)

Now, as to the question whether the *musnad ileha* of *hai* should be called *mubteedaa* or *ism*, it needs to be pointed out that the grammarians of Arabic refer to *mubteedaa* as *mubteedaa* because it is the initial item in the clause. If it were the case that in clauses with verbs too the *faael* was the initial item, there would be no ground for calling *mubteedaa* *mubteedaa*. But in Urdu, *faael* too occurs clause-initially,[12] hence no specific value can be attached to this fact where the *musnad ileha* of a nominal clause is concerned. For this reason we hesitate to refer to the *musnad ileha* of a nominal clause as *mubteedaa* on the only criterion that it occurs clause-initially. So far as we are concerned we would prefer to refer to this (element, R.H.) as *ism*. (*ibid.*)

The various strands running through this argument can be stated as follows: the label *mubteedaa* is rejected by Fateh Mohammad because (a) it is not applied consistently to all clauses with the verb *honaa* in them but only to those which have the present tense form of the verb; (b) in Arabic this label is applied only to the *musnad ileha* of what Fateh Mohammad classifies as clause type one, in which there is 'absolutely no verb'; this clause type 'does not occur' in Urdu since some form of the verb *honaa* is required for the realization of some feature of the clause; and, lastly, (c) the very meaning of the term *mubteedaa* is unsuited for making a distinction between the grammatical subject of clauses whose process is signified by *honaa* as opposed to those whose process is signified by some other verb; the sequential criterion does not apply.

It has to be granted that taken individually these three arguments put forward by Fateh Mohammad Khaan are valid, yet his resolution of the problem has been generally ignored. The reasons for this are as follows. The distinction between *hai* and *thaa* pointed out by Fateh Mohammad Khaan seems to have been abandoned by the Urdu grammarians. In fact, it has not been possible for me to trace a grammar of Urdu, in which *honaa* is assigned to two different primary classes of word according to whether it is in the present tense or in the past tense. There seems to be a tacit agreement, therefore, that *honaa* in one of its senses is a lexical verb no matter what tense may be signified by any given form of it, from which it followed that there were no clauses in Urdu which replicated clause type one of

---

[12] In fact this should be taken to mean "in clauses with unmarked theme, *faael* is always clause-initial" if the word *faael* is interpreted as grammatical subject. Any other interpretation of this statement by Fateh Mohammad would not be true in all cases.

Arabic (at least in their surface manifestation). The labels *ism* and *mubteedaa*, as labels for transitivity function in the clause, could therefore not be distinguished from one another so far as Urdu was concerned. Here only one label was needed. *ism*, both in Arabic and Urdu, was employed to label a word class, i.e. noun; *mubteedaa* was therefore less confusing and seems to have been universally adopted. The motivation for the choice of this item as a label in Arabic might very well have been the one cited by Fateh Mohammad Khaan; it would however be absurd to think that the sequence criterion was regarded as the defining one by Urdu grammarians: no grammarian faced with a string such as *xuubsurat laRki hai laRkaa nahī* (beautiful girl is boy not=it's the girl who is beautiful not the boy) would consider *xuubsurat* as carrying the function of *mubteedaa*, even though the item occurs clause-initially. An even more interesting example would be a particular type of relational clause exemplified by, say, *rashiid ko kariim beewaquuf lagtaa hai* (Rashiid to Kariim idiot seems is=Kariim seems an idiot to Rashiid), in which the function of *mubteedaa* is assigned to *Kariim* and not *rashiid*. It is therefore safe to assume that in Urdu grammars the term *mubteedaa* came to mean not 'that which constitutes the beginning of the clause' but 'that participant to which some circumstance is ascribed'. Again, like *xabar*, the term *mubteedaa* is less delicate than either attribuand or identified, since it subsumes both. A comparable term in English would be 'ascribed participant'.

4.0. If the relational clause is characterised as one whose process signifies intensional relation and 'calls for' two elements one of which carries the function of 'ascribed participant' and the other that of 'circumstance ascribed', then the following may be regarded as an agnate set of such clauses:

(16)   laRkee nee laRki ko xuubsurat paayaa.
          boy nee girl to beautiful found
          the boy found the girl beautiful.

(16a)   laRki xuubsurat paai gai.
          girl beautiful found was
          the girl was found beautiful.

(16b)   laRki xuubsurat lagi.
          girl beautiful seemed
          the girl seemed beautiful.

(16c)   laRki xuubsurat thi.
          girl beautiful was
          the girl was beautiful.

While most Urdu grammars have explicitly stated the relationship existing between clauses (16) and (16a), I have not found any account of how the remaining two clauses are to be treated so far as their relationship to the other two clauses is concerned. There is only an agreement regarding the basic fact that they should all be treated as *jumlaa xabariyaa* (relational clause). However, some indication can be found in the treatment of the non-relational paradigm such as the following:

(17)   naukar nee caaval tolee.
        servant nee rice weighed
        the servant weighed the rice.
(17a)   caaval tolee gaee.
        rice weighed was
        the rice was weighed.
(17b)   caaval tulee.
        rice got-weighed
        the rice got weighed.

Both (16) and (17) would be regarded as active clauses, the definition of the active being 'that clause the actor of whose process is known'. In our terminology, the actor in the non-relational and the 'ascribing participant' in the relational clause are 'known' in an active clause and these transitivity functions are associated with the grammatical subject of the clause. Both (16a) and (17a) would be regarded as passive clauses, the definition of the passive being 'that clause the actor of whose process is not known'.[13] This definition of the passive for Urdu is more accurate than has been realized by some recent grammarians of Urdu and Hindi. It has been assumed that as in English, the actor of the process (the grammatical subject of the active clause) may be inserted into the passive as an 'agentive adjunct'.[14] This observation is correct only to the extent that a clause such as *naukar see caaval tolee gaee* (servant by rice weighed was = the rice was weighed by the servant) is not ungrammatical but it is doubtful whether it could be regarded as a passive agnate of (17). The insertion of the agentive adjunct in clauses of the type

[13] I have not gone into any details concerning the syntactic similarities of the grammatical subject in types (16)–(19); in the discussion of these four types the term 'actor' is used (or 'dynamic participant') for the participant function associated with the grammatical subject of an active clause. If we were to think of the terms dynamic and passive participant as contrasting with each other, it would be seen that wherever we have the use of lexical *honaa*, the participant function associated with the grammatical subject of the clause is the 'passive' one. A detailed discussion of the implications of such an analysis would require another paper.
[14] So far as I can see *agentive* is used here as in Fillmore (1968), the only difference being that I use the term *agentive adjunct* only when the dynamic participant is signified by an adjunct and is not associated with the grammatical subject, that is, I do not use 'agent' for attributor, actor, perceiver, etc., if these functions are associated with the grammatical subject of the clause.

(17a) has the effect of introducing an element of potentiality into the clause; that is to say, the clause cited last should be translated idiomatically as *the servant was able to weigh the rice* and not as *the rice was weighed by the servant*. So far as (16a) is concerned the insertion of the agentive adjunct is totally unacceptable here,[15] since there is no such clause in Urdu as *laRkee see laRki xuubsurat paai gai* (boy by girl beautiful found was = the girl was found beautiful by the boy). The restriction on the selection of the feature 'potential' can, however, not be explained by the clause being relational since a relational clause such as *laRki see kamraa saaf kiaa gayaa* (girl by room clean done was = the room was made clean by the girl) is acceptable. Instead this restriction has to be explained by reference to another primary system which is applicable to all major clauses in Urdu. The terms of this system are 'volitional' and 'non-volitional'; every major clause in Urdu must have one of these features in addition to the feature relational or non-relational. Consider the following examples:

(16)   laRkee nee laRki ko xuubsurat paayaa.
(17)   naukar nee caaval tolee.
(18)   laRki nee kamraa saaf kiyaa.
        girl nee room clean did
        the girl made the room clean.
(19)   naukar nee eek baks paayaa.
        servant nee one box found
        the servant came across a box.

A volitional clause[16] may be characterized semantically as one the process of which is such that it could be undertaken voluntarily; (17) and (18) are examples of such clauses. The non-volitional clause may be semantically characterized as one the process of which is such that it could not be undertaken voluntarily; rather it is a process that 'happens' to some one/thing; (16) and (19) are examples of such a clause.

Since the process of the non-volitional clause is one that happens to some one and is not undertaken voluntarily, we find that the selection of the feature causative is not permitted to such clauses. The feature causative

[15] The non-agentive passive agnate of type (16) and (19) is usually employed for (i) an assertion that is habitual, e.g. in *aisi kahaaniyãã muxrib-ee-ixlaaq maani jaati haĩ* (such stories are considered immoral); (ii) an assertion that, naturally enough, takes the dynamic participant as known either through the co-text or through the immediate extra-linguistic situation.
[16] A distinction of this kind is recognized by Halliday (1968). The term volitional corresponds roughly to his term 'actional' and the non-volitional to his 'superventive'. I have avoided the use of actional for the volitional type of process since according to one view a clause such as *bacca giraa* (the child fell) may be seen as one in which *bacca* is involved in some kind of activity.

for Urdu may be characterized generally as 'causing some one to undertake an action' from which it follows that the process of the clause is to be of the volitional type if external causation is to be introduced. Thus it is possible to say *maalik nee naukar see caaval tolvaayee* (master nee servant by rice caused-to-weigh = the master made the servant weigh the rice) and *m̃aa nee laRki see kamraa saaf karvaayaa* (mother nee girl by room clean caused-to-do = the mother made the girl make the room clean) while both **maalik nee naukar see eek baks pavaayaa* (master nee servant by box caused-to-come-across = the master made the servant come across a box) and **m̃aa nee laRkee see laRki ko xuubsurat pavaayaa*[17] (mother nee boy by girl to beautiful caused-to-consider = the mother made the boy consider the girl beautiful) are unacceptable. Given the characterization of the causative and the non-volitional process, it must follow that verbs which signify the latter process may not be selected in imperative clauses. So while both *caaval tolo!* (rice weigh = weigh the rice) and *kamraa saaf karo!* (room clean do = make the room clean) are possible grammatical clauses, both *laRki ko xuubsurat paao!*[18] (consider the girl beautiful) and *baks paao!* (come across a box) are unacceptable. It is suggested here that the feature volitional also controls the selection of the feature 'potential'; only those clauses can have the feature 'potential' which also have the feature 'volitional'. The reasons for the unacceptability of **laRkee see laRki xuubsurat paai gaii* (the boy was able to find the girl beautiful) are the same as those which account for the unacceptability of clauses such as **laRkaa laRki ko xuubsurat paa sakaa* (the boy was able to find the girl beautiful), **hawaa patta hilaa saki* (the wind was able to move the leaf), **laRki ghabraa saki* (the girl was able to get confused), **aadmi mar sakaa* (the man was able to die), etc.

On the basis of these observations it would appear to me that the characterization of passives such as (16a) and (17a) as clauses in which the actor remains unknown is correct. I shall refer to passives of this type as 'non-agentive passive'.

---

[17] In the deep grammar the only exception to this rule would be found if the causer was some supernatural power such as *xudaa* (God) but only if we were to regard *maalik nee naukar see caaval tolvaayee* (the master caused the servant to weigh the rice) and *maalik kee hukm see naukar nee caaval tolee* (according to the order of the master, the servant weighed the rice) as having the feature causative at some point in their deep grammar. The non-volitional verb itself may never be causative in its own structure.

[18] There are certain clauses in Urdu which in their surface structure resemble the imperative but have a non-volitional verb, e.g. jio! (live!) *xush raho!* (remain happy!) *duniyaa aur uqbaa mẽe cain paao!* (find peace in this world and in the other!). These clauses are not imperative; in fact they may be perceived as elliptical. Their contextual function is to greet or to curse, so that some such verbalizing clause as *duaa karti hũ* (I pray), *xwaahish-mand hũ* (I desire), etc., are always implied. It would appear to me that the non-volitional feature and certain restrictions on imperative structures are very closely related.

4.1. Clauses of the type (17b) *caaval tulee* have some times been described as active intransitive clauses. Such an analysis would not distinguish (17b) from:

(20)   bacca soyaa.
          child slept
          the child slept (i.e. went to sleep).

There are, however, grounds for doubting whether the points of dissimilarity between (17b) and (20) are not just as important as – or, perhaps more important than – the points of similarity. It is true that every active volitional clause, whether 'transitive' or 'intransitive', may be seen as standing in a causal relation to an agnate causative. Thus we have pairs such as:

(17i)   maalik nee naukar see caaval tulvaayee.
(17)   naukar nee caaval tolee.
(20i)   m$\widetilde{aa}$ nee baccee ko sulaayaa.
          mother nee child to caused-to-sleep
          the mother caused the child to sleep.
(20)   bacca soyaa.

It is possible to think of (17) and (20i) as sharing a certain similarity in the sense that both can be interpreted as *x nee kuch kiaa jis kaa asar y par paRaa* (*x* did something the effect of which fell upon *y*); in (17) *x* would be *naukar* and *y caaval*; in (20i) *x* would be *m$\widetilde{aa}$* and *y bacca*. From this it would follow that (17b) *caaval tulee* stands in the same relation to (17) as (20) does to (20i), so that (17b) and (20) would both be regarded as active non-causative and intransitive. To be sure some differences between the clauses would be noticed, but these would be explained by the fact that there exists an animate vs. inanimate distinction between the grammatical subjects of the clauses, and this would explain why, for instance, we may say *bacca sonee par majbuur huaa* (child to sleep on obliged became = the child was obliged to sleep) but not **caaval tulnee par majbuur huee* (the rice was obliged to get-weighed).

There is, however, a defect in this reasoning. The distinction of animate vs. inanimate grammatical subject is certainly relevant to the syntactic organization of the language but at this particular point this distinction does not appear to me to be the crucial one. Consider a clause such as:

(21)   m$\widetilde{aa}$ nee baccee ko piiTaa.
          mother nee child to beat
          the mother beat the child.

This clause could be interpreted in the same general way as (20i) and (17): *m$\widetilde{aa}$ nee kuch kiaa jis kaa asar baccee par paRaa* (the mother did something the effect of which fell upon the child), therefore a clause such as *bacca piTaa* should stand in the same relation to the above as the two pairs considered above. Since the grammatical subject of the latter clause is animate it should be possible to say **bacca piTnee par majbuur huaa* (the child was obliged to get-beaten); but this clause is unacceptable. The clauses *bacca piTaa* and *caaval tulee* are more like each other than the clauses *bacca piTaa* and *bacca soyaa*. Since the verbs *tolnaa*, *sulaanaa* and *sonaa* as well as *piiTnaa* all signify a volitional process, these verbs can be selected in imperative clauses independently or in an embedded form. Thus we have a set such as the following:

(17ii)   caaval tolo.
          rice weigh
          weigh the rice.
(17iii)   naukar see kaho kee woh caaval tolee.
          servant to say that he rice should-weigh
          ask the servant to weigh the rice.
(20ii)   baccee ko sulaao
          child to cause-to-sleep
          cause the child to sleep.
(20iii)   mãã see kaho kee woh baccee ko sulaaee.
          mother to say that she child to cause-to-sleep
          ask the mother to cause the child to sleep.
(22ii)   baccee ko piiTo.
          child to beat
          beat the child.
(22iii)   mãã see kaho kee woh baccee ko piiTee.
          mother to say that she child to should-beat
          ask the mother to beat the child.

The verb *sonaa*, as is evident from the above examples, is more like *tolnaa* and *piiTnaa* than it is like *piTnaa* or *tulnaa*. There are no such clauses as **naukar see kaho kee woh caaval ko tulee* or **mãã see kaho kee woh baccee ko piTee* nor is it possible to say *tulo* or *piTo* as an imperative (see footnote 18).

In the preceding section it has been pointed out that the feature imperative may be selected only if the clause has the feature volitional. It is however not true that all volitional clause types can have the feature imperative; consider that it is impossible to say **caaval tolaa jaao* (to be weighed the rice) or **soyaa jaao* (to be slept). The feature imperative may be selected only if the clause is both volitional and active; thus both (17ii) and (22ii) are acceptable. Both these clauses are active transitive; the rule however applies to intransitive clauses as well, thus to correspond to (20) we have an imperative clause *so-o !* (sleep). And here, again, we find *sonaa* more like *tolnaa* and *piiTnaa* than like *tulnaa* and *piTnaa*.

In Urdu, all major clauses whether they are volitional or non-volitional, relational or non-relational, transitive or intransitive have the option of active vs. non-agentive passive. So that in addition to (16a) and (17a), we have the following clauses:

(18a)   kamraa saaf kiyaa gayaa.
room clean done was
the room was made clean.

(19a)   baks paayaa gayaa.
box found was
a box was found.

(20a)   soyaa gayaa.
slept was
was slept (i.e. sleeping was done).

If *sonaa* and *tulnaa* are both treated as intransitive verbs, we would expect to find a corresponding passive for *tulnaa* in the manner of *sonaa*. There, however, does not exist any such passivized form of the verb, the item *tulaa gayaa* or *piTaa gayaa* being unacceptable.

The above reasons seem to me to be sufficient for emphasizing the dissimilarity between clause types (17b) and (20). In fact, some traditional Urdu grammars recognize this distinction. Thus Haq points out that there are certain verbs in the language which in their 'shape' resemble the intransitive but are in their meaning, in fact, passive. To quote him:

Consider *aaTaa tulaa* (the flour got weighed). It is clear that the flour cannot get weighed by itself; the weigher must be some other entity. So how can *aaTaa* be regarded as the *faael*? In fact the clause was (meant, R.H.) *aaTaa tolaa gayaa* (the flour was weighed); similarly (we have, R.H.) *kapRee silee* (the clothes got sewn), *rupyee baTee* (money got distributed) and *darwaaza khulaa* (the door got opened), *lakRi gaii* (the wood went) etc. etc. (*ibid.*, p. 143).

In all these examples the grammatical subject would be referred to by the label *qaaem-muqaam-ee-faael* (standing-place-of-actor i.e. officiating actor) on the assumption that *faael* is to be interpreted as performer of the process. This same label is used to refer to the grammatical subject of (17a) and (19a), the grammatical subjects of (16a) and (18a) being referred to as *mubteedaa*.

The solution of regarding (17b) as a type of passive appears to me to be more attractive since it immediately makes explicit the relationship of the clause to (17) and also distinguishes it from (20), which as has been pointed out is necessary if what we are interested in is a semantically motivated grammar of the language. I shall refer to this type of passive as 'processive passive'. The processive passive may be informally characterized as 'a clause the process of which is seen as taking place independent of the actor, attributor or identifier'. The grammatical subject of such clauses, therefore, carries the transitivity function of affected, attribuand or identified.

4.2. From the above characterization it follows that clause (16b) *laRki xuubsurat lagi* and (17b) *caaval tulee* can be regarded as the processive passive related to (16) and (17) respectively; the process in these clauses is seen as independent of actor and attributor as if *tulnaa* were a process capable of taking place without a participant other than *caaval* and *lagnaa* were a process which could take place without a participant other that *laRki*. The processive passives related to (18) and (19) would be:

> (18b)   kamraa saaf huaa.
>   room clean became
>   the room became clean.
> (19b)   eek baks milaa.
>   one box got-found
>   a box got found.

The use of the lexical verb *honaa* in the sense 'to become' is realizationally related to the selection of the feature processive in relational clauses which have the feature volitional. Thus we have clauses such as *kariim sadar huaa* (example (7)) and *bacci taiiyaar hui* (little-girl ready became = the little girl got ready). Traditionally, the verb *honaa* with the meaning *to become* has been regarded as one which could occur in an intransitive active clause. The reasons for this are easy to understand: like (20) *bacca soyaa*, a clause such as:

> (23b)   bacci taiiyaar hui.

may be seen as one which is only potentially related to an active clause such as:

> (23)   kisi nee bacci ko taiiyaar kiyaa.
>   somebody nee little-girl to ready made
>   somebody made the little girl ready.

in the same manner as *bacca soyaa* is only potentially related to a causative *mãa nee baccee ko sulaayaa*. Semantically, it is possible to view both (20) and (23b) as clauses in which causation external to *bacca* and *bacci* is not needed. Consequently we may say *bacca xud see soyaa* (the child slept by

himself) and *bacci xud see taiiyaar hui* (the little girl got ready by herself).
There are however certain differences between (20) and (23b). If the latter is a
relational clause, no active member of it will be acceptable without the
attributor. The examples of active relational attributive clauses so far presented in this paper will bear witness to this fact; however, in all these examples the two participants selected are distinct entities, since this is the unmarked case. It should be noted however that it is by no means necessary
that they be two distinct entities (extra-linguistically). There is a well-defined
category[19] of transitive clauses in which the affected participant may be
realized by a reflexive pronoun, e.g. *aurat nee xud ko tolaa* (the woman
weighed herself). The attribuand is a special case of affected and may be
realized by such a pronoun, as in:

(23i)   bacci nee xud ko taiiyaar kiyaa.
         little-girl nee herself to ready made
         the little girl made herself ready.

It is, however, not possible to say *baccee nee xud ko sulaayaa* (the child made
himself sleep) or *bacci nee xud ko dauRaayaa* (the little girl made herself run)
for the obvious reason that there is no affected participant to be realized in
the clause. The following clause:

(23a)   bacci taiiyaar ki gaii.
         the little girl was made ready.

will be invariably regarded as the non-agentive passive agnate of the active
clause (23) but not of (23i). I would suggest that the non-agentive passive
agnate of the latter clause would be *xud taiiyaar huaa gayaa* (herself ready
become was = herself was got ready). Note the similarity between *laRki see
kamraa saaf kiyaa gayaa* (cf. (18a)) and *bacci see xud taiiyaar huaa gayaa*
(little-girl by herself ready become was = herself was got ready by the little
girl). In both cases the attribuand function is associated with the grammatical
subject of the clause and the attributor is signified through the agentive
adjunct; further, in conformity with all volitional intransitive passive clauses
with agentive adjunct, the feature of potentiality is relevant to the semantics
of the clause.

If the above suggestion is accepted, then *honaa* in the sense 'to become,

[19] There are restrictions on the selection of the feature 'reflexive' but the details of these
need not concern us here. The main point is that although extra-linguistically the process
of (23i) may not be seen as involving two distinct entities, there is a syntactic 'requirement'
for a participant attribuand (or more generally 'affected') so that *bacci nee taiiyaar kiyaa*
(the girl caused to be ready) will not be interpreted as (23i).

to get' would always be associated with the selection of the feature passive in relational volitional clauses. If such a clause is non-reflexive, the verb would be associated only with the processive passive as in (18b); if the clause is reflexive, it would be associated both with the non-agentive and processive passive, since the processive passive agnate of (23i) would be the clause *(bacci) xud taiiyaar hui* ((little-girl) herself got ready). Unlike (23b) *bacci taiiyaar hui*, this clause is totally unambiguous; it could be related to (23i) only, not to (23).

4.3. It will be seen from the examples discussed so far that if a clause is active and non-causative, then the actor of the non-relational and the attributor and identifier of the relational clause share certain syntactic potentialities. From now on, I shall refer to all these three functions by a less delicate term 'the dynamic participant'. In effect, the dynamic participant function is always associated with the grammatical subject of such clauses. The non-agentive passive is characterized by the fact that the dynamic participant of the process remains unknown; in the case of volitional clauses there exists a clause type which in its surface structure resembles the non-agentive passive except that here the dynamic participant can be signified through the agentive adjunct. This clause type is the passive agnate of an active clause with the feature 'potential'. These categories have been exemplified by the following clauses:

    (17a)   caaval tolee gaee.
               the rice was weighed.
    (18a)   kamraa saaf kiyaa gayaa.
               the room was made clean.
    (23ia)   xud taiiyaar huaa gayaa.
               herself was got ready.
    (17ai)   naukar see caaval tolee gaee.
               the servant was able to weigh the rice.
    (18ai)   laRki see kamraa saaf kiyaa gayaa.
               the girl was able to clean the room.
    (23iai) bacci see xud taiiyaar huaa gayaa.
               the girl was able to get ready by herself.

The first three of the above examples are non-agentive passive without the feature potential; the last three have the feature potential. All six have the features volitional, transitive and passive.

The processive passive is characterized as one in which the process is viewed as if it could take place without the intervention of the dynamic participant, although extra-linguistically this is not the case. The type may be exemplified by:

(16b)   laRki xuubsurat lagi.
        the girl seemed beautiful.
(17b)   baks milaa.
        a box got-found.
(18b)   caaval tulee.
        the rice got weighed.
(19b)   kamraa saaf huaa.
        the room got clean/became clean.

In all four clauses the process in fact 'requires' a participant other than the one associated with the grammatical subject of the clauses, while in the active intransitive clauses of the type *bacca soyaa* (the child slept) and *buDDhaa maraa* (the old man died) there is no such obligatory 'requirement'.

The reasons for making a distinction between the active intransitive and the passive processive have already been offered (see Section 4.1 above). It is, however, not the case that two distinct syntactic categories have to be totally distinct semantically. Thus the active and the passive members of a paradigm share certain semantic similarities while the causative and the transitive clause types may be seen as having one similar semantic component in the sense that in both causation is external to the affected participant.[20] As a matter of fact, one may maintain that the move from causative to non-causative is in some way similar to the move from transitive to intransitive, just as the move from active to passive is in some way similar to the move from volitional to non-volitional. If the non-volitional process is a process that happens to someone without any volition on his part, then those processive passive types for which there exists no option 'reflexive' can be seen as some-what close in their meaning to non-volitional intransitive active clauses such as *buDDhaa maraa* (the old man died). Examples (16b)–(19b) belong to this type of processive passive. If, on the other hand, we look at the volitional processive passive type for which there exists the option 'reflexive', this may be seen as close in its meaning to volitional intransitive active clauses such as *bacca soyaa* (the child slept) since one component of the meaning of the latter clause is the same as that in *bacci xud see taiiyaar hui* (the little girl got ready by herself). This seems reasonable since reflexive causation (using caus-ation in its most general sense) is equal to no external causation and since the absence of external causation can in general be related to intransitivity.

[20] This point is discussed in greater detail by Halliday (1968, Section 9.1). That two differ-ent sets of systemic options may share some component(s) of meaning is interesting since it will have direct relevance to semantics and also, probably, to stylistics.

4.4. It has been pointed out that so far as the 'true' non-agentive passive is concerned, it has no mechanism for signifying the dynamic participant of the agnate active (see Section 4.0). The same holds true for the volitional non-reflexive clauses of the processive type; thus if we have a clause such as (cf. (17b)) *naukar see caaval tulee* (the rice got weighed by the servant) and (cf. (18b)) *laRki see kamraa saaf huaa* (the room got made clean by the girl), these clauses have the same element of meaning in them which has been related to the feature 'potential'. As for the non-agentive passive so here too, the non-volitional clauses show a difference from the volitional ones: in the non-volitional processive type the dynamic participant of the agnate active may be signified through an adjunct without entailing any sense of potentiality; thus we may say (cf. (16b)) *laRkee ko laRki xuubsurat lagi* (the girl seemed beautiful to the boy) and (cf. (17b)) *naukar ko eek baks milaa* (a box got found to the servant).

The position implicitly taken in this rather lengthy discussion is that *honaa* in the sense 'to become' is in some respects syntactically like the verbs *tulnaa*, *lagnaa* and *milnaa*; in these said respects, then, the semantics of *honaa* is like that of the last three verbs. That there is a regular phonetic similarity between *tolnaa* and *tulnaa* but not between *karnaa* and *honaa* seems to me to be irrelevant in the context of this discussion.

4.5. If the passive for Urdu is generally defined as a clause in which the dynamic participant of the agnate active may not be associated with the grammatical subject, then a clause such as (16c) *laRki xuubsurat thi* presents some interesting problems. There is no doubt that the grammatical subject here is *laRki*; the question that may be debated is whether or not it also carries the transitivity function of dynamic participant. The view may be taken that this is a subcategory of non-volitional relational active clause; if so it could at once be related to:

(16)   laRkee nee laRki ko xuubsurat paayaa.
(24)   buDDhaa maraa.

so that (16) and (16c) would resemble each other by virtue of the fact that both have the features non-volitional and relational; to distinguish the two we would have to maintain that (16) is a clause in which the relational process can be more delicately described as 'perception', whereas this would appear to be not true of (16c). The latter clause would resemble (24) by virtue of the fact that, in both, the process happens to the participant associated with the grammatical subject of the clause; the two could be distinguished from each other on the ground that (16c) is relational, whereas (24) is not. Further we would have to maintain that if a clause is non-volitional there exists another option namely that it may either have the feature 'existential' or 'actional', so that at a certain degree of delicacy both (16) and (24) would have the feature actional whereas (16c) would have the feature existential.

If, however, the comments made earlier regarding the points of semantic similarity between distinct syntactic categories (see Section 4.3) are conceded, it may be maintained that the relational use of *honaa* in clauses of the type (16c) and (19c) *kamraa saaf thaa* are in fact maximally passive so that they share one component of the meaning of the non-volitional; at the same time since relational clauses may not be 'causative' this clause type ((16c) and (19c)) is also the least causative of the clause types, and thus shares one component of the meaning of 'intransitive'. The advantage in regarding (16c) as a member of the paradigm (16)–(16b) would be that the clause could be still regarded as related to a clause of perception, for in fact it is not true that (16c) has no element of perception in it. We have to assume that in the deep grammar of the clause the feature of perception is 'present' in order to account for the unacceptability of the following sentence:

(25)   *kariim rashiida ko xuubsurat paataa hai magar kariim kee liyee
        Kariim Rashiida to beautiful finds is but Kariim for
        rashiida xuubsurat nahĩ hai.
        Rashiida beautiful not is
        Kariim finds Rashiida beautiful but for Kariim Rashiida is not
        beautiful.

The anomaly here is of the same nature as in *mãã nee baccee ko piiTaa magar bacca nahĩ piTaa* (the mother beat the child but the child did not get beaten); if the active clause is true then the other clause must be false and vice versa. When we have a sentence such as *laRki koi xaas xuubsurat nahĩ magar laRkee ko xuubsurat lagti hai* (the girl is not particularly beautiful but she seems beautiful to the boy), this clause can be treated as not anomalous only on the assumption that for some other perceiver/attributor the *laRki* is not beautiful but so far as *laRkaa* is concerned he perceives her as beautiful. Such clauses as *aap kee liyee to har laRki koh-ee-qaaf ki pari hai* (for you every girl is a fairy from the Caucasian mountains) and *karnee walee kee liyee har kaam aasaan hai* (for one who wishes to act every action is easy), *xudaa kee liyee Gariib amiir baraabar haĩ* (for God the rich and the poor are equal), *meeree liyee tum aaj bhi baccee ho* (for me you are still a child) are all frequent and acceptable utterances in the language and for all these clauses the nominal with the post-position *kee liyee* can be shown to be the same as the dynamic participant of the active agnates of these clauses. In view of this close relationship between clause types (16) and (16c) it appears desirable to regard the latter as a member of the same paradigm as that to which (16) belongs. Let us now tentativily suggest that (16c) is a 'stative passive'[21] agnate of (16); the process of a stative passive may, in this context, be characterized generally as the process of existence in a perceived state. The verb *honaa* in the sense 'to be' is the only verb in the language which may be used for signifying the process of a clause with the set of syntactic options 'non-volitional, relational and stative passive', and as such its meaning may be exhaustively stated by reference to these options. The verb *honaa* (to be) signifies a process which happens to someone (cf. option non-volitional); it signifies a process that is relational so that basically in its semantics it 'needs' the ascribing participant, the ascribed participant, and the circumstance ascribed; being realizationally related to a stative passive, it is at the furthest remove from active, so that the process is least causal in character; in the manner of other passives, the process appears as if it required no dynamic participant (of which ascribing participant is a special case) but simply pertains to the affected one (of which ascribed participant is a special case).

4.6. Clauses of the type (16c) are in fact statements of opinion, either personal, e.g. in *laRki xuubsurat hai* (the girl is beautiful) or general, e.g. in *laRkiyãa sharmiili hotī haĩ* (girls are usually shy) or technical, e.g. in *Tinkcar aayoDiin zahriilaa hotaa hai* (tincture iodine is poisonous). The post-position *kee liyee* (for) can also be used in volitional benefactive clauses to signify the 'beneficiary', e.g. in *naukar nee baavarci kee liyee caaval tolee* (the servant weighed the rice for the cook); when *kee liyee* occurs in clause type (16c) the nominal to which it is attached does not have the function of beneficiary. Since the basic contextual function of this clause type is to make a statement, the phrase *in the opinion of* + *attributor* (attributor *ki raaee mẽe*) may be substituted for *for* + *attributor* (attributor *kee liyee*) without leading to any change in the relationship of the participants of the clause. Thus the clauses *laRkee*

---

[21] The term 'stative' as used here is, probably, roughly comparable with Lyons' (1968) usage, and perhaps it is as closely related to 'static'. The opposition dynamic vs. static, Lyons suggests, is relevant to the verb vs. adjective distinction (*ibid.* p. 437). The same is true of stative and action verbs (*ibid.* p. 325) "... there are certain stative verbs in English which do not normally occur in the progressive form .... This aspectual difference between stative verbs and verbs of action is matched by a similar difference in English adjectives .... The possibility of free combination with the progressive aspect correlates with a number of other important features in English syntax: most notably, with the potentiality of occurrence in answer to a question like *what did she do? what is she doing? ...*." If this criterion were applied to Urdu a large sub-category of the non-volitional verbs would have to be regarded as 'stative' for we may not say **laRki ciix sun rahi hai* nor may we offer the response *laRki nee eek ciix suni* (the girl heard a cry) to the question *laRki nee kyaa kiyaa?* (what did the girl do?). The same applies to the pair **laRkaa baks paa rahaa hai* (the boy is coming across a box) and *laRkee nee eek baks paayaa* (the boy found a box). For Urdu the term stative passive as used in this article means 'the predication of existence regarding some participant and/or circumstance'.

kee liyee laRki xuubsurat hai and *laRkee ki raaee mẽe laRki xuubsurat hai*
have the same transitivity selection. Note that it is impossible to have a clause
such as **laRkee ki raaee mẽe laRkee kee liyee laRki xuubsurat hai* (in the
opinion of the boy the girl is beautiful for the (same) boy) while the clause
baavarci ki raaee mẽe naukar nee usi kee liyee caaval tolee (in the opinion
of the cook the servant weighed the rice for him (the cook)) is acceptable.
The following discussion will throw some light on the selection of *kee liyee*
in stative passive clauses.

It is now tentatively assumed that (16c) *is* a member of the non-volitional
relational paradigm. Are its characteristics shared by (18c) *kamraa saaf thaa*?
It has been shown that sentence (25) is unacceptable; it is however perfectly
possible to say:

> (26)   laRki nee saaree din kamraa saaf kiyaa magar phir bhi kamraa
>   girl nee whole day room clean did but even then room
>   saaf nahĩ thaa.
>   clean not was
>   the girl had been making the room clean all day but even then
>   the room was not clean.

Unlike (25), the above example has no illogicality or anomaly; both the
clauses of the sentence may be true at once. Now if (16) and (18) are compared, it will be found that in the former the attribute is perceived as if it were
'present in the attribuand'; that is, it is impossible for a perceiver to 'find'
an attribute in an attribuand and yet not to regard it as existing in the
attribuand. In (18) the attribute is not seen as existing in the attribuand but as
one which the attributor's action makes the attribuand acquire. We may refer
to these two kinds of attribute as 'depictive' and 'resultative' respectively.
The attribute in volitional relational clauses is always of the latter type; in
accordance with its semantics only non-durational adjectives (i.e. those which
signify a non-permanent quality) may function as attribute in such clauses.[22]
The semantics of the resultative attribute also accounts for the acceptability
of (26); it is logically possible to undertake the process of making an attribuand acquire an attribute without actually achieving this end. On the other
hand, the achieving of this end will always imply that for some attributor
now the attribute is 'present in the attribuand'. Thus clauses of the type (18c)
genuinely face in two directions; they may be shown to be implicationally

---

[22] This should be regarded as a statement of the general tendency. One can think of
grammatical clauses in which the attribute is resultative though realized by a durational
adjective as in *is kriim nee bahot si aurtõ ko hasiin banaayaa hai* (this cream has made lots
of women beautiful) or *rozaana ki jhak-jhak nee us ko bad-mizaaj banaa diyaa* (these daily
altercations made him irritable) (!). It would appear that the grammatical subject in such
cases has to be inanimate and may be interpreted as 'cause' rather than as 'perceiver'.

related to the volitional relational clause or to the non-volitional non-relational clause. So we may construct a set of clauses such as the following:

(18)   laRki nee kamraa saaf kiyaa.
(18a)   kamraa saaf kiyaa gayaa.
(18b)   kamraa saaf huaa.
(18c)   kamraa saaf thaa.
(18d)   kamraa saaf milaa.
(18e)   kamraa saaf paayaa gayaa.
(18f)   kisi nee kamraa saaf paayaa.

It has been pointed out that clauses of the type (18f) are ambiguous (cf. example (14), Section 3.3 above), because of the lexical multivalence of the verb which may be interpreted as 'consider' or 'come across'. When it has the former meaning the processive passive verb corresponding to it is *lagnaa* or *maaluum honaa* (to seem); in the latter sense the processive passive verb is *milnaa*. (18f) is used here as an example of a non-volitional non-relational clause which may be paraphrased as *kisi nee kamraa paayaa aur kamraa saaf thaa* in the same manner as *naukar nee baks TuuTaa paayaa* may be paraphrased as *naukar nee baks paayaa aur baks TuuTaa thaa* (the servant found the box and the box was broken). One component of the meaning of a non-volitional non-relational clause with attribution can be readily seen as follows: to the dynamic participant a process happens which involves an affected participant and the latter is perceived by the former participant as 'having an attribute'. Thus attribution in a non-volitional non-relational clause may be regarded as depictive; by contrast in volitional non-relational clauses attribution is generally resultative, so that if we have *darzii nee kurtaa choTaa siyaa* (the tailor sewed the shirt small) the clause may be paraphrased as *darzii nee kurtaa is tarah siyaa kee woh choTaa ho gayaa* (the tailor sewed the shirt so, that it became small). Strictly speaking the attribute *choTaa* in the preceding example combines both result and manner. I shall ignore this complication for the time being and concentrate only on the resultative part of the meaning of the clause.

It has been pointed out that certain volitional clauses may have the feature benefactive and the beneficiary participant has usually the post-position *kee liyee* attached to it, e.g. *naukar nee baavarci kee liyee caaval tolee* and *darzii nee kisi kee liyee kurtaa siyaa* (the tailor sewed the shirt for some one) where *baavarci* and *kisi* have the function of beneficiary. On the same analogy it is possible to say:

(27)   laRki nee kisi kee liyee kamraa saaf kiyaa.
        girl nee somebody for room clean did
        the girl made the room clean for some one.

(27) differs from (18) only in one respect: the former has the feature benefactive whereas the latter does not have such a feature. Consequently a clause such as *kisi kee liyee kamraa saaf hai* (the room is clean for some one) is potentially ambiguous; it may mean that *kisi ki raaee m̃ee kamraa saaf hai* (in somebody's opinion the room is clean) or *kamraa kisi kee isteemaal kee liyee saaf hai* (the room is clean for somebody's use). In the non-volitional relational clause where the selection of the option benefactive is not permissible (there being no such clauses as *the boy found the girl beautiful for somebody*) *laRki kisi kee liyee xuubsurat hai* cannot be regarded as ambiguous; the phrases *attributor kee liyee* and *attributor ki raaee m̃ee* are interchangeable.

4.7. Two facts follow from the above discussion: (i) clause type (18c) is related to clause type (18) and (ii) by indirect implication it is also related to clause type (16); hence if we say:

(28)   laRki nee kamree ko saaf samjhaa magar laRki ki raaee m̃ee
         girl nee room to clean thought but girl of opinion in
         kamraa saaf nahĩ thaa.
         room clean not was
         the girl considered the room clean but in the girl's opinion the
         room was not clean

we are faced with the same kind of illogicality which was encountered in (25). Thus it appears that those stative passive clauses in which the attribute is realized by a non-durational adjective can be seen as simultaneously related to non-volitional relational clauses, to the volitional relational clauses and to the non-volitional non-relational attributive clauses. Thus if we are interested in the derivational history of a clause *laRki xush thi* (the girl was happy), it matters very little, it would seem, whether we claim it to be derived from *kisi nee laRki ko xush samjhaa* (some one thought the girl happy) or from *kisi nee laRki ko xush paayaa* (somebody found the girl happy) or from *kisi nee laRki ko xush kiyaa* (somebody made the girl happy). I would maintain that if we make an effort to consider the clause as derived chiefly from one of these three types, we will be distorting some facts about it. It is suggested that clauses of the type (18c) may be seen as a type in which certain features get neutralized, which to a large extent explains why they have not been traditionally shown as related to specific clause paradigms of the language. Thus while if we relate (18c) to the non-volitional relational clause of perception the attribute may be viewed as depictive, if we relate it to the volitional relational one it may be viewed as the result of an activity.

5.0. So far for the volitional non-relational clause of the type (17) *naukar* *nee caaval tolee* a paradigm has been set up which in general terms corresponds to the paradigms for (16), (18) and (19). The question arises if the option of stative passive is available to clause type (17). Let us consider:

(17c)   caaval tulee huee haĩ.
         rice weighed become are
         the rice is weighed.

It is suggested that (17c) is different from:

(20iv)   bacca soyaa huaa hai.
         child slept become is
         the child is still sleeping.

This difference lies in the function of *tulee huee* and *soyaa huaa*. Other examples of the type (17c) would be *kurtaa rãgaa huaa hai* (the shirt is dyed), *kursi TuuTi hui hai* (the chair is broken), *duudh ublaa huaa hai* (the milk is boiled), *farsh dhulaa huaa hai* (the floor is washed) and so on; examples of the type (20iv) would be *laRki leeTi hui hai* (the girl is still lying down), *naukar baRi deer see gayaa huaa hai* (the servant has been gone for a long time), and so on. The items *tulee huee, rãgaa huaa, TuuTi hui* etc. may be regarded as having the function of an attribute in the clause type (17c), so that it is possible to co-ordinate these items with a situationally appropriate adjective with the entire adjectival complex functioning as attribute in the clauses *caaval tulee huee aur saaf haĩ* (the rice is weighed and clean), *duudh taazaa aur ublaa huaa hai* (the milk is fresh and boiled), *kursi TuuTi hui aur gandi hai* (the chair is broken and dirty); items such as *soyaa huaa* and *gayaa huaa* etc. cannot be co-ordinated with any adjectives in clause type (20iv); thus clauses such as **bacca thakaa aur soyaa huaa hai* (the child is tired and still sleeping) or **laRki leeTi hui aur biimaar hai* (the girl is still lying down and ill) are unacceptable.

5.1. Three points emerge from a consideration of type (17c): (i) if the clause *caaval saaf hai* (the rice is clean) is regarded as a relational attributive clause, then there is reason to consider (17c) as a clause having the same features; (ii) if (17c) is regarded as a relational attributive clause, the attribute *tulee huee* would be like the attribute in (18c): both result from the undertaking of a volitional process; and (iii) if *caaval tulee huee haĩ* is a relational attributive clause and is still regarded as a member of the paradigm of (17), then we have a case where by the time we arrive at this particular member of the paradigm, the features of the paradigm as a whole no longer apply to it. While (17)–(17b) are volitional (17c) may not be regarded as having such a feature; while (17)–(17b) are non-relational, we have shown that (17c) may be regarded as relational; and finally while (17)–(17b) are non-attributive the type under focus has to be regarded as attributive.

5.2. It can be readily seen that the above is, in fact, the inevitable logical result of the approach taken in the discussion of (18c) with reference to (18f) and (18e), where, it might be recalled, (18c) was treated as a relational clause while the types (18f) and (18e) were considered to be non-relational. Further it was pointed out that a particular category of the stative passive type is, as it were, the genuine meeting ground for many different paradigms (see Sections 4.6–4.7 above). The ground is now clear to take a further step: if it is the case that a particular type is related to so many basically different types, then it is also the case that it is not related specifically to any one particular type. The clauses which have been labelled stative passive may then be regarded as the most neutral type of clause in the language; that is to say, they represent a category for the semanticization of which such basic options as causative vs. non-causative, volitional vs. non-volitional, transitive vs. non-transitive, active vs. passive and relational vs. non-relational are, in fact, somewhat irrelevant. A given instance of such a category will no doubt be relatable to a given permissible set of the above options, both by sharing some of the syntactic potentialities of the clause type which has the said set of systemic features and by showing a constant logical implicational relationship to it. The instances which could be most readily related to other clause types would be marked neutral clauses, i.e. marked in respect to some feature which is exclusively related to a particular category. Thus given *caaval baavarci kee liyee tulee huee haĩ* (the rice is weighed for the cook) it is possible to relate it to a volitional benefactive such as *kisi nee baavarci kee liyee caaval tolee* (some one weighed the rice for the cook). The systemic option of relational vs. non-relational is said to be irrelevant to the neutral clause type because such clauses do not in fact have an 'option': each instance of this type may be treated as relational if intensional relation is not confined to the specific types discussed above, namely that of attribute-attribuand and identity and identified; in other words if it could be extended to include such relations as location-localized and possession-possessed, then all the following would be instances of relational clause:

(29)   laRki xush hai.
        girl happy is
        the girl is happy.

(30)   woh DaakTar hai.
        he doctor is
        he is a doctor.

(31)   baks kamree mẽe hai.
         box room in is
         the box is in the room.
(32)   laRki kee paas eek baks hai.
         girl of near one box is
         the girl has a box.

It is in this sense that *honaa* 'to be' may be regarded as a connecting word
(or as 'copula') in that its primary function in these cases is to relate the
circumstance ascribed to the ascribed participant. It is immaterial that *hai*
in (32) has to be translated as *has* in English; in all four cases the semantics
of *honaa* for the Urdu clauses is identical: it is an item which signifies the
process of existence which is predicated of the ascribed participant and of the
circumstance ascribed: both exist and both exist in a given relationship to
each other.

6.0. Examples (29)–(32) are instances of the neutral type of clause. They
are distinguished from each other by having a distinct feature. Thus (29) is
attributive, (30) is equative, (31) is locative and (32) is possessive; of these
the first two categories have been discussed in some detail. One might question whether it is valid to set up a systemic option for the neutral clause
type whose terms are attributive, equative, locative and possessive so that if
the clause is attributive it may not be equative and if it is either, then it
may not be locative and if it is any of the latter three categories then it may
not be possessive. It might be argued that since we have:

(33)   laRki landan mẽe xush hai.
         girl London in happy is
         the girl is happy in London.
(34)   haamid kee paas laahaur mẽe kaii makaan haĩ.
         Haamid of near Lahore in many houses are
         Haamid has many houses in Lahore.
(35)   woh haspataal mẽe sab see qaabil DaakTar hai.
         he hospital in all of able doctor is
         he is the ablest doctor in the hospital.

the option locative should not be regarded as being in contrast with the
options attributive (cf. (33)) or possessive (cf. (34)) or equative (cf. (35)).
It is suggested that such a view could be taken only if the semantic function
of *landan mẽe*, *laahaur mẽe* and *haspataal mẽe* is not taken into consideration;
in other words they could be regarded as having the function of the locative
if we were defining locative only by reference to the post-position *mẽe, par,*

etc. The locative may be characterized as that phrase which signifies the place in some relation to which the process takes place; the specific relation is, in general, signified by the post-position attached to the place-signifying noun, thus in *bacca kamree mẽe soyaa* (the child slept in the room) the process of sleeping takes place in the room, with *mẽe* signifying the specific relation of the process to the place signified by the noun *kamraa*. Similarly in *woh kamree mẽe see niklaa* (he came out of the room), *mẽe see* signifies the specific relation in which the process of *nikalnaa* stands to the location *kamraa*. If so defined, the function of the locative is simply to signify a localization relation; it may not signify condition or part-whole relations. In (33), however, we find that *landan mẽe* has precisely the function of signifying condition, so a near paraphrase of the clause may be *cũkee laRki landan mẽe hai is liyee xush hai* (because the girl is in London therefore she is happy). If the verbal group of the clause had a modal construction *hoti hai* (usually is) signifying a 'habitual occurrence' then we could have paraphrased it as *jab laRki landan mẽe hoti hai to xush hoti hai* (when the girl is in London, she is happy), whereas even if we have a clause such as *bacca kamree mẽe sotaa hai* (the child usually sleeps in the room) we may not interpret it as *when the child is in the room, he sleeps*. The function of *landan mẽe* in (33), if the verbal group has a modal construction, is the same as that of *javaani mẽe* in the following:

(36)   javaani mẽe gadhaa bhi xuubsurat hotaa hai.
        youth in donkey too beautiful usually-is
        even a donkey is beautiful in youth.

It may be noted here that in a clause such as *kisi nee laRki ko kamree mẽe xaamosh paayaa* (somebody found the girl silent in the room), the clause is paraphrased as *kisi nee laRki ko kamree mẽe paayaa aur woh xaamosh thi* (somebody found the girl in the room and she was silent) and not as *kisi nee laRki ko paayaa aur woh kamree mẽe xaamosh thi* (somebody found the girl and she was silent in the room). Thus the domain of the locative in the last clause mentioned above does not extend over the attribute.

The interrogative locative employed in non-polar interrogative clauses is *kahãa* (where). However, in the written form the following is an ambiguous clause:

(20) (v) bacca kahãa soyaa?
          child where slept
     (i) where did the child go to sleep?
     (ii) the child has certainly not gone to sleep.

In interpretation (i) the function of the item *kahãa* is that of an interrogative

locative; it calls for a specification of place of action. *kahãã* alone is the 'new'
part of the message; the other elements of the message are known. Consequently in speech *kahãã* is the item that would carry the greatest amount of
prominence; that is to say, it will function as a 'tonic' syllable.[23] This is a
constant characteristic of the interrogative locative. Usually an interrogative
locative immediately precedes the verbal group; this is the unmarked order
of occurrence for an interrogative locative, as shown by the above example
as well as by *laRki nee kitaab kahãã paRhi?* (where did the girl read that
book?). Again, if *kahãã* functions as an interrogative locative in the latter
clause, it will carry the tonic. In interpretation (ii) of (20v) the tonic will be
carried by some other item than *kahãã*. If it is carried by *bacca*, the implication is that some one else has gone to sleep but not the child; if it is carried
by *soyaa*, the implication is the child is doing something else, not sleeping.
In the latter case, the information may also be carried by reversing the
sequence of the verbal group and the item *kahãã*, so that the clause would
read *bacca soyaa kahãã*. But here another distinction operates: if the tonic
is carried by *soyaa* the implication is that by contrast the child did something
else; if it is carried by *kahãã*, no contrast is intended so that there is only
emphatic negation regarding the process. When *kahãã* signifies emphatic and/
or contrastive negation, its place in sequence can be varied in many ways in
agreement with what part of the message is being negated and/or is contrastive. This is not true of the interrogative *kahãã*. When *kahãã* signifies
emphatic and/or contrastive negation, it may or may not carry the tonic
according to whether it is functioning contrastively or not. It stands to
reason therefore that when *kahãã* has the most unmarked place in sequence
as in *laRki nee kitaab kahãã paRhi* (girl nee book where did-read), the
distinction in the two meanings of the clause is made through the selection
of the tonic. So that if *kahãã* is tonic, the clause is locative interrogative, if
some other item is tonic then the clause is contrastive, negative and emphatic. Thus:

(37)   laRki nee kitaab *kahãã* paRhi?
        where did the girl read the book?
(38)   laRki nee *kitaab* kahãã paRhi.
        the girl certainly did not read the *book*.

are distinct in their meaning. Now consider the following pair:

(33a)   laRki xush *kahãã* thi.
(33b)   laRki *xush* kahãã thi.

The distinction in meaning here is not parallelled by the distinction between

---

[23] For the terms tonic, given, new, contrastive and emphatic see Halliday (1967a).

(37) and (38). (33a) may be translated as *the girl certainly* wasn't *happy* with the tonic on the verbal group, so that there is an emphatic negation of the process here as would be the case if the tonic had been carried by *paRhi* in (37) or (38). (33b) may be translated as *the girl certainly wasn't happy*, with the tonic on the attribute, so that there is a contrastive emphatic negation and we may interpret the clause as 'whatever else the girl might have been she certainly wasn't happy'. In fact *kahãa* in its interrogative locative meaning may not be used in clauses of the type (33). This discussion provides us with well-motivated reasons for the statement that if a neutral clause type has the feature attributive, it may not have the feature locative; these features are mutually exclusive and can therefore be regarded as terms in the system. When in clause type (33) there occurs a phrase which in its structure contains a place name, its function is to specify (by indirect means) the time during which a said attribuand had a specific attribute. That is why it is difficult, if not impossible, to find an appropriate context for a clause such as *laRki landan mẽe zahiin thi* (the girl was intelligent in London). This is not to deny that the place-name phrase may have other functions in such a clause type, e.g. in *is mulk mẽe laRkiyãa xuubsurat hoti haĩ* (in this country girls are usually beautiful) where *is mulk mẽe* has the function of modifying *laRkiyãa* so that it is possible to say *is mulk ki laRkiyãa*. My purpose is not to go into the detailed description of the environments in which such place-name phrases have different functions, but simply to point out that a locative feature does not co-occur with the feature attributive in the neutral clause type.

6.1. That the equative and the attributive features are mutually exclusive is probably demonstrated sufficiently in the discussion of the relational clauses. In *kariim qaabil DaakTar hai* (Kariim is a capable doctor), *qaabil* and *DaakTar* do not have two separate functions, so that the clause may not be paraphrased as *kariim qaabil hai aur kariim DaakTar hai* (Kariim is capable and kariim is a doctor) but rather as *kariim DaakTar ki haisiyat see qaabil hai* (Kariim is capable as a doctor). The function of *qaabil* is to modify the (identity) noun *DaakTar* and the entire group *qaabil DaakTar* functions as the identity ascribed to the identified. Thus it is justifiable to regard equative and attributive features as terms in the same system.

6.2. The question that arises at this point is whether the feature locative and equative are also mutually exclusive so that in (35) *woh haspataal mẽe sab see qaabil DaakTar hai* (he is the ablest doctor in the hospital) the place-name phrase *haspataal mẽe* can be shown to be not locative. Unlike (33), the clause here may not be paraphrased as *cũkee woh haspataal mẽe hai is liyee sab see qaabil DaakTar hai* (because he is in the hospital therefore he is the ablest doctor) or *jab woh haspataal mẽe hotaa hai to sab see qaabil DaakTar hotaa hai* (when he is in the hospital he is the ablest doctor). Indeed, if the latter were a possible paraphrase, it would be also possible to say that when he comes out of the hospital he is no longer the ablest doctor in the hospital which would be manifestly absurd. In fact then we have to regard *haspataal mẽe* as a modifying phrase; it constitutes a part of the complex group *haspataal mẽe sab see qaabil DaakTar* and the entire group has the function of identity, despite the fact that the item may occur discontinuously, e.g. in *haspataal mẽe woh sab see qaabil DaakTar hai* (in the hospital he is the ablest doctor). It is clear that the relationship here is not that of location-located but that of part-whole. This relation of part-whole is internal to the nominal group functioning as identity and does not dominate the clause. Thus a possible close paraphrase of (35) is *woh haspataal ka sab see qaabil DaakTar hai* (he is the ablest doctor of the hospital). It is not the case that the locative relation 'gets converted into' part-whole relation through the process of nominalization. Thus given (31) *baks kamree mẽe hai*, its nominalization will not be *kamree kaa baks* but *kamree mẽe kaa baks* (*box of the room* and *box of in the room*, literally). Other examples of the type (35) would be *woh hamaaree halqee mẽe hardil-aziiz shaaer hai* (he is a popular poet in our circle), *woh is kaalij mẽe lekcarar hai* (he is a lecturer in this college), *woh kisi shahar mẽe jaj hai* (he is a judge in some city), and so on.

In the manner of (33), the possibility of introducing an interrogative locative[24] in clause type (35) does not exist; here too the item *kahãa* could be used to signify emphatic and/or contrastive negation. Thus if the feature equative 'appears' in the deep grammar of the neutral clause, this will imply that neither the feature attributive nor locative may be 'present'. One means of making this environmental restriction explicit is to say that the features attributive, equative and locative form terms in the same system so that the selection of one option in the clause restricts the selection of the other two options.

6.3. If the locative is a phrase which signifies the place in some relation to which a process occurs, then (34) *haamid kee paas laahaur mẽe kaii makaan haĩ* may not be regarded as a clause with the feature locative in it, since the process of possession is independent of the locational relation signified by *laahaur mẽe*. In other words it is not the case that *haamid laahaur mẽe nahĩ hai magar haamid kee paas laahaur mẽe kaii makaan haĩ* (Haamid is not in Lahore but Haamid has many houses in Lahore) is either illogical or false,

---

[24] Perhaps this fact is relevant to English syntax as well. A clause such as **where are you the president?* or **where are you the doctor?* is ungrammatical, whereas clauses such as *which society is he the president of?* are grammatical.

while a sentence such as *haamid kee paas laahaur mẽe kaii makaan haĩ magar woh makaan laahaur mẽe nahĩ haĩ* (Haamid has many houses in Lahore but those houses are not in Lahore) is clearly illogical and one constituent clause of the sentence must be false if the other is true. Thus in (34) the domain of *laahaur mẽe* is seen to extend only over *kaii makaan*; note that the clause may be paraphrased as *haamid kee paas kaii makaan haĩ jo kee laahaur mẽe haĩ* (Haamid has many houses which are in Lahore). The location-localized relation therefore is clearly group-internal; that is to say it is not at the rank of clause that the locative has been selected but at the rank of that group which has the function of 'possession' in the clause. A comparable situation exists in the clause *woh baRaa mehnti laRkaa hai* (he is a hard-working boy) where the relation of attribute-attribuand in *baRaa mehnti laRkaa* is group-internal; the clause itself is equative, not attributive.

As in (33) and (35), so here too, the possibility of introducing an interrogative locative[25] in the clause does not exist; the item *kahãa* when used in such a clause type signifies emphatic and/or contrastive negation. The source of the ambiguity in clauses such as *aap kee biwi bacce kahãa haĩ* (your of wife children where are) is dicussed below (see Sections 8.0–8.1).

6.4. If the arguments put forward in Sections 6.0–6.3 are accepted, clauses (29) and (33) would be regarded as having the feature attributive, (30) and (35) would be regarded as having the feature equative, (32) and (34) as having the feature possessive; (31) *baks kamree mẽe hai* alone would be a clause with the feature locative. The domain of the locative here extends over the entire clause. No such paraphrases are possible as *jab baks thaa to kamree mẽe thaa* (when the box existed then was in the room), *cũkee baks thaa is liyee kamree mẽe thaa* (because the box existed therefore was in the room), *baks thaa jo kee kamree mẽe thaa* (the box existed which was in the room) or *kamree kaa baks thaa* (the box of the room existed).

In fact the reason for regarding the neutral clause type[26] as essentially relational is precisely this: the ascribed participant and the circumstance ascribed in such a clause cannot be 'separated' from each other, as if the predication of existence without the 'state of existence' were totally impossible. Thus (29) *laRki xush hai* does not mean *laRki hai* (a girl exists) and

---

[25] Again it may be noted in passing that the same applies to English; clauses like *where do you have a pen? *where do you have a brother? *where do you have eyes? *where does he have intelligence?* are all unacceptable. In Urdu since the equivalent of *where* has two functions one of which is permissible in the possessive clause, the clauses with *kahãa* are not unacceptable; they simply do not have the locative meaning.

[26] That there may be clause types which can be potentially related to more than one paradigm is perhaps implicit in Halliday's (1968) treatment of nuclear clause type as well as in his discussion of the superventional and actional clauses.

xush hai (happy is), nor does (32) mean *eek baks hai* (a box exists) and *laRki kee paas hai* (the girl has). Logically or extra-linguistically it may be a fact that an ascribed participant has to exist in order for it to be in a state, but so far as Urdu language and its syntax is concerned, this logical extra-linguistic 'fact' is of no consequence. That being the case, what is the description of *kariim hai* (Kariim is), or *baks hai* (a box is) etc.? The answer, in my opinion, is that such clauses are always elliptical and such ellipsis is decoded either by reference to the co-text or to the immediate context of situation. Thus the clause *kariim hai* may function as an answer to such questions as *kaun biimaar hai?* (who is ill?), *kamree mee̋ kaun hai?* (who is (there) in the room?) and *kaun DaakTar hai?* (who is the doctor?) etc., where both for the encoding and decoding of the clause *kariim hai*, the items *biimaar*, *kamree mee̋*, and *DaakTar* are relevant. In other words for the deep grammar of the clause, one of the four terms from the system just discussed will always be relevant. A question like *kariim hai?* is not to be decoded as *does Kariim exist?* but rather as *is Kariim here?* in which case the tonic would be carried by the verb *is* (hai); or as *is it Kariim who is ill/a doctor?* in which case the tonic would be carried by *kariim*. If for *kariim* we substitute an inanimate noun (or any noun that can function as 'possession' in the language) such as *baks hai* it may function as an answer to a question with the feature locative, attributive, equative or possessive; equally, given the right intonation it may function as a question with one of these features. One could maintain that in Urdu there exists no verb with the scope of the verb *exist* in English. This raises a question regarding the clause *xudaa hai* (God exists).[27] I suggest that the peculiarity of this clause arises from the selection of the item *xudaa*. This item, as is perhaps befitting given the belief of the speech community, over-

---

[27] The question that arises here is of the clause type *eek laRki thi* (there was a girl) in which the sequence of verb and noun may be reversed so that the verbal group is 'included' within the group (nominal) as in *eek thi laRki*. Both the types have generally the limited function of starting a fictional narrative. In my opinion they may not be interpreted as *a girl existed*, or *there existed a girl*. Such a clause may have a locational phrase in it as *kisi mulk mee̋ eek laRki thi* or *eek thi laRki kisi mulk mee̋* (there was a girl in some country). The locational phrases which may occur with *xudaa hai* are severely limited; the following clauses represent the total of the location phrases available to it: *xudaa har ⁱagah hai* (God is everywhere), *xudaa na masjid mee̋ hai na mandir mee̋; insaan kee dil mee̋ hai* (God is neither in the mosque nor in the temple; he is in man's heart) (!). This restriction does not apply to *eek laRki thi*. Secondly, usually the clause following the latter one in the narrative can, on the grounds of intonation, be shown to be related to it in some kind of modificational function; thus *eek laRki thi us kaa baap waziir thaa* (there was a girl; her father was a prime minister). When we have a string of clauses *eek laRkaa hai; woh mujhee rozaana pareeshaan kartaa hai* (there is a boy; he teases me every day), the clauses can be related to each other by the substitution of *jo* for *woh*. In the previous example *us* may be replaced by *jis*, without changing the meaning of the utterance in either case. It would seem to me that the use of *honaa* in these clauses is no more existential than it is in other stative passive clauses.

rides all syntactic distinctions that can be made so that we have clauses such as *xudaa nee kariim ko do beeTee diyee* (God gave Kariim two sons), *xudaa nee murdee ko jilaayaa* (God caused the dead (person) to live) and even *xudaa kee hukm see laRkee nee laRki ko xuubsurat paayaa*[28] (according to the will of God, the boy found the girl beautiful), and so on. It would be somewhat pointless to make rules for the description of these clauses as also for *xudaa hai*[29]; one rule suffices, namely that in Urdu *xudaa* is capable of anything and everything.

7.0. The neutral clause type has been characterized as one which can be potentially related to different clause types. This was exemplified in the discussion of the attributive and the equative neutral clauses. Does this characterization also hold true of the possessive and the locative? Let us first examine the possessive neutral clause.

The characterization of the possessive clause as one in which there exists a possessor-possession relation is highly generalized since it is possible to establish at least four subtypes of relation as exemplified by the following clauses:

(39)   kariim kee eek bhaai hai.
         Kariim of one brother is
         Kariim has a brother.
(40)   kariim kee baRi daulat hai.
         Kariim of lots-of wealth is
         Kariim has a lot of wealth.
(41)   kariim kee do ãakhẽe haĩ.
         Kariim of two eyes are
         Kariim has two eyes.
(42)   kariim kee aql hai.
         Kariim of intelligence is
         Kariim has intelligence.

In (39) the relation between *kariim* ('possessor') and *eek bhaai* ('possession') may be more specifically described as kin-to-kin relation. In (40), the relation between kariim ('possessor') and *baRi daulat* ('possession') may be more specifically regarded as owner-property relation. In (41), the relation between *kariim* ('possessor') and *do ãakhẽe* ('possession') may be described as a whole-

---

[28] See Section 4.1 above for the relationship between the causative and the non-volitional clauses.

[29] See Yamuna Kachru (1968): "... the verb *ho* is used as a complementless verb in only very special contexts, asserting the existence of some being or thing; the following philosophical sentence is an example of this: *iishwar hai* (God exists or God is)".

part relation, while in (42) *kariim* and *aql* may be seen as standing in a qualified-quality relation. Of these only (40) is alienable possession, the remaining are all 'inherent' or 'in-alienable' possession. The possessor in all
the above cases is an animate noun; when the possessor is animate the post-
position *kee/kee paas* (of, of near) occurs as the marker of this transitivity
function. Both post-positions are multivalent, that is, they may function as
markers in other structures either at clause rank or at group rank (see Section
8.1 below). All four specific types of possession exemplified above are available to clauses in which the possessor is animate; if, however, the possessor
is inanimate only the whole-part and qualified-quality relations are available,
as can be exemplified by the following:

(43)   is kamree mẽe do khiRkiyãa haĩ.
         this room in two windows are
         this room has two windows.

(44)   is kapRee mẽe kuch aib hai.
         this material in some defect is
         this material has some defect (in it).

(43) is like (41) a clause in which there exists a whole-part relation; (44) is
like (42) a clause in which there exists qualified-quality relation. If our concern was only to describe (41)–(44), without relating them to any other clause
types in the language, then it would be possible to view all four as cases of
whole-part relation. (44) and (42) are however relatable to the attributive
clause so that (42) may be regarded as giving more or less the same information as is conveyed by *kariim aqlmand hai* (Kariim is intelligent) while (44)
stands in the same relation to *yee kapRaa aibdaar hai* (this material is defective), whereas neither (41) nor (43) can be related to an attributive clause.
Such clauses as *yee gaaee dumdaar hai* (this cow is with-a-tail) and *kariim
do aakhõ waalaa hai* (Kariim is with-two-eyes) or *yee kamraa khiRki waalaa
hai* (this room is with-a-window) are perceived as odd, if not totally ungrammatical.

As can be seen from (43) and (44), the post-position *mẽe* (in) occurs as
the marker of possessor function. *mẽe*, needless to say, is multivalent and
in addition to this function, it may be used either to signify the locational
function of a noun or the time function, e.g. in *kamree mẽe* in (31) and *din
mẽe* in a clause such as *is kaarxaanee mẽe din mẽe baRaa shor hotaa hai*
(there is a lot of noise in this factory during the day), where the first occurrence
of *mẽe* signifies location and the second time duration. It is easy to see how
the surface similarities of (43) and (31) may be construed as implying a deep
grammar similarity between the locative and the possessive (see footnote 30).

7.1. Clauses (39)–(42) may be potentially related to a non-volitional non-relational active clause type, as is exemplified by the following:

(39i)   kariim eek bhaai rakhtaa hai.
         Kariim one brother owns is
         Kariim owns a brother.

(40i)   kariim baRi daulat rakhtaa hai.
         Kariim lot-of wealth owns is
         Kariim owns a lot of wealth.

(41i)   kariim do ãakhẽe rakhtaa hai.
         Kariim two eyes owns is
         Kariim owns two eyes.

(42i)   kariim aql rakhtaa hai.
         Kariim intelligence owns is
         Kariim owns intelligence.

It is irrelevant that the English translations of these clauses sound 'odd'; in Urdu given the right context, these clauses are used without any perception of 'oddity' about them. Thus when we have *laRkaa eek nahĩ chee bahnẽe rakhtaa hai; aisee laRkee ko laRki deenaa munaasib nahĩ* (the boy owns not one but six sisters; it is not right to give a girl (in marriage) to such a boy) or *ai bahan! ãakhẽe rakhti ho yaa baTan jo tumhẽe kuch nazar hi nahĩ aataa* (O sister! do you own eyes or buttons that nothing ever gets seen by you) or *tum bhi to aql rakhtee thee; apni aql see kaam liyaa hotaa* (you too owned intelligence! you should have used your own intelligence), none of the clauses with the feature possessive in these sentences is seen as 'odd'. That clause types (39i)–(42i) do not occur very frequently is not being denied; simply the point is being made that they are all grammatical and acceptable and that there is no oddity in their use, and that they are related to (39)–(42).

7.2. It has been suggested that a clause such as:

(45)   kariim kee paas eek kitaab hai.
        Kariim of near one book is
        Kariim has a book.

is potentially related to a benefactive clause[30] such as:

(46)   kisi nee kariim ko eek kitaab di hai.
        somebody nee Kariim to one book gave is
        somebody has given Kariim a book.

Certainly there exists a constant logical relationship of implication (effect/

---

[30] Lyons (1967), pp. 390–96; also Lyons (1968), p. 368; also Allen (1964), pp. 337–43.

result-cause) between (45) and (46). However it is doubtful whether the benefactive feature as such is at the basis of such a relation. (45) can still have a result relation with a non-benefactive clause such as:

(47)   kariim nee kutub-xaanee see eek kitaab curaai hai.
        Kariim nee library from one book stolen is
        Kariim has stolen a book from the library.

Similarly the pair *kariim nee musiiqi par eek kitaab xarridi hai* (Kariim has bought a book on music) and *kariim kee paas musiiqi par eek kitaab hai* (Kariim has a book on music) are potentially related as cause and effect, and there seems no reason to think that the benefactive is the only clause type which could stand in a causal relation to the possessive.

Like (40), the possessive relation in (45) can be regarded as that of owner-property. Whereas it is true that some benefactives can be related to such a clause type, it is not true of the other possessive types, unless we thought of *xudaa* or some item signifying supernatural power as the benefactor. Thus while both (40) and (45) may be potentially related to (40ii) and (46) respectively:

(40ii) kariim kee waaldeen nee kariim ko baRi daulat di hai.
        Kariim of parents nee Kariim to a-lot-of wealth gave is
        Kariim's parents have given Kariim a lot of wealth.
(46)   kisi nee kariim ko eek kitaab di hai.

the benefactive is in general not a feature which would be related to (39), (41) and (42). If clauses (39)–(42) are all regarded as cases of possessive type, then the case for the benefactive being related to the feature possessive cannot be argued successfully, at least so far as Urdu is concerned.

7.3. Taking (39)–(44) as the various sub-types of the possessive neutral clause one may enquire about each: what other clause types are these potentially related to? (39) which is a kin-to-kin relationship can only be related to a clause such as (39i). We ignore *xudaa nee us ko eek bhaai diyaa hai* (God has given him a brother) as not very relevant since it does not reflect a general syntactic tendency in the language; that is, it is not the case that benefactive clauses as such are related to (39). A very small sub-category of these in which the benefactor participant has to be characterized by its lexical properties may be so related; there is no such clause as *maã nee us ko eek bhaai diyaa hai* (the mother has given him a brother). It is perhaps justifiable to maintain that clauses with kin-to-kin relationship form a special category in most languages; thus while in English *he has a brother* may be seen as related by its meaning to some such clause as *his mother has two sons*, it is not clear how this meaning relation can be formalized in the syntactic description of the language, except through the interrelationship of the kinship items as elements of lexis in the language. In Urdu too, it is probably not true that (39) can be potentially related to paradigms of different clause types. To relate (39) to *us ki m͠aa kee eek beeTaa huaa* (a son was born to his mother) we would have to set up a body of ad hoc rules – ad hoc in the sense that the kind of syntactic and implicational relationship postulated in this case would probably not be reflected anywhere else in the syntax of the language.

7.4. As has been indicated by the discussion in Sections 7.1–7.2, for a clause type with the owner-property relation both volitional and non-volitional clauses are relevant. Although the feature benefactive is by no means necessarily related to such a clause, in a given case it may be so related, as is shown by the examples above. A non-benefactive volitional clause potentially related to (40) may be cited: *kariim nee baRi daulat banaai hai* (Kariim has made a lot of wealth) would be such a clause; like (40ii), it has the implication *kariim has a lot of wealth*, but unlike (40ii) it does not have the feature benefactive.

The volitional non-benefactive clause *kariim nee baRi daulat banaai hai* stands in a cause relation to the volitional relational clause *kariim kee baRi daulat hui* (kariim of a-lot-of wealth became = kariim came to have a lot of wealth). This cause-effect relationship also exists between *laRki nee kamraa saaf kiyaa* (the girl made the room clean) and *kamraa saaf huaa* (the room became clean). However, the resemblance between the two pairs is partial: while both members of the latter pair have the relational feature, in the former pair this feature is present only in the processive passive *kariim kee baRi daulat hui* (kariim came to have a lot of wealth). On the other hand, the relationship existing between *kariim nee baRi daulat banaai hai* and *kariim kee baRi daulat hai* (kariim has a lot of wealth) is very closely par-allelled by that obtaining between *naukar nee caaval tolee h͠ai* and *caaval tulee huee h͠ai* (the servant has weighed the rice and the rice is weighed, respectively). Members of both pairs stand in cause-effect relation; the active member (the cause) in both cases is non-relational, while the neutral type clause in both pairs, related as result to the active one, has the relational feature. Finally the surface structure shows certain similarities: the affected participant in the neutral type in both pairs is associated with the grammatical subject of the clause, namely, *baRi daulat* and *caaval*.

7.5. Clause type (41) resembles (39) in that it can only be shown to be related to the type (41i) or to a benefactive in which the benefactor participant is some supernatural power. It has been pointed out that (41) and (43) can both be regarded as whole-part relation, the distinction being simply that in (41) the possessor is animate while in (43) it is inanimate. Even if we were to grant that a small specific subcategory of the benefactive can be shown to be related to (41), this is in fact not true of (43); the latter clause is not related to a benefactive clause. It can however stand in a cause-effect relation to:

(48)   kisi nee kamree mẽẽ do khiRkiyãã lagaai haĩ.
        somebody nee room in two windows fixed is
        somebody has fixed two windows in the room.

The latter is a volitional non-benefactive clause; *kamraa* may not be regarded as a beneficiary participant here any more than it may be so regarded in a relational volitional clause such as *laRki nee kamraa saaf kiyaa* (the girl made the room clean). It is significant, perhaps, that the verbs *deenaa* (to give) and *bheejnaa* (to send), equivalents of which in most languages may be regarded as signifying an inherently benefactive process, when used in a clause type represented by (48) lead either to ungrammaticality or to a meaning which can be readily perceived as having no overt selection of the beneficiary in it; thus consider:

(49)   *kisi nee kamree mẽẽ do khiRkiyãã di haĩ.
        somebody nee room in two windows gave is
        somebody has given two windows in the room.
(50)   *kisi nee kamree mẽẽ do khiRkiyãã bheeji haĩ.
        somebody nee room in two windows sent is
        somebody has sent two windows in the room.

The unacceptability of (49) and (50) does not arise from the selection of the post-position *mẽẽ*; one may maintain at least for these cases that the ungrammaticality arises because of covert selection of beneficiary in an environment where ellipsis is not permissible. If however one uses the post-position *ko* (to) which is normally associated with beneficiary function of a specific kind, the clauses become even more ungrammatical in that there would then exist more than one reason for their ungrammaticality. In the following:

(51)   maĩ nee darwaazee ko dhakkaa diyaa.
        I nee door to push gave
        I gave the door a push.

the verb *deenaa* is used as a pro-verb, with *dhakkaa* functioning as process-range. It has been shown [31] that an item functioning as action-range may not be replaced by a wh-interrogative item without changing the pro-verb. Thus for *I gave the door a push*, the non-polar interrogative is not *what did you

[31] See Huddleston *et al.* (1968, p. 26).

give the door but *what did you do to the door?* This observation also applies to (51); in Urdu we cannot say **aap nee darwaazee ko kyaa diyaa* (which corresponds to the former of the clauses above) but rather *aap nee darwaazee kee saath kyaa kiyaa* (what did you do with reference to the door?). Other arguments may be offered to show that neither (51) nor (48) could be regarded as benefactive; consider:

(48i)   *jo maĩ nee kamree mẽe lagaayaa woh yeh khiRkiyãã thĩ.
        what I fixed to the room were these windows.

(48ii) *jo maĩ nee us laRkee ko diyaa woh yeh kitaab thi.
        what I gave that boy was this book.

(48iii) jisee maĩ nee woh kitaab di woh yeh laRkaa thaa.
        the one to whom I gave that book was this boy.

(51i)   *jo maĩ nee darwaazee ko diyaa woh dhakkaa thaa.
        what I gave the door was a push.

(48iii) which is the only clause above with the feature benefactive is related to a clause such as *maĩ nee woh kitaab is laRkee ko di thi* (I had given that book to this boy); that in some sense *kitaab* in this clause and *khiRkiyãã* in (48) are alike is shown by the fact that both (48i) and (48ii) are unacceptable. Let us then assume that (43) is not even potentially related to a volitional benefactive clause; rather it is related to a volitional relational clause such as (48). The clause is considered to be relational because the process here 'requires' at least three participants, *kisi* (actor), *kamraa* (possessor: whole) and *khiRkiyãã* (possession: part), so that in *khiRkiyãã lagaa di gaiĩ?* (Have the windows been fixed?) the implication is that they were fixed *to* something and that somebody was doing the fixing.

I would suggest that although (43) itself is ambiguous (see Section 8.0 below) (48) may not be regarded as ambiguous with reference to the features possessive and locative. It is in fact an accident that the process stands in the *in* relation to the noun *kamraa* for the simple reason that it is a place noun. The following clause representing the type (48) is not ambiguous:

(52)   kisi nee baks mẽe Dhaknaa lagaayaa.
        somebody fixed the lid to the box.

It would be absurd to suggest that (52) is a locative clause, in the sense in which the term locative is being used here.

The whole-part type of possessive may be seen as (a) not locative and (b) as not related to a benefactive; instead it is related to a volitional relational non-benefactive clause (e.g. (48), (52)) to which it stands in a result relation in somewhat the same way as *caaval tulee huee haĩ* is related to *kisi nee caaval tolee haĩ*. In certain cases, type (43) may also be seen as related to a non-volitional clause. Consider the following pair:

(53)   masjid mẽe caar miinaar hotee haĩ.
         a mosque has usually four minarets.

(53i)   aap har masjid mẽe caar miinaar paaẽe gee.
         you will find four minarets in every mosque.

It is probably the case that such a relationship exists often if the neutral
clause type has a verbal group which signifies 'habitual occurrence'.

7.6. (42) and (44) are distinct in their deep grammar only by virtue of the
fact that in (42) possession involves an animate possessor whereas in (44)
it involves an inanimate one. As already indicated these clauses are closely
related in their meaning to the relational attributive clause. Thus the following:

(42i)   maĩ nee kariim kee zaraa bhi aql nahĩ paai.
         I did not find Kariim to have any intelligence.

(42ii)   maĩ nee kariim ko zaraa bhi aqlmand nahĩ paayaa.
         I did not find Kariim intelligent in the least.

may be regarded as fairly close in their meaning for the obvious reason that
the quality-qualified relation is very close to the attribute-attribuand relation.
A significant fact here is that in type (42) the quality noun is one which signifies
a durational (hence often 'inherent') quality. There are no such clauses as
laRki kee Gam hai (the girl has sorrow) or *laRki kee xushi hai* (the girl has
happiness). (However, see Section 9 below.) This being the case these clauses
can be related only to the relational non-volitional ones such as (42i) and
(42ii). In the former case the type may be regarded as having the features
non-volitional, relational, possessive (qualified-quality); in the latter case the
clause has the feature attributive instead of the feature possessive.

The clause type (44) too is related to a relational clause such as:

(44i)   maĩ nee us kapRee mẽe aib paayaa.
         I nee that material in defect found
         I found some defect in that material.

(44ii)   maĩ nee us kapRee ko aib-daar samjhaa.
         I nee that material to defective considered
         I considered that material defective.

As can be seen whenever the neutral clause type is related to a non-volitional
relational clause the implicational relationship is not that of effect and cause,
but simply that in the latter case (i.e. (42i), (42ii), (44i) and (44ii)) the commentator whose opinion is presumably also expressed in the neutral clause,
is selected overtly with the function of dynamic participant in the clause
whereas in the latter (i.e. (42), (44)) this is not made explicit.

There is however a difference between (42) and (44); if the quality noun in (44) is of the type that may be described as 'transient' (i.e. it is a quality which may be acquired and/or lost) then the clause may be seen as standing in a cause relation to a corresponding neutral type. Consider:

(54)   is kamree meẽ baRi xushbu hai.
         this room in big perfume is
         there is a beautiful perfume in this room.[32]

(54i)   kisi nee is kamree meẽ baRi xushbu ki hai.
         somebody nee this room in big perfume done is
         somebody has made the room have a beautiful perfume.

Here (54) may be seen as standing in a result relation to a volitional clause (54i). This relationship is not possible for a neutral clause type such as *gulaab meẽ baRi xushbu hoti hai* (the rose has a beautiful perfume) for obvious reasons. Other clauses of the type (54) would be *kamree meẽ andheeraa hai* (it is dark in the room), *kaii Galaafõ par dhabbee thee* (there were stains on many covers), *is baalTi meẽ cheed hai* (there is a hole in the bucket) and so on. All these can be related to a volitional clause and all will stand in the result relation to such a clause.

7.7. The neutral locative type may again be seen as related to both the volitional and the non-volitional clause types. Consider:

(55)   kisi nee kamree meẽ eek baks paayaa hai.
         somebody nee room in one box found is
         somebody has found a box in the room.

(56)   kisi nee kamree meẽ eek baks rakkhaa hai.
         somebody nee room in one box put is
         somebody has put a box in the room.

The relationship of the locative to clause type (56) (which is volitional) has already been pointed out by Lyons (1968). That (55) and (31) *kamree meẽ eek baks hai* (there is a box in the room) are related may perhaps be shown by the illogicality of a sentence such as *baks kamree meẽ nahĩ thaa magar kisi nee kamree meẽ eek baks paayaa hai* (there was no box in the room but somebody has found a box in the (same) room). This relationship cannot be attributed to the selection of the locative in the two clauses of the sentence since it is perfectly logical to say *us nee kamree meẽ baks nahĩ paayaa leekin usi kamree meẽ woh baks thaa* (he did not find the box in the room but the (same) box was in that (same) room). *To find (paanaa), to come across*

---

[32] Unlike the English clause the Urdu one is not ambiguous; the Urdu clause may not be interpreted as: there is an object in this room; the name of the object is 'perfume'.

(paanaa), *to spot* (deekhnaa) all imply a locative just as much as the verb *to put* (rakhnaa) does. There seems no a priori reason for thinking that whatever is somewhere *was put* or *was sent* there by someone unless that category of someone includes the supernatural powers. It appears to me that once we include such super-natural powers as 'actors', the case for *put* type clause (i.e. volitional ones) becomes somewhat weaker, since the relationship postulated between a put-clause and the neutral locative is, truly speaking, no longer of sufficient significance. The verbs *put, come, go, throw* etc. may be regarded as forming a subset of that class of verbs which signifies volitional process. Without the postulation of some super-natural power as actor, it is not easy to see how a volitional clause with these verbs would be related to locatives such as *suraj aasmaan kee nisf par hai* (the sun is at the zenith (of the sky)), *hindustaan tibbat kee junuub mẽe hai* (India is to the South of Tibet), *tumhaaree piichee tumhaari parchaaĩ hai* (behind you is your shadow), *landan mẽe kaii hazaar DaakTar haĩ* (there are thousands of doctors in London). Thus while it has to be granted that there are cases of the neutral locative, which are potentially related to a volitional clause, there are also neutral locatives which cannot be so related in any significant sense. On the other hand, most neutral locative clauses may be related to non-volitional clauses, with verbs such as *to spot* (i.e. to see accidently), *to come across*, *to find* etc. These non-volitional verbs are at least as 'inherently' locative as are the volitional ones cited above; further there is the extra-linguistic fact that whatever is somewhere has not always been *put* or *sent* there though it is true that whatever is *spotted* somewhere always must have been there at the time of being *spotted* etc.

7.8. My conclusion, then, is that for most neutral clause types there exists the possibility of establishing some constant implicational relationship with more than one paradigm. The details of the relationship may vary from type to type but where it does exist, it shows a constant syntactic similarity apart from the meaning relation. It is probably this characteristic that baffles all efforts made to establish the neutral type as the member of one given paradigm alone. Perhaps what we require is a grammar in which simultaneous relationships may be built in without causing any inconsistencies in the description, since it would appear that in most languages we shall encounter some type which will show this particular characteristic of the neutral clause type in Urdu. I would suggest that a description in which the deep grammar of an item under focus is based upon its syntagmatic characteristics will handle this aspect only poorly.

8.0. In this section two clause types are examined which are, in fact, ambiguous though often treated as simply a possessive or a locative. The two clauses are:

(43)   is kamree mẽe do khiRkiyãa haĩ.

(57)   aap kee biiwi baccee kahãa haĩ.

(43) is potentially ambiguous; it may be interpreted as (i) there are two objects in this room and these objects are 'windows' or as (ii) the windows form part of this room. In the first case it resembles a locative such as (31); in the second case it resembles a possessive such as (41). The fact that in isolation (43) would most often be interpreted as having a possessive meaning implying part-whole relation is yet another indication of how much extra-linguistic information goes into the interpretation of language. One makes use of one's knowledge that very few people are in the habit of keeping windows (the objects that have not been fixed to any place yet) while prob-ably every room has at least one window as a part of it. But were we engaged in the construction of a house, it would be not too far-fetched to say to our assistant *us kamree mẽe do khiRkiyãa haĩ, unhẽe uThaa laao!* (there are two windows in that room, fetch them here!). Such a sentence would be absurd if the clause (43) were always to be interpreted as a possessive type and could not be interpreted as a locative in certain environments.

In Urdu for certain number words we have a corresponding 'inclusive' number, e.g. *do* (two), *donõ* (both); *tiin* (three), *tiinõ* (all three); *caar* (four), *caarõ* (all four). The difference between *do kursiyãa uThaa laao!* (bring two chairs) and *donõ kursiyãa uThaa laao!* (bring both the chairs) is that in the latter case the objects signified by the nominal group are known (definite) whereas in the former case they are not known (indefinite). When the noun signifies an unknown single entity, the modifier *eek* (a, an) precedes it and often, in accordance with the function of *eek*, we find a complex modification *eek koii* (a some) as in *eek koii laRki saRak par cali jaa rahi thi* (some girl was walking along the street); when the noun signifies a single known entity the modifier *eek* can only be selected as a numeral *one* (contrasting with *two*, *three*, etc.) or to show contrast (one as opposed to the other). In both cases *eek* will carry the tonic. Thus we have the following clauses:

(58) (i)   kamree mẽe *eek* baks thaa (do nahĩ).
           there is *one* box in the room (not two).

(ii) *eek* baks kamree mẽe hai (duusraa kahĩ aur hai).
           one box is in the room (the other is somewhere else).

(iii) kamree mẽe eek *baks* hai.
           there is a box in the room.

(58iii) represents the unmarked sequence of the indefinite located vis à vis the location. The unmarked sequence of the definite located vis à vis location is as represented by (31) *baks kamree mẽe hai* with the tonic carried by the item *kamree* (or more accurately by the first syllable of it). When therefore we have a clause such as:

(59)   meez par *kitaab* hai.

the clause is to be interpreted as *the* book *is on the table* and has a contrastive feature. Corresponding to (31) we have a clause:

(59i)   donõ baks kamree mẽe haĩ.
            both the boxes are in the room.

And corresponding to (59) we would have a clause *meez par donõ kitaabẽe haĩ* (both the *books* are on the table), where the tonic would be carried by the second syllable of *kitaabẽe*; the clause has the same kind of contrastive information as in (59). Accordingly if corresponding to (43) we have:

(43a)   kamree mẽe donõ khiRkiyãa haĩ.

with the tonic carried by some part of *khiRkiyãa*, this implies that both the windows are there but something else is not.

The use of the inclusive number as a modifier for a noun in a nominal group functioning as possession at clause rank is not permissible, so that neither (43a) nor (43b) would be ambiguous:

(43b)   donõ khiRkiyãa kamree mẽe haĩ.
            both the windows are in the room.

The unmarked sequence of possessor-possession at the clause rank is as exemplified by (43) in one of its senses, i.e. the possessor precedes the possession. When the sequence is reversed, the clause has a contrastive implication. These two facts account (a) for the unacceptability of:

(60)   *kariim kee donõ ãakhẽe haĩ.
            Kariim has both eyes (or both the eyes).
(60i)   *kursi mẽe donõ hatthee haĩ.
            the chair has both the arms.

(b) they account for the distinction in meaning between:

(60ii)   caar laRkiyãa kariim kee haĩ hamiid kee nahĩ.
            it is Kariim who has four daughters not Hamiid.
(60iii)   dum jaanwar kee hoti hai insaan kee nahĩ.
            it is animals who have tails not human beings.

and the unmarked possessives such as *kariim kee caar laRkiyãa haĩ* (cf. (60ii) above: Kariim has four daughters) and *jaanwar kee dum hoti hai* (cf. (60iii):

animals have tails). (43) being ambiguous has all the forms available to the locative as well as those available to the part-whole possessive.

8.1. The ambiguity of (57) *aap kee biiwi baccee kahãã haĩ* arises from the multivalence of *kahãã* and *kee*. It may be interpreted either as a locative interrogative or it may be interpreted as an emphatic and/or contrastive negative. *kahãã* has been discussed earlier (see Section 6.0); it may mean either *where* or *(but) surely not*. The possessive relation can be selected either at the clause rank as exemplified in the above discussion, or it may be selected at the group rank as in *meeree bhaaii ki beeTi* (my brother's daughter). At the group rank, except for the pronominals *maĩ* and *tum* (*I* and *you* in its familiar function), all items having the function of possessor must have a post-position; the post-position shows number gender concord with the possession so that we have *kariim ki biiwi* (Kariim's wife; the marker *ki* in concord with singular feminine noun '*wife*') *kariim kaa beeTaa* (Kariim's son; the marker *kaa* in concord with singular masculine noun) and *kariim kee bhaai bahan* (Kariim's brother and sister; the marker *kee* in concord with group complex, gender mixed i.e. one group masculine one feminine); *kariim kee beeTee* (Kariim's sons; *kee* in concord with plural masculine) and *kariim ki beeTiyãã* (Kariim's daughters; *ki* in concord with plural feminine). So far as the discussion here is concerned the three uses of *kee* are relevant; it may now be seen that the *kee* in (57) can be interpreted in two ways: either it signifies a possessive relation at the clause rank in which case *kahãã* has a non-locative function as in the sentence *aap kee biiwi baccee kahãã haĩ itnaa baRaa makaan lee kee kyaa karẽe gee* (but you *don't* have wife and children what are you going to do with such a big house), or it signifies a possessive relation at the group rank (where the group functioning as possession is of a complex structure with a feminine and a masculine noun co-ordinated) as in the sentence *aap kee biiwi baccee kahãã haĩ bahot dinõ see un see mulaaqaat nahĩ hui* (where are your wife and children, I haven't met them for a long time). Clauses in which possession noun is singular are unambiguous in this respect whether the possession relation obtains at the group rank or at the clause rank. *aap ki laRki kahãã haĩ* (where is your daughter?) would be interpreted unambiguously as a locative interrogative clause with the possessive relation obtaining at the group rank; by comparison *aap kee laRki kahãã hai* (but you *don't* have a daughter) will be interpreted as an emphatic negative possessive clause (i.e. here the possession relation obtains at the clause rank). The same applies respectively to *aap kaa beeTaa kahãã hai* (where is your son?) and *aap kee beeTaa kahãã hai* (but surely you don't have a son). If the possession is a plural but feminine noun, then again this ambiguity would not take place, e.g. in *aap ki beeTiyãã kahãã haĩ* (where are your daughters?) which is locative interrogative with possession obtaining at the group rank and *aap kee beeTiyaa kahaa hai* (but surely you don't have daughters), which is emphatic negative with possession obtaining at the clause rank. In the remaining cases the ambiguity of the type exemplified by (57) will exist and would be resolved, in speech by reference to the phonological pattern of the clause, in writing by reference to the co-text. The characteristic of these clauses may be taken as yet another indication of the fact that at clause rank the features possessive and locative are not selected within the same clause in the neutral type.

9.0. There are at least two other categories in which the verb *honaa* is regularly used; in fact no other verb is available except some form of *honaa* (with some specific meaning) to this category. Two examples are presented here:

(61)   keraaee-daar ko takliif hui.
        tenant to inconvenience happened
        the tenant suffered inconvenience.

(62)   keraaee-daar ko takliif hai.
        tenant to inconvenience is
        the tenant faces inconvenience.

Both (61) and (62) may be seen as related to *kisi nee keraaee-daar ko takliif di* (somebody caused the tenant inconvenience). In general 'verbs' such as *takliif deenaa* (to cause inconvenience), *ummiid rakhnaa* (to keep hope i.e. to hope), *shor karnaa* (to make a noise), *balwaa karnaa* (to cause riot) etc. have been regarded as *feel-ee-murrakkab* (compound verbs).[33] I would argue that in all these cases we have a complex of process-range + pro-verb, where the process-range is realized by the nominal 'bit' and the pro-verb by the verbal 'bit'. This is not to deny that there are compound verbs in the language

---

[33] Haq (*ibid.*, p. 150): "Compound verbs are formed in two ways: (i) with the help of other verbs, which are called 'auxiliary verb' and (ii) by 'arranging' verbs with adjectives and nouns [in a particular order, R.H.]". From this definition it is clear that Haq is contradicting his own statement regarding the *naaqis* verbs; secondly he is not making a distinction between a verbal group such as *aayaa hotaa* ((if) had come), a group which has the feature conditional, and *muqarrar kiyaa* (appointed) which is like *khaayaa* a simple past; further he makes no distinction between *waada kiyaa* (made a promise) and *muqarrar kiyaa*, although the syntactic potentialities of *waada* and *muqarrar* are very distinct. Yamuna Kachru (1966) makes a distinction between conjunct verb and compound verb; an example of conjunct verb for Yamuna Kachru is *band karnaa* (to shut; literally, shut to do) which is like *saaf karnaa* (clean to do i.e. to clean). The conjunct verb is "translatable by a one-word English verb" (*ibid.*, p. 59); example of a compound verb would be *aa gayaa* (has arrived) as opposed to *aayaa* (arrived) (derived from the list of examples in Yamuna Kachru; *ibid.*, p. 53). According to this approach the conjunct verbs could also be compound, e.g. *band kar diyaa* (has shut) as opposed to *band kiyaa* (shut (past)). It is clear that many confusions will arise from this.

such as *muqarrar karnaa* (to appoint), *qaraar deenaa* (to consider), *maaluum karnaa* (to discover), and so on.[34] The genuine compound verbs, such as represented by the latter list all have this in common: the two bits of the group may not appear without the other; moreover the first word of such compound verbs cannot be assigned to any known class of word, since they do not function as nouns, adjectives or adverbs, etc. By contrast the item realizing process-range can function as noun and may accept modification and qualification in the manner of other nouns, e.g. *aap ki takliif ki xabar sun kar mujhee baRaa afsos huaa* (I was sorry to hear the news of your trouble) or *guzishtaa saal kee balwee mẽe bahot log maree* (many people died in last year's riot).[35]

The difference between the two is also apparent at the clause rank. In general it is the case that verbs of the former category have in their paradigm a member such as (62), whereas this is not the case with the latter set. Below are provided some tentative suggestions regarding three sub-types of clauses with pro-verb and process+range selection in them.

9.1. There is a certain process type in Urdu which always requires an animate affected participant. Examples would be *kisi nee kisi ko takliif di hai* (somebody has caused somebody inconvenience), *kisi nee kisi ko DāaTaa* (somebody scolded somebody), and *kisi nee kisi ko tassali dilaaii* (somebody consoled somebody); in all these cases *kisi ko* may not be replaced by *kisi ciiz ko* (to something); that is to say, the affected participant has to be animate.[36]

---

[34] More accurately one might say that the first word (of what to my mind are not 'compound verbs' on some superficial criterion of whether there are two graphic words or only one) may not appear except in company with the verb associated with certain choices; thus in the processive passive the verb *huaa/hui* (with auxiliaries or without according to the options being realized by the verbal group) must occur with *muqarrar* as in *woh sadar muqarrar huaa* (he got appointed president), *woh sadar muqarrar ho gayaa hai* (he has got appointed president).

[35] Thus while we have *darwaazaa band karo* (shut the door) we may also have a group such as *band darwaazaa* (shut door i.e. closed door); while we have *takliif di* (caused inconvenience) we also have *aap ki takliif* (your inconvenience), *is tarah ki takliifẽe* (inconveniences of this kind). But in the case of the compound verb (which is distinct from compound verbal group) we have *is aadmi ko sadar muqarrar karo* (appoint this man president) but not **muqarrar aadmi* (appoint man); instead we should say *muqarrar shuda aadmi* (appointed become man, i.e. the appointed man) or *muqarrara waqt* (appointed time); nor do we have **aadmi kaa/ki muqarrar* (the man's appoint).

[36] The dynamic participant in the active agnate need not be animate; consider *in waaqeaat nee us ko baRaa sadmaa pãuhcaayaa* (these events caused him great sorrow), *aap ki mohabbat nee mujhee taqwiyat di hai* (your love has given me strength) and *is mashiin nee mjuhee baRaa aaraam diyaa* (this machine has given me a lot of rest, i.e. it has helped me greatly). These clauses may be seen as resembling the ones quoted in footnote 22 above; there appear to be restrictions so far as the verb+process-range of the type discussed in Sections 9.2 and 9.3 is concerned, the details of which are too complicated to go into here.

I shall refer to this type of process as 'complex process type'; *takliif deenaa* (to cause inconvenience), *Dãã Tnaa* (to scold) and *tassalli dilaanaa* (to console) signify such a process type. When the process of the clause is of this type and the verb selected belongs to the category pro-verb as in *takliif deenaa* and *tassalli dilaanaa* (to console), then the paradigms of such clauses will have, apart from the active and the non-agentive passive, two members corresponding to (61) and (62), where for the type (61) we may retain the term processive passive and for (62) may be used the term stative passive. Clauses such as *laRki ko Gam hai* (the girl has sorrow) (see Section 7.6), *laRki ko xushi hai* and *laRki ko tassalli hai* all represent type (62) and are related to the clause type mentioned above, to which they stand in a result relation. In their meaning such clauses are close to the qualified-quality possessive type, since the process range is usually realized by some abstract noun involving some perception. To this set may also be related clauses such as *laRki takliif mẽe hai* (the girl is in trouble), *laRki inteezaar mẽe hai* (the girl is waiting) and so on.

9.2. Not all clauses with a pro-verb and process-range have the complex process type. One set has the function contextually of verbalization (Halliday, 1968); verbs of this category are usually *rakhnaa* and *karnaa* (*to keep* and *to do*) and the process-range is potentially a verbalizing noun e.g. *ummiid*, *xwaahish* (desire), *tammannaa* (wish). The verbalized may be a rankshifted clause functioning as an immediate constituent of the matrix clause or of a nominal group. Examples of each are presented below:

    (63)   laRki ko ummiid thi kee woh kaamyaab ho gi.
            the girl had hoped that she would succeed.
    (64)   laRki ko apni kaamyaabi ki ummiid thi.
            the girl had the hope of her own success.

Both (63) and (64) may be shown to be related to either of the two clause types below:

    (63i)   kisi nee laRki ko ummiid dilaaii thi kee woh kaamyaab ho gi.
           somebody had given the girl to hope that she would succeed.
    (63ii) laRki nee ummiid ki thi kee woh kaamyaab ho gi.
           the girl had hoped that she would succeed.

The process of the first clause here may be seen as a complex transitive type, that of the second as intransitive; in both cases it is of the type verbalization. (63i) is not a benefactive clause except in that general sense in which all complex process type clauses may be seen to be benefactive. The clause type

(63) and (64) may be seen to be related to the relational attributive clause type; only two rules suffice for the mechanical conversion of one into the other, if one were interested in carrying out such mechanical conversion. These are (i) delete *ko*; (ii) for the process-range nominal substitute a lexically related adjective (i.e. instead of *ummiid* write *ummiid-waar*; instead of *xwaahish* write *xwaahishmand*; instead of *itmiinaan* write *mutmaiin*, and so on and so forth). When these rules are followed we have the following:

(63a)   laRki ummiidwaar thi kee woh kaamyaab ho gi.
         the girl was hopeful that she would succeed.
(63b)   laRki apni kaamyaabi ki ummiidwaar thi.
         the girl was hopeful of her own success.

where the matrix clause *laRki ummiidwaar thi* is essentially like *laRki xuub-surat thi*. (63a–b) may also be seen as closely related to the qualified-quality type of possession; this is not surprising since the latter is itself easily relatable to a relational attributive. The motives for assigning different labels to:

(65i)   kariim kee samajh hai.
         Kariim has maturity (mental).
(65ii)   kariim samajhdaar hai.
         Kariim is mature.
(66i)   kariim ko xwaahish hai…
         Kariim has the wish…
(66ii)   kariim xwaahishmand hai…
         Kariim is desirous…

are to my mind primarily syntactic; semantically the two members of each are very close to each other.

9.3. If one considers the clauses:

(62i)   kisi nee keraaee-daar ko takliif di.
         somebody caused the tenant inconvenience.
(63i)   kisi nee laRki ko ummiid dilaaii…
         somebody gave the girl to hope…
(63ii)   laRki nee ummiid ki…
         the girl did hope…

in one respect they are all like (51) *maĩ nee darwaazee ko dhakkaa diyaa*; the active nonpolar interrogative corresponding to all of these will have the pro-verb *karnaa* (i.e. some of it); moreover, the post-position *kee saath* would be attached to the affected participant *keraaee-daar* (62i) *laRki* (63i) and *darwaazaa* (51) in all such non-polar interrogative clauses. Thus we have *kisi nee keraaee-daar kee saath kyaa kiyaa* (what did somebody do to the tenant), *kisi nee laRki kee saath kyaa kiyaa* (what did somebody do to the girl). In (63ii) where *laRki* must be regarded as a dynamic participant the post-position *kee saath* cannot be attached to it. The non-polar interrogative would be *laRki nee kyaa kiyaa?* (what did the girl do?). The interesting point here is that if one postulates that the latter clause is a non-polar interrogative corresponding to (63ii), one is faced with the fact that the question would in all probability never get the response (63ii) except in a grammar, which fact may be attributed to the grammarian's great passion for symmetry.

If now we compare (63ii) with:

(67)   baccõ nee kamree mẽe baRaa shor kiyaa.
          the children made a lot of noise in the room.

we find that (67) may stand as a probable response to a question:

(67i)   baccõ nee kamree mẽe kyaa kiyaa?
          what did the children do in the room?

just as *laRki nee kyaa kiyaa* may get the response:

(68)   laRki nee eek kurtaa siyaa.
          the girl sewed a shirt.
(69)   laRki nee eek meez banaaii.
          the girl made a table.

One of the things that is in common to both the last-mentioned clauses here is that the process may be seen as one of creation, where the affected participant may more delicately be labelled 'effectum' (Fillmore, 1968). If the process is creative, the effectum may not be thematized in the following manner:

(68i)   *jo laRki nee siyaa woh *kurtaa* thaa.
          what the girl sewed was a shirt.
(69i)   *jo laRki nee banaaii woh *meez* thi.
          what the girl made was a table.

(67) is similar to (68) and (69), the following clause being unacceptable.

(67ii)   *jo baccõ nee kiyaa woh *shor* thaa.
          what the children made was a noise.

Since (68) and (69) are transitive clauses, it may be thought that (67) too is a transitive clause, with *shor* functioning as effectum. But now consider:

(68ii)   jo kurtaa laRki nee siyaa woh yeh waalaa thaa.
          the shirt that the girl sewed was this one.

(69ii)   jo meez laRki nee banaaii woh yeh waali thi.
          the table that the girl made was this one.

But we cannot say *jo shor baccõ nee kiyaa woh yeh waalaa thaa (the noise that the children made was this one). It might be rightly thought that since shor is not a count noun it cannot be replaced by waalaa, but the clause *jo shor baccõ nee kiyaa woh yeh thaa (the noise that the children made was this) is also ungrammatical. The ungrammaticality of the clause does not stem, it would appear, from the fact that the effectum shor is abstract. The clause jo baat laRki nee kahi woh yeh thi (the comment that the girl made was this) is grammatical; equally it is possible to say jo raaee laRki nee di woh yeh thi (the opinion that the girl gave (i.e. expressed) was this). One of the differences between shor and baat/raaee is that while the former is a mass noun, the latter two are count ones; they are both abstract. However ummiid and takliif are like baat and raaee; both are abstract count nouns. We may, however, not say:

(70)   *jo ummiid laRki nee ki woh yeh thi.
          the hope that the girl did was this.
(71)   *jo takliifẽẽ kisi nee keraaee-daar ko dĩ woh yeh thĩ.
          the inconveniences that somebody caused the tenant were these.

It would appear that shor is at once like kurtaa and meez in (68) and like ummiid and takliif in (62i) and (63ii); it functions as process-range hence it cannot be thematized like baat or kurtaa but behaves like ummiid and takliif. Both (62) and (63ii) are related to a transitive with complex process such as:

(62i)   kisi nee keraaeedaar ko takliif di.
(63i)   kisi nee laRki ko ummiid dilaaii.

but if the process-range is such that it may be described as the 'creative' one then whether a complex process clause corresponding to it exists or not, it is possible to have a stative passive of the type exemplified by (67). Thus while we have:

(72)   kisi nee bacci see rozaa rakhwaayaa.
          somebody caused the girl to keep fast (i.e. to fast).
(72i)   bacci nee rozaa rakkhaa.
          the girl kept fast (i.e. fasted).

There is no such clause as rozaa hai (fast is = there was a fast). But clauses such as shor thaa (there was a noise), balwaa thaa (there was a riot), miilaad thaa (there was a religious gathering) are all possible. In such passives the dynamic participant of the corresponding active clause need not appear and since there is no affected participant (unless *shor* is regarded as one, the arguments against which have been provided above), the nucleus of the clause may be considered to be composed of process-range + *honaa* (the pro-verb). Such clauses, however, always seem to imply a locative. So *baRaa shor thaa* (there was a lot of noise) implies *there was a lot of noise somewhere* and *miilaad thaa* implies *kahĩ miilaad thaa* (there was a religious gathering somewhere) and so on.

9.4. In general the meaning of *honaa* associated with the processive passive of the type discussed in this section such as *keraaeedaar ko takliif hui* (the tenant was faced with a lot of inconvenience), *laRki ko ummiid hui* (the girl came to have the hope), and *shor huaa* (noise took place) may be stated as 'some process took place and is stated as if it took place of its own accord without intervention from any participant', the meaning of the stative passive such as *keraaeedaar ko takliif thi, laRki ko ummiid thi* and *baRaa shor thaa* may be stated as 'the predication of the existence of whatever the process-range signifies such that the latter is always in relation to some participant or circumstance'.

No doubt the meanings offered here for *honaa* are highly generalized, but it is to be doubted if the meaning derived from the syntactic categories is ever of very specific nature, except in the case of structure markers.

10.0. The clause types with the verb *honaa* discussed in this article (which incidentally do not exhaust all possible uses) are as follows:

(73)	laRki xuubsurat hai.	(cf. examples (1) and (16)–(16c))
(74)	kamraa saaf hai.	(cf. examples (18)–(18f))
(75)	kamraa saaf huaa.	(cf. examples (18)–(18f))
(76)	kariim sadar hai.	(cf. examples (18)–(18f))
(77)	kariim sadar huaa.	(cf. examples (18)–(18f))
(78)	caaval tulee huee haĩ.	(cf. example (17))
(79)	kariim kee eek bhaaii hai.	(cf. example (39))
(80)	kariim kee baRi daulat hai.	(cf. example (40))
(81)	kariim kee baRi daulat hui.	(cf. example (40))
(82)	kariim kee do ãakhẽe haĩ.	(cf. example (41))
(83)	kariim kee aql hai.	(cf. example (42))
(84)	is kamree mẽe do kursiyãa haĩ.	(cf. example (43))
(85)	is kapRee mẽe kuch aib hai.	(cf. example (44))
(86)	baks kamree mẽe hai.	(cf. example (31))
(87)	xudaa hai.	(cf. example (31))
(88)	kariim hai.	(cf. example (31))

(89)	aap kee biiwi baccee kahãã hai.	(cf. example (57))
(90)	keraaeedaar ko takliif thi.	(cf. example (62))
(91)	keraaeedaar ko takliif hui.	(cf. example (61))
(92)	laRki ko ummiid thi.	(cf. example (63))
(93)	LaRki ko ummiid hui.	(cf. example (63))
(94)	shor huaa.	(cf. example (67))
(95)	shor thaa.	(cf. example (67))

Wherever these clauses are related to any paradigm,[37] it would appear that either we would have to recognize two active members in the same paradigm or we would have to treat them as some form of passive.[38] Sub-groups of these 23 clauses may be made according to which feature is under consideration; thus all uses of *honaa* for which the past tense is realized by the form *huaa/hui* have the feature processive passive (i.e. this is the label used in this article); these stand in a result relation to their active agnate; clauses (73)–(75), (83), (85), (90), (92) may be seen as forming one sub-group on the ground that they could be regarded as the source for the derivation of the attribute-attribuand relation at the nominal group rank. Within this, (83), (85), (90), and (92) may be seen as closely related to each other since in some sense the possession of an attribute is implied. To go on would be tedious. Perhaps it would be appropriate to end with the Urdu sentence *jo hai so hai* (whatever is there is there) which cannot be interpreted as *whatever exists exists.*

APPENDIX

1. The word-class membership of *honaa* was a subject of controversy for Urdu grammarians as indicated incidentally by the quotation from Fateh Mohammad Khaan in Section 3.4 of this paper. In fact, it would be more

---

[37] That implicational relationship is in some sense reflected in syntactic relationship of items may not be questioned. There are, however, no criteria, to my knowledge, for regarding one set of implicational relations as more relevant than another. The effort to relate a clause to a given clause paradigm, it would appear, has to be based not only on the 'presence' of a particular type of implicational relation but (and, perhaps primarily), because some of the syntactic characteristics are shared by the clause under focus with the paradigm to which it is being related. I have not gone into details regarding this aspect at every point but even the surface structure of the items which I have shown to be related to each other will display the kind of syntactic similarities which may be established.

[38] This finding would agree with Lyons' (1968) statement that the uses of *be* copula are 'stative'. Instead of dynamic vs. stative process as a two term opposition I have maintained here that we have a move from dynamic to stative; the active and/or causative of any paradigm is the maximally dynamic member while its stative passive is the maximally passive member, with the result that the *honaa* associated with the processive passive can at once be related to the dynamic and the stative types.

accurate to say that the controversy centred round the items *hai, thaa, ho* (is, was, be) etc. rather than the form *honaa* itself. This state of affairs arose directly from the crucial definition offered for the primary word-classes. According to traditional Urdu grammars, the words of the language could be exhaustively classified into three primary categories: particle, noun, and verb.

A particle, to quote Fateh Mohammad Khaan, is that "which conveys no definite meaning by itself. Particles are used for establishing relations between other words. You can understand nothing [of, R.H.] what the speaker wants to say from *see* (from/by/with/to), *meẽ* (in/of)...", etc., until they are used in company with some other words between which they establish some relation (*Misbaah-ul-Qawaaid*; Part I, p. 20). On the other hand both noun and verb are classes of words, any one member of which may even in isolation signify something definite. "The difference between noun and verb is only this: the former cannot signify time, whereas the latter *must* signify some discrete time. Thus when we say *aanaa* (to come), in this word there is no definite indication of time and *that is why it is a noun*. But when we say *aayaa* (came), *aataa hai* (comes) or *aaee gaa* (come will = will come), then time is definitely and compulsorily indicated" (*ibid.*). Elsewhere Fateh Mohammad Khaan is careful to emphasize that the signifying of time is not 'accidental' to the members of the word-class verb; every member of this class, he maintains, should be potentially capable of signifying any of the three points on the time scale, namely past, present and future. Thus a noun such as *kal* (the day adjacent to today, i.e. either *tomorrow* or *yesterday*) is not a verb because it has no potentiality of signifying present, and in any given instance can signify either past or future.

2. It followed from this definition of noun and verb that the item *honaa* itself was universally regarded as belonging to a specific sub-class of noun labelled *ism-ee-masdar* (noun-of-infinitive; *masdar* literally means 'that which constitutes the source' so that *ism-ee-masdar* is that sub-class of noun which functions as the source for verb). On the other hand, while the grammarians were agreed that the forms *thaa* and *ho* (*gaa*) (*was* and (*will*) *be*) belonged to the verb class, they disagreed regarding the class-membership of *hai* (is), some of them maintaining that all derived forms of *honaa* belonged to the verb class, while others maintaining that all derived forms except *hai* (is) belonged to verb class; *hai* in their opinion was a particle (with the function of connecting two words). As pointed out by Fateh Mohammad Khaan (see quotation in Section 3.4 of this paper) the latter view was the result of making Urdu language fit the descriptive categories set up for the analysis of Arabic. The Arabic clause *zaidun aalimun* (Zaid learned = Zaid is learned) could be called an 'unmarked' clause following Lyons' suggestion (Lyons, 1968); that is to say, it is a clause which has an unmarked selection of tense, aspect and mood. Like some other languages of the world, the unmarked relational clause in Arabic 'does not have a verb': there is no segment in the clause such that it may be said to belong to the word-class verb. Those Urdu grammarians who followed the Arabic tradition therefore refused to treat *hai* in such unmarked Urdu clauses as a verb word, preferring to label it a connector. The controversy, however did not last long; the very definition of the verb making it impossible to allow this analysis of *hai* (is). Once *hai* (is) was accepted as belonging to the word-class verb, it 'became' a fact that unlike Arabic, all relational clauses in Urdu must have a verb. The verb may be selected overtly or covertly.

3. It would be a mistake to think that Fateh Mohammad Khaan's concern with overt and covert selection of the verb is a concern with superficial matters, without any implications for the description of the language. The position taken by him may be reformulated as follows: in Urdu and Persian all relational clauses 'must have' a verb; that is to say, systemically the feature relational is 'present' and is realized partially by the selection of a suitable item from the word-class 'verb'. An item realizing a given feature may not be present in substance within the string under focus, but if the deep grammar of a language is related to its semantics, the presence of the given systemic feature and hence of the item realizing it has to be postulated. If in answer to the question (i) *who is ill?* we have a clause such as (ii) *my brother's daughter*, the latter cannot be regarded as a clause without attribute and verb except in the most superficial sense. Thus both clauses (i) and (ii) 'have' a verb, the former has it overtly, the latter covertly.

These observations are so patently obvious and so widely accepted that one seldom bothers to spell them out. However, the implications of the feature of ellipsis or 'deletion' are not equally patently obvious. It is suggested here that the environments in which ellipsis of a particular type is permissible can be stated by reference to the interrelations existing in the system network of a given language; these too form 'rules' in the integral description of the language although they may not be as obvious as the rules which prohibit a clause such as *my brother's daughter ill laughed. Despite the fact that there is a lot in common in the description of the Arabic clause *zaidun aalimun* (Zaid (is) learned) and the Urdu one *zaid aalim* (Zaid learned) it is not a fact that both these clauses have deletion; or if we say that both of them have deletion we must mean two different things by the word 'deletion'. The view taken here is that the Arabic clause has no deletion; in accordance, mark that there is no obligation for the Arabic clause to be anaphorically related to any preceding language; this clause can constitute a text on its own. The speaker of Arabic does not have a set of rules which enumerate the

environment in which alone this so-called 'deleted version' may be grammatical for the simple reason that there is no real contrast of deletion vs.
non-deletion here. In the case of *zaid aalim*, we have predicate-ellipsis and it
is obligatory for this clause to be anaphorically or cataphorically related to
some specifiable clause forming part of the larger text in which this elliptical
clause occurs; unlike the Arabic clause it may not constitute a text on its own.
The speaker of Urdu has a set of rules which enumerate the environment in
which a relational predicate-elliptical clause will be regarded as both grammatical and appropriate and this environment is not identical with that in
which the non-elliptical version would be appropriate. There is no doubt
that these rules have to be built into a grammar which rises above the
description of the simple sentence. If these rules are regarded as belonging
to the sphere of performance and not of competence, I can only say that
I know of no instance of performance which is independent of competence
except the uninteresting cases of memory lapse, etc.

4. It has been suggested by Lyons (1968) that the verb *be* may not be
regarded as an element in the deep grammar of some languages, since its
'principal function' is to realize certain particular syntactic options. I would
suggest that no individual lexical item of a given language may be regarded
as an element in the deep grammar of that language, unless grammar is to be
interpreted as "the total description of the language including syntax, lexis
phonology and phonetics". It appears to me that an individual lexical item is
related to the deep grammar only by virtue of its realizational potentialities
with reference to some syntactic option(s). In this respect *be* is not different
from *eat* or *drink*. There is however a significant difference between *be* and
eat or *drink*. If I may confine myself to Urdu and English alone, this difference
may be stated as follows. At a particular degree of delicacy in the syntactic
description of these languages, we arrive at a verb class which has only one
member in it, namely, *be*. On the other hand, no matter how delicate a
syntactic description of these languages is made, we shall never arrive at a
verb class such that its only member is *eat* but not *drink*; that is to say,
unless we introduce some ad hoc or non-syntactic grounds for sub-classifica-
tion, these two verbs will appear as members of the same most delicate verb
class. Since the sub-categorization of a class is based upon the potentiality
of the said sub-category to realize a set of syntactic options uniquely, it
follows that some component(s) of the meaning of all items in a given sub-
category is 'the same'. Whenever we have an item which forms a unique
member class (i.e. the class contains no item but this one), the meaning of
the item may be stated exhaustively by reference to the set of systemic options
which the item is capable of realizing; in other words, there is no 'lexical
residue' for which one must account. The reason for this is quite obvious:

since the category consists of only one member and is itself based upon a set of systemic options, the question of lexical contrast does not exist as it does in the case of *eat* or *drink*. The meaning of the item can be stated solely by reference to the semantics of the set of systemic options relevant to the sub-category. It could therefore be cogently argued that the item *be*, like *a*, *the*, *this*, *that*, etc., which all form unique member classes at the most delicate stage of grammatical description, should not be treated as elements in the *deep lexis* of these languages and that they are far more grammatical than are items such as *eat*, *two*, *boy*, *girl*, etc. This position is implicit in Halliday (1966) and Sinclair (1966).

5. It is significant that neither those Urdu grammarians who treated *hai* as a connecting particle nor those who treated it as a verb along with *thaa* etc. ever questioned the fact that there is need to recognize at least one complete verbal paradigm derived from *honaa* which belonged to that sub-class of verb known as *feel-ee-imdaadi* (auxiliary verb). Thus arose the curious situation that while there was disagreement regarding the class membership of *haĩ* in *yeh laRkiyãã sharmiili haĩ* (these girls are shy), no such problem arose regarding the description of *haĩ* in *laRkiyãã sharmiili hoti haĩ* (girls are (usually) shy) where it was unanimously treated as an auxiliary.

Recently it has been suggested that in many languages all occurrences of the verb *be* may be regarded as some kind of auxiliary. To quote Lyons (1966) again "there appears no reason to regard S (the 'copula') as a lexical class in English (or in the Indo-European languages generally). The 'verb *to be*' in sentences of the kind we are considering [the sentences under consideration are *Mary is beautiful* and *Mary is a child*, R.H.]... may be regarded as a 'dummy carrier' of tense, mood, aspect, and number in 'surface' structure (roughly comparable with the '*do*-auxiliary' in negative, interrogative and emphatic sentences...)". Lyons' 'dummy carrier' may be seen as in some sense corresponding to "an item representing a unique member class, arrived at by reference to the syntactic options it may realize". It is true, by definition, that all such items, at the most delicate stage of the description of the language are shown as belonging to a class which contains no items that may contrast with it lexically. Thus although in the first instance we may think of *a* and *the* as belonging to the same word class as other modifiers such as *frequent*, *normal* and *usual*, there comes a stage at which the former two represent two separate delicate sub-classes of the class 'modifier'. On this analogy *be* should be separated from the other lexical verbs but whether this implies that therefore it should be treated as an auxiliary seems to me to be a separate question. At least in Urdu, it is not true that *honaa* alone is a verb which represents a unique member set; in one of its senses (i.e. the possessive) the item *rakhnaa* would also constitute such a set and it would indeed pose many problems to think of *rakhnaa* in this sense as an auxiliary on the ground that its function is simply to realize certain syntactic options. Further, so far as Urdu is concerned, the treatment of all verbs derived from *honaa* as auxiliary will pose a problem: if the fully grammatical copula *be* is regarded as an auxiliary, it would still have to be differentiated from that *be* which has traditionally been regarded as auxiliary since the syntactic potentialities of these two *be* would not be identical. The *be* copula-auxiliary will be the only auxiliary in the language that will share some potentialities of the lexical verbs of the language. Consider that while it is possible to say *laRkaa qaabil thaa aur laRki hasiin* (the boy was capable and the girl beautiful), the sentence **laRkaa khaanaa khaataa thaa aur laRki paani piiti* (the boy was eating the food and the girl drinking water) is ungrammatical. The copula-*be* may be 'deleted' in any kind of branching but the auxiliary-*be* can be deleted only in certain very restricted environments. Again the clause *thee hi kahãa itnee log* (there *were*n't many people) is grammatical but the clause **thee hi kahãa log caltee* (people *did*n't (usually) walk) is ungrammatical; it is possible to use the copula-*be* 'thematically' as the first of the last two examples shows; it is not possible to use just the auxiliary-*be* in this manner; thus it is ungrammatical to say **thee hi kahãa itnee log hotee* (there *were*n't (usually) many people). These examples show some of the differences between the auxiliary and the copula-*be*. Consider now the sentences *laRkaa qaabil thaa aur laRki hasiin* (the boy was capable and the girl beautiful) and *laRkee nee caaee pi aur laRki nee kaafi* (the boy drank tea and the girl coffee); the conditions under which the lexical verb may be deleted are the same whether the verb is copula-*be* or *piinaa* (drink). Similarly compare *thee hi kahãa itnee log* (there *were*n't many people) and *khaayaa hi kahãa us nee khaanaa* (he *did*n't eat any food); again the rules regarding the thematization of the verbal group remain the same irrespective of whether the lexical element of the verbal group is realized by a (fully) lexical verb like *khaanaa* (to eat) or by a fully grammatical one like *honaa*. These appear to me to be strong reasons for carefully examining the suggestion that all occurrences of *be* should be regarded as some kind of auxiliary; at least so far as Urdu is concerned this solution does not seem to me to carry much weight. Often characteristics are cited which are supposedly specific to the copula *be* and not shared by other 'lexical' verbs. One such characteristic is that the continuous tense would seem to be not permissible with copula *be*, clauses such as *she is/was being beautiful* being odd. This observation will apply equally to a large number of relational verbs as well as to some superventive ones, since clauses such as *the boy is/was coming across a man, the girl is/was hearing a shriek, I am/was owning a house* are all odd. Even more interesting is the case of *I am finding the girl attractive*, where it is very much open to question whether the verbal group *am finding* is to be interpreted semantically as "process being carried out at the moment of speaking".

Sociological Research Unit,
University of London Institute of Education

BIBLIOGRAPHY

Abercrombie, David: 1967, *Elements of General Phonetics*, Edinburgh U.P.

Allen, W. Sidney: 1964, 'Transitivity and Possession', *Language* **40**, 337–43.

Fillmore, Charles J.: 1968, 'The Case for Case', in *Universals of Linguistic Theory* (ed. by Bach and Harms), Holt, Rinehart and Winston, New York, N.Y.

Halliday, M. A. K.: 1966, 'Lexis as a Linguistic Level', in *In Memory of J. R. Firth* (ed. by Bazell, Catford, Halliday, and Robins), Longmans, London.

Halliday, M. A. K.: 1967a, *Intonation and Grammar in British English*, Mouton, The Hague.

Halliday, M. A. K.: 1967b, 'Notes on Transitivity and Theme in English, 1', *JL* **3**, 1.

Halliday, M. A. K.: 1967c, 'Notes on Transitivity and Theme in English, 2', *JL* **3**, 2.

Halliday, M. A. K.: 1968, 'Notes on Transitivity and Theme in English, 3', *JL* **4**, 2.

Harter, Choudhry and Budhraj: 1960, *Hindi Basic Course*, Reprint, Center for Applied Linguistics, Washington.

Haq, Maulvi Abdul: *Qawaaid-ee-Urdu*, Taj Publishing House, Delhi.

Hasan, Ruqaiya: 1968, *Grammatical Cohesion in Spoken and Written English*, Part 1 (Programme in Linguistics and English Teaching, Paper 7), Longmans, London.

Huddleston, R. D., Hudson, R., Winter, E. O. and Henrici, A.: 1968, *Sentence and Clause in Scientific English*, University College London, Communication Research Centre.

Kachru, Yamuna: 1966, *An Introduction to Hindi Syntax*, University of Illinois, Urbana, Ill.

Kachru, Yamuna: 1968, 'The Copula in Hindi', in *The Verb 'Be' and Its Synonyms* (ed. by John W. M. Verhaar), *FL*, Supplementary Series, Vol. 6.

Lyons, John: 1966, 'Towards a 'Notional' Theory of 'Parts of Speech'', *JL* **2**, 2.

Lyons, John: 1967, 'A Note on Possessive, Existential and Locative Sentences', *FL* **3**.

Lyons, John: 1968, *Introduction to Theoretical Linguistics*, Cambridge University Press, Cambridge, England.

Mohammad Khaan, Maulvi Fateh: 1945, *Misbaah-ul-Qawaaid*, Parts I, II. Barqi Press, Rampur.

Sinclair, J. McH.: 1966, 'Beginning the Study of Lexis', in *In Memory of J. R. Firth* (ed. by Bazell, Catford, Halliday, and Robins), Longmans, London.

R. B. LEES

THE TURKISH COPULA

Many linguistic problems have been raised by copula constructions in English and other languages. English *be* is very irregular and is used in two auxiliary constructions, an existential construction with *there*, and two cleft-sentence constructions; it may be a verb, a particle, or a transformational insert with no semantic interpretation; and it may be connected with constructions in *have*, the genitive, and others.

In Hebrew, too, there are many unanswered questions revolving about the copula: are there verbless sentences in the present tense or deleted copulas; what are the existential particles *yeš* and *ʾein* which appear only in present tense; and what are the pronoun-like forms in *h-* with non-pronoun-like 4-way agreement just like so-called present-tense verb forms (or participles)?

In Turkish there are again many interesting questions one can raise about copular constructions and perhaps some surprising conclusions one may have to accept after study. The copula is suppletive and complemented by forms of the verb *ol-* 'become', as in other languages; again there seem to be verbless sentences in present tense; adjective + personal suffix seems to be parallel to verb + tense + personal; there are 3 different negative forms – verbal, existential, and copula; there are some ambiguities in meaning between 'be' and 'become', but not everywhere; and there are complex verb-phrases containing forms of both *ol-* and the copula.

To understand some of these features of Turkish syntax we shall first have to become familiar with some simple sentence components.

Predicate-adjective sentences in present tense contain only a personal suffix which agrees with the subject NP:

(1)   Sen zengin-sin.[1]
        thou rich   personal
        'You're rich.'

In the negative a particle intervenes between the predicate and the personal suffix:

(2)   Sen zengin değil-sin.
                    not
        'You're not rich.'

---

[1] Hyphens connect morphemes within the same word.

In the interrogative a different particle intervenes:

(3)   Sen zengin mi-sin?
        'Are you rich?'

Finally, the two may be combined:

(4)   Sen zengin degil mi-sin?
        'Aren't you rich?'

When such a sentence is in another tense, such as the Quotative past, a third morpheme intervenes in addition to the tense-suffix; it is often enclitic, in isolation from the preceding word it has the form *i-*, and after a vowel is enclitically *-y-*:

(5)   Sen zengin i-miş-sin.
        'You're said to be rich.'

We call the particle *i-* the *Copula*. In the negative and the interrogative again *değil* and *mi* intervene:

(6)   Sen zengin değil i-miş-sin.
        'You're said not to be rich.'
(7)   Sen zengin mi-y-miş-sin?
        'Are you said to be rich?'

In the ordinary past tense in *-di* there are a few differences characteristic of this tense (and, in part, of one other 'tense', the conditional in *-se*), namely, the personal endings are reduced to a secondary form and another irregularity noted below:

(8)   Sen zengin i-di-n.
        'You were rich.'
(9)   Sen zengin degil i-di-n.
        'You weren't rich.'
(10)   Sen zengin mi-y-di-n?
        'Were you rich?'

When the tense is future, the verb *ol-* must appear, apparently in place of the copula:

(11)   Sen zengin ol-acak-sın.[2]
                     future
        'You'll be rich.'   OR   'You'll become rich.'

[2] The vowels of suffixes, subject to the rules of vowel-harmony, alternate either among i/ı/u/ü if high, or between e/a if low. There may also be other alternations in vowels or consonants. None of these assimilations is relevant to the topic of this paper.

and the sentence is ambiguous. Moreover, in the negative the verb-stem itself is rendered negative with the suffix -*me*, implying that the particle *değil* is used only with the copula itself:

(12)   Sen zengin ol-mı-yacak-sın.
        'You won't be rich.'   OR   'You won't become rich.'

The interrogative seems to be regular:

(13)   Sen zengin ol-acak mı-sın?
        'Will you be rich?'   OR   'Will you become rich?'

Next, tenses may be combined; we cite here only the case of the Future plus Past. The Future is a participle from *ol-*, the Past is on the copula:

(14)   Sen zengin ol-acak i-di-n.
        'You were to be rich.'   OR   'You were to become rich.'

The negative uses a negative verb-stem in the participle:

(15)   Sen zengin ol-mı-yacak i-di-n.
        'You weren't to be rich.'   OR   'You weren't to become rich.'

Finally, we consider parallel cases of sentences containing verbs with object-complement, here in the Momentary present tense:

(16)   Sen paked-i gönder-iyor-sun.
              package send   momentary
        'You're sending the package.'
(17)   Sen paked-i gönder-mi-yor-sun.
        'You're not sending the package.'
(18)   Sen paked-i gönder-iyor mu-sun?
        'Are you sending the package?'

In form they are just like the predicate-adjective sentences in *ol-*. However, in verbal sentences (including those in *ol-*, of course) in the Past tense, the interrogative particle cannot intervene between the tense-morpheme and the personal suffix in its secondary form:

(19)   Sen paked-i gönder-di-n.
        'You sent the package.'
(20)   Sen paked-i gönder-di-n mi?
        'Did you send the package?'

Thus, we see that the copula is a defective stem *i-* and its paradigm is filled out by the verb *ol-* 'become'. Moreover, the negative differs – a particle *değil* is inserted for the copula type, but for the verbal type an infix -*me*- is inserted.

Now, the copula *i*- has only the following 4 forms:[3]

(21)   Zengin i-di-n.   'You were rich.'   (Past)
        Zengin i-miş-sin.   'You're said to be rich.'   (Quotative)
        Zengin i-se-n,...   'If you're rich, ...'   (Conditional)
        Zengin i-ken, ...   'While being rich, ...'   (Gerund)

The interrogative shows an affix -*mi*- before the copula, but it shows an irregularity with the past-tense -*di*, namely, the latter (along with the conditional tense -*se*) takes secondary, reduced forms of the personal suffixes, and the interrogative *follows* tenses plus secondary personal on participles (though not on the copula).

If we construe (1) Adjective+copula to be parallel in form to a verb-phrase, and (2) present-tense Adj+*i*- to be parallel to momentary- and aorist-tense verb phrase (these present tenses are semantically neutralized in the copula), and (3) simplex forms to be parallel to complex forms, like

(22)   Sen paked-i gönder-miş ol-acak ol-sa-y-dı-n, ...
        'If it were the case that you will have sent the package, ...'

then we may assume a deleted present-tense copula in the form of (1) and (16) above, and we may also assume that the *ol*- of (11) is a replacement for *i*- (since *i*- has no future-tense form).

Thus, it appears that verbal sentences are just participles plus the copula. We may then go on to construe these as parallel to ordinary copula sentences of the form NP+NP+Cop, as in:

(23)   Sen çiftçi-sin.
        'You're a farmer.'

This strange conclusion is not entirely new; some grammarians in the past have spoken of the nominal character of Turkish verb-phrases, but the evidence has never been clearly stated or examined. There are several independent observations on the structure of Turkish sentences which corroborate the conclusion:

(1) There is a somewhat rarer, though grammatically impeccable construction which combines a participle with the negative copula, as in:

(24)   Sen paked-i gönder-ecek değil-sin.
        'They'll never catch yóu sending that package!'

---

[3] Among the forms which the copula cannot take are the Momentary -*iyor*, Aorist -*er*, Future -*yecek*, Necessitative -*meli*, and Optative -*ye* tenses, verbal nouns, gerunds, infinitive, etc.

which contrasts with the regular negative future

(25)   Sen paked-i gönder-mi-yecek-sin.
         'You won't send the package.'

The included participle can even itself be negative, as in

(26)   Sen paked-i gönder-mi-yecek değil-sin.
         'You're not the kind who wouldn't send the package!'

This construction lends much weight to the presumption that the ordinary verbal sentence in *gönder-ecek-sin* 'You'll send it', is only the surface form of an underlying *gönder + yecek + i + Tns + sin*. The identity of the underlying Tns morpheme must be reconstructed from the contrasts between the form *gönder-ecek-sin* and the other possible copula forms *gönder-ecek-ti-n* = = *gönder-ecek i-di-n* 'You were to send it' (since all the copula forms are normally pronounced enclitically), *gönder-ecek-miş-sin* 'They say you're going to send it', *gönder-ecek-se-n* 'If you're going to send it, ...', and *gönder-ecek-ken* 'While (you) send it later, ...' (non-finite gerund without personal suffix). The tense appears to be non-past, non-conditional, and we can say that it is the 'architense' Present, a neutralization between aorist and momentary.

(2) All forms of the verb-phrase with *ol-* are semantically ambiguous between the two meanings 'be' and 'become' except those in tenses which the copula *i-* can take, in which cases they are interpreted only as 'become'. We can capture this nicely by allowing some (so-called copular or equational) verbs, in particular the verb *ol-* itself, to take as complement an adjective-phrase. We then interpret underlying *ol-* as 'become' and the *ol-* which substitutes for the copula in its forbidden tenses and non-finite verbals as 'be'.

(3) In non-finite embedded sentences, as for example relative clauses inside of noun-phrases, a form of *ol-* regularly appears with either of two forms: a verbal noun in *-yen* for present tense when the subject of the relative clause is coreferent to the head noun of the dominating noun-phrase; and a verbal noun in *-dik* for present or past tenses, when the subject of the relative clause is not the pivot noun. Thus, we have

(27)   Adam paked-i gönder-iyor.
         'The man is sending the package.'
         paked-i gönder-en adam...
         'The man who's sending the package...'
         Adam-ın gönder-dig-i paket...
         'The package which the man $\begin{Bmatrix} \text{is sending} \\ \text{sent} \end{Bmatrix}$ ...'

[The -*i* suffix on *paket* is for definite verbal objects; the -*ın* on *adam* is the genitive, and the associated -*i* suffix on *gönderdik* is the 3rd-pers. possessed.]

If now the underlying embedded sentence is in any other tense, such as the Necessitative in -*meli*, although there is no overt copula in the underlying sentence, the derived relative clause is construed with the verbal-noun form of *ol*-:

(28)   Adam paked-i gönder-meli.
        'The man has to send the package.'
        Paked-i gönder-meli ol-an adam...[4]
        'The man who has to send the package...'
        Adam-ın gönder-meli ol-duğ-u paket...
        'The package which the man has to send...'

In complex verb-phrases like those of (14) and (22) we appear to have participles recursively embedded within copular verb-phrases, all intermediate copulas going to forms of *ol*-. The participialized verb-phrase is itself a noun-phrase, a predicate of the copula. Thus, a complex predicate-phrase like

(22)   Sen paked-i gönder-miş ol-acak ol-sa-y-dı-n, ...
        'If it were the case that you will have sent the package, ...'

is actually understood something like

     'If you were someone who might be someone who will be someone who sent the package...'

Incidentally, despite the irregularities of the past-tense forms, we may still treat cases of -*di* exactly like other participles since there are actually cases of complex predicate-phrases with intermediate forms in -*di*, as e.g.,

(29)   Sen paked-i gönder-di-y-di-n.
        'You had already long since sent the package.'

Also cases in conditional-tense -*se* are all normally final in the sequence since they are non-main-clause embeddings; but the counterfactual conditional is irregularly constructed in Turkish with the conditional inside of the past, -*se*+*i*+*di*-, as

(30)   Sen paked-i gönder-di-y-se-n, ...
        'If you sent the package, ... (then it must be there)' (factual conditional)
        Sen paked-i gönder-se-y-di-n, ...
        'If you sent the package, ... (it would be there, but you didn't)' (counterfactual)

and the past-tense counterfactual conditional has a past participle inside of the conditional:

(31)   Sen paked-i gönder-miş ol-sa-y-dı-n, ...
        'If you had sent the package, ...'

---

[4] Exactly parallel in form to:
        Çiftçi ol-an adam ...
        'The man who is a farmer ...,'
again supporting the view that *pakedi gönder-meli* is a participal noun-phrase.

Since simple rules to express all these regularities would permit the free choice of any tenses on indefinitely many intervening participles as well as on the final copula, there will be a number of semantically uninterpreted combinations of tenses and infinitely many embeddings with no uses. There is no reason to treat these as syntactic gaps rather than semantic.

The copula sentences we hypothesize are now parallel to the following more familiar types of copula sentences:

(32)	NP+NP+Cop	Sen çavuş-sun.	'You're a sergeant.'
		Sen çavuş-tu-n.	'You were a sergeant.'
	NP+AP+Cop	Sen genç-sin.	'You're young.'
		Sen genç-ti-n.	'You were young.'
	NP+Loc+COP	Sen Fransa-da-sın.	'You're in France.'
		Sen Fransa-da-y-dı-n.	'You were in France.'

In the latter type of copula sentence the subject NP must in general be definite before the locative nominal. When it is indefinite, as in many languages there is a special form for the sentence, in Turkish an existential construction:

(33) * Bir paket masa-da.
 Masa-da bir paket var.
 'There's a package on the table.'
 Masa-da (hiç)bir paket yok.
 'There's no package on the table.'
 Masa-da bir paket var-dı.
 'There was a package on the table.'
 Masa-da (hiç)bir paket yok-tu.
 'There wasn't any package on the table.'

Here the copula predicate contains an existential particle *var*, and in the negative this is replaced by another morpheme *yok*. However, in tenses or non-finite forms which the copula itself does not otherwise have *ol-* replaces the copula and the existential particles are deleted:

(34) Masa-da bir paket ol-acak.
 'There'll be a package on the table.'

This existential construction corresponds in other languages to

	Turkish	English	German	French	Russian	Hebrew
copula	i-	be	sein	être	byt,	(hovei) l'hiyot
exist.	var i-	there be	es geben	il y avoir	yest,	yeš

Now, in Turkish the existential copula sentence is also used for another construction, the possessive:

(35) Sen-in   paked-in   var.
       genitive   possessed
'You have a package.'
Sen-in paked-in var-dı.
'You had a package.'
Sen-in paked-in ol-acak.
'You'll have a package.'

One could take the possessor in the genitive case to be subject and the possessed NP to be the copula predicate, parallel to the genitivization of the subject of certain nominalizations, in Turkish as well as in English. And thus we have another confirmation of our claim that Turkish sentences are all copular (as distinguished from, say, the verbal trend in Indo-European):

	Turkish	English	German	French	Russian
possession	NP$_1$-in NP$_2$-si var	NP$_1$ have NP$_2$	NP$_1$ haben NP$_2$	NP$_1$ avoir NP$_2$	NP$_1$ imet, NP$_2$

However, in Hebrew the construction is much more like the Turkish, using the dative case in place of the genitive: le-NP$_1$ yeš NP$_2$. (In all the above cases the first NP is the possessor.)

For these existential sentence types in Turkish we can then assume that there is a rule to front the Locative NP and another to genitivize the possessor NP (and simultaneously add the possessed suffix on the following NP required with all genitives in Turkish).

Finally, as in other languages, there is also a third subtype of existential sentence with just one NP, as in

       İn-   ecek   var mı?
       descend   future ppl.
       'Is there anyone who wishes to get off (at the next station)?' (conductor in bus)

If the deictic element semantically implied in such sentences (e.g., 'Does anyone want to get off (from *this* bus)?') is represented in the underlying form, then this type is an ordinary Locative existential; otherwise, we shall need a *var*-predicate consisting of a single NP subject (in the example itself an intransitive participle from the verb *in*- 'descend').

I have drawn a rough contrast between Indo-European and Turkish sentence-types at a perhaps not very abstract level of representation. It seems to show that while in IE the copular notions of identity, class inclusion, and attribution, and the notion of possession are all assimilated to that of verbal action, *be* and *have* being expressed in the form characteristic of verbs, in Turkish the verbal notions are all expressed statically as attributions in copular form.

I suppose that a deeper analysis would reveal that much the same semantic distinctions are made by speakers of all languages. And perhaps a study of these *is* a way to approach the 'laws of thought' 'innate ideas', 'man's view of his world'. And Whorf's notion that the arbitrary syntactic organization of one's language conditions one's world view (if that's what he meant) *is* indeed very hard to free of emptiness. Yet, if the basic notions underlying the copula sentence and the verbal sentence are so different, as one would suppose, one wonders *why* there are languages which collapse the expressions of these in one direction and other languages which collapse them in the opposite way.

APPENDIX. ROUGH SKETCH OF THE RULES PROPOSED

Base

$$S \rightarrow NP + Pred + Prs$$

$$Pred \rightarrow \left\{ \begin{array}{cc} NP & (var) \\ AP & \end{array} \right\} Cop$$

$$NP \rightarrow \left\{ \begin{array}{ll} D \quad (S) \quad N & \\ VP & \\ Pred & /\_ + Cop \end{array} \right\}$$

$$VP \rightarrow (Adv) \quad (NP) \quad V$$

$$Cop \rightarrow i + PPL$$

Transformations

i.   Existential fronting

$$_S[NP_1 \quad _{Pred}[NP_2 + var + Cop]_{Pred}]_S \Rightarrow$$
$$_S[NP_2 + NP_{1\,Pred}[var + Cop]_{Pred}]_S$$

ii.   Participle shift

$$_{Pred}[_{NP}[_{VP}[X + V]_{VP}]_{NP} \quad _{Cop}[i + PPL]_{Cop}]_{Pred} \Rightarrow$$
$$_{Pred}[_{NP}[_{VP}[X + V]_{VP}PPL]_{NP}]_{Pred}$$

iii.   Copula Replacement

$$i \Rightarrow OL/\_ \left\{ \begin{array}{l} PPL + Cop \\ FUT, \quad NEC, \quad OPT \end{array} \right\}$$

iv.   Existential deletion

$$var \Rightarrow \emptyset /\_OL$$

v.   Negative Placement Rules

var ⇒ yok
değil/_+i+PPL
V ⇒ V$_{neg}$

vi.   Interrogative placement

mi/_+i+PPL

vii.   Present-tense copula deletion

$$i+ \begin{Bmatrix} \text{MOM} \\ \text{AOR} \end{Bmatrix} ⇒ ∅$$

viii.   Secondary Personal Suffixes

$$\text{Prs} ⇒ \text{Prs}_{\text{II}}/ \begin{Bmatrix} \text{PST} & \text{(mi)} \\ & \text{CND} \end{Bmatrix} +\_$$

ix.   Interrogative shift

mi + Prs$_{\text{II}}$
1   2   ⇒   2   1

Tel Aviv University

CHARLES A. FERGUSON

VERBS OF 'BEING' IN BENGALI, WITH A NOTE ON AMHARIC

0. INTRODUCTION

This study resumes an old interest of the author. In 1945 he read a paper on 'The Bengali verb "to be"' at the annual meeting of the Linguistic Society of America. The paper attempted a description of the Bengali equivalents of the English verb 'to be' based on Zellig Harris's method of analysis which groups morpheme alternants on the basis of complementary distribution and formal similarity (Harris, 1942). The paper was never published, but some years later the findings were utilized in the paper 'Clause negation in Bengali' read at the Linguistic Institute in Seattle in 1963 and the Congress of Orientalists in Delhi in 1964. The findings were corrected and extended by Julia Sableski in her article in *Language* 'Equational sentences in Bengali' (Sableski, 1965). The Foundations of Language series has provided the stimulus for reworking the material in somewhat greater depth.[1]

The present study attempts a clear presentation, at the level of observational adequacy (Greenberg, 1970), of a body of information about Bengali copulative and existential expressions together with some related material on verb auxiliaries and other phenomena. No attempt is made to present the information in a unified theoretical framework, and only a minimum of general semantic, syntactic, and phonological material on Bengali is given. Nevertheless, it is hoped that enough information is provided so that theoreticians of various persuasions may at least get a feeling for the way this piece of Bengali works and some notion of how to incorporate it in a total grammar of the language.

The study also offers some tentative observations on the structure of verbs of 'being' in general and the ways such structures change through time. These observations include the presentation of a limited amount of information about Amharic verbs of 'being'.

Bengali is a major world language, spoken by some 120 million people in India and Pakistan, an official language of both countries, and the vehicle

[1] Some of the research reported here was supported by the Language Universals Project of Stanford University, National Science Foundation grant GS-1880. The study has benefited from comments made by members of the project staff, but they do not necessarily agree with the positions taken, and the author takes full responsibility for the approach as a whole and any errors of fact or interpretation which are in it.

Verhaar (ed.), The Verb 'Be' and its Synonyms 5, 74–114. All Rights Reserved.
Copyright © 1972 by D. Reidel Publishing Company, Dordrecht-Holland.

of a rich body of literature. It is an Indo-European language, one of the modern Indo-Aryan languages of South Asia, and has a distinctive alphabet of the devanagari type. Bengali is the usual medium of instruction up through the secondary schools in West Bengal (India) and East Pakistan, and it is used to a considerable extent in higher education. Like other major languages, Bengali offers a wide range of regional and social dialects, colloquial and literary levels, historical and contemporary texts (S. K. Chatterji, 1926; Chowdhury, 1960; Dimock, 1960; S. Chatterji, 1962). Also there is a grammatical tradition in Bengali and scholars of other countries have studied various aspects of the language and its literature (Čižikova and Ferguson, 1969, give a bibliographical review).

The linguistic material presented here is limited to Standard Colloquial Bengali (SCB), the widespread norm of educated conversation in both West Bengal and East Pakistan, used also to an increasing extent as the language of writing. It would have been desirable, even for full analysis of the SCB material, to examine related information from other varieties, such as the literary *sadhu bhasa*, some of the more divergent local dialects, and some older texts, but such an extension was beyond the scope of the monograph. The sources of the material presented were chiefly sentences from Page's textbook (Page, 1934) and sentences elicited from Mrs Ranu Basu, a speaker of SCB currently residing at Stanford. All examples, whether taken from Page, other published works listed in the references, or elicited directly, were checked or re-checked with Mrs Basu.

1. FIRST LOOK

If we examine Bengali sentences which are translation equivalents of English sentences containing the verb 'to be' in its copulative and existential uses, we find two common counterparts of English 'be'. One is the absence of overt morphemic material, the other the presence of the verb *ach-*. Some tendency to a contrast in meaning between the two is apparent, since the sentences with *ach-* tend to have existential value while the sentences without it (so-called 'equational sentences') tend to have copulative meanings. The contrast is not clear-cut, however, and some sentences may be said either with or without *ach-* with no change in basic meaning. Accordingly it seems natural to assume that the sentences without *ach-* have an underlying copula (*ach-*) which is deleted under certain conditions. This is in fact the conclusion drawn by Y. Kachru in the course of her very informative study of the syntax of the Hindi copula (Kachru, 1968). On the basis of Bengali and Telugu versions of three sample sentences she concluded: "Hence, even in these languages [i.e., Bengali and Telugu], the 'equational' sentences will have to be derived from copula sentences in the present tense." (p. 45.)

More extensive investigation of Bengali sentences will, however, quickly reveal the problems of such a simple, natural hypothesis. In the first place, most equational sentences are negated by the inflected negative copula *nɔ-*, while all *ach-* sentences are negated by the invariable negative existential verb *neĭ*. In the second place, when equational sentences and *ach-* sentences are changed to other tenses than present, at least two verbs of 'being' are possible counterparts, usually with a clear difference of meaning between them. Finally, in subordinate clauses of certain kinds there is a complex pattern of suppletions and neutralizations of various copulative and existential expressions.

The two verbs which appear most often as counterparts to *ach-* and zero copula in non-present tenses and in subordinate clauses are *hɔŏa*, 'be, become,' and *thaka*, 'be, stay.' It would seem appropriate to look for minimal contrasts among the four element ∅, *ach-*, *hɔŏa*, and *thaka* in order to reach at least a preliminary hypothesis about their lexical identity. Fairly satisfactory frames of minimal contrast can be found, and we shall use here sentences in which *chele* 'boy' is the subject and *bhalo* 'good' is the complement. The following four sentences are grammatical:

(1)   cheleṭi bhalo.
        The boy is good (in character).

(2)   cheleṭi bhalo ache.
        The boy is well (in health).

(3)   cheleṭi bhalo hɔĕ.
        (a) The boy gets well.
        (b) The boy becomes good.

(4)   cheleṭi bhalo thake.
        (a) The boy stays well.
        (b) The boy stays good.

The corresponding negative sentences are:

(5)   cheleṭi bhalo nɔĕ.
        The boy isn't good.

(6)   cheleṭi bhalo neĭ.
        The boy isn't well.

(7)   cheleṭi bhalo hɔena.
        (a) The boy doesn't get well.
        (b) The boy doesn't become good.

(8)   cheleṭi bhalo thakena.
        (a) The boy doesn't stay well.
        (b) The boy doesn't stay good.

These eight sentences suggest that the situation is more complex than our first hypothesis, but they do not take us very far toward understanding the syntax and semantics of 'being' in Bengali. For example, the contrast between (1) and (2) and between (5) and (6) might be attributed to the homonymy between a $bhalo_1$ 'good' and a $bhalo_2$ 'well'. Also, sentences (3), (4), (7), and (8) might be regarded as unrelated to the sentences of 'being'.

Let us now examine one kind of subordinate clause, the present-tense protasis with *jodi* 'if' of conditional sentences. Here are the if-clauses corresponding to our original four sentences:

(9)   cheleṭi jodi bhalo hɔě,...
        (a) If the boy is good,...
        (b) If the boy gets well,...
        (c) If the boy becomes good,...
(10)   cheleṭi jodi bhalo thake,...
        (a) If the boy is well,...
        (b) If the boy stays well,...
        (c) If the boy stays good,...

Each of these clauses taken out of context is ambiguous three ways, although the (c) reading in each instance seems less likely or 'natural' than the others since goodness in character is generally regarded as a more permanent kind of condition than good health. Bengali has an alternative construction for the protasis of conditional sentences: a conditional participle in -*le* which is not inflected for person. If this is used there is the same pattern of replacement, i.e., *hole* for zero and *thakle* for *ache*.

(11)   cheleṭi bhalo hole,...
        (a) If the boy is good,...
        (b) If the boy gets well,...
        (c) If the boy becomes good,...
(12)   cheleṭi bhalo thakle,...
        (a) If the boy is well,...
        (b) If the boy stays well,...
        (c) If the boy stays good,...

Here again the readings labeled (c) are relatively unlikely, although possibly (11c) is somewhat more natural than (9c) while (12c) seems even less likely than (10c).

The corresponding negative conditional clauses to examples (9)–(12) have the inverted position of the negative characteristic of certain kinds of sub-

ordinate clauses, i.e., the negative -na which is normally suffixed to the verb
appears as a na preceding the verb. Thus, the corresponding negatives of
(9)–(12) are:

(13)   cheleṭi jodi bhalo na hɔĕ,...
(14)   cheleṭi jodi bhalo na thake,...
(15)   cheleṭi bhalo na hole,...
(16)   cheleṭi bhalo na thakle,...

Examples (9)–(16) make it clear that the structural description of sentences
containing zero copula or ach- must involve the verbs hɔŏa and thaka in some
way. Accordingly the presentation here will be reminiscent of the treatments
of Malayalam and Kurukh in this series, in which several verbs of 'being'
are discussed along with equational sentences, rather than the treatments of
Hindi, Kashmiri, and Mundari, which operate with a single copula and its
deletion under certain conditions.[2]

2. GENERAL ASSUMPTIONS

The presentation of data here is based on a number of assumptions widely
held (explicitly or implicitly) by linguists of various schools. A number of
these assumptions are spelled out here for the sake of clarity.

   a) Every language has major word classes characterized by semantic,
syntactic, and phonological features.

   b) Every language has a major word class of nouns which is formally
definable on the basis of syntactic and phonological phenomena in the
language; such nouns typically denote "persons, places, and things" and
typically exhibit such categories as definiteness and countability.

   c) Every language has a formally definable major word class of verbs,
which typically denote actions or states of being and exhibit such categories
as tense and negation.

   d) Every language has at least one set of forms or constructions whose
primary function (or one of several major functions) is to denote existence,
generally with respect to a location in space or time, but in the limiting case
existence apart from specific location. In other words, every language has an
existential element such as a verb or particle, and the denotation of existence

---

[2] The various systems of verbs of 'being' in Modern Indo-Aryan languages – and indeed
for Modern South Asian languages in general – meɪit comparative study typologically
and diachronically. The most comprehensive treatments to date have generally been
concerned primarily with etymology, i.e. the history of the words themselves (e.g. Turner,
1936).

is never merely a marginal function of something else. Examples: French *il y a*, Hebrew *yeš*, Chinese *zai*.

e) Every language has at least one set of forms or constructions whose primary function (or one of several major functions) is to denote copulative relationships (e.g., identity, equivalence, class membership, class inclusion, attribution of property). In other words, every language has at least one copula or copulative construction, even if this is a zero of some kind which clearly contrasts with other elements commutable with it. Examples: French *être*, Hebrew ∅ (zero), Chinese *shi*.

f) In a given language the grammatical categories of the verb (e.g., person, voice, mood, tense, negation) may be carried to a greater or lesser extent by auxiliary verbs or particles which co-occur with the verb. In an extreme case these categories may be carried by a dummy morph which has no apparent lexical meaning at all.

g) There is a tendency for the existential, copulative, and verb-category-carrying dummy elements of a language (a) synchronically to interpenetrate in complex patterns of formal suppletion, semantic overlapping, and partial homonymy, and (b) diachronically to merge, split, and otherwise restructure among themselves.

In addition to these, two further assumptions are made here which may not be shared by so many linguists, and one of the purposes of this study is to offer some evidence in favor of them. They are:

h) There are severe limitations on the kinds of synchronic patterns and diachronic restructurings which may occur in existential-copulative-auxiliary systems, and such patterns and changes are related to syntactic characteristics of a very general typological nature. In other words, a particular pattern of constructions of 'being' tends to reflect the general syntactic character of the language, and changes in the pattern tend to form part of general typological shifts.

i) Tenseless or present-tense copulative expressions connecting nouns are more likely to vary diachronically between zero and overt morphemic marking than other copulative expressions or existential and auxiliary expressions. On the one hand, the N_1 *is* N_2 construction is the most likely place for optional omission and eventual full deletion, and, on the other hand, when the language has a zero copula, this same construction is the most likely place for the appearance of a new copulative marker.

3. SKETCH OF BENGALI

Basic information about SCB suitable as background for study of the existential-copulative-auxiliary system of 'being' may be found in Ray (1966),

Ferguson and Chowdhury (1960), and Ferguson (1964). Here only a few essential points will be given.

Bengali sentences typically have SOV order, i.e., the subject and object precede the verb, and in general modifiers precede their heads (e.g., adjective-noun, relative clause-noun). Bengali nouns have case suffixes and post-positions, verbs have tense and person endings, and auxiliary verbs follow the main verb. The combined category of person and respect-grading has five terms: first person ('I, me'); three levels of second person ('you'), commonly called 'inferior', 'ordinary', or 'honorific'; and two levels of third person ('he, she, they'), 'ordinary' or 'honorific'. Verbs have distinct forms for four of these 'persons', the second and third person honorific always being identical, e.g., *bɔlen* 'you (hon.) say, he (hon.) says.' The verb has no distinction in number, e.g., *boli* 'I say, we say'. Pronouns have distinct forms for all five persons and singular-plural distinction throughout, e.g., *tui, tumi, apni*, singular 'you', inferior, ordinary, honorific; *tora, tomra, apnara*, plural 'you'. Neither pronoun nor verb has distinction of gender; the third person pronouns are identical with the demonstrative adjectives *e* (near), *o* (far), *se* (neutral), and *se* as pronoun has an inanimate *ta* 'it, that.'

Verbs have eight inflected 'indicative' tenses (present, past, future, present continuous, past continuous, perfect, perfect past, conditional) and two inflected imperative tenses (present, future); they have four invariable non-finite forms: a conjunctive in *-e*, a conditional conjunctive in *-le*, an infinitive/present participle in *-te*, and a verbal noun/passive participle in *-a*, which has a partially independent variant form in *-ba*.

Nouns have four cases: an 'absolute' or 'direct' case without ending, which is used for subject and indefinite direct object; a genitive in *-r* which is used to indicate possession and reference; an objective in *-ke*, used for definite direct object, indirect object, and 'inner' objects ("they named *the city* Calcutta"); and a locative-instrumental in *-e* which is used for place in which, place to which, and certain agentive and instrumental uses. Postpositions normally take the genitive but a few take other cases.

SCB has a set of 'definitives' which serve as numeral classifiers and definitizing suffixes. Number in the noun is indicated chiefly by the addition of these definitives, some of which are singular (e.g. *-ṭa, -khana*), others plural (e.g. *-gulo, -ra*). A noun without one of these suffixes is unmarked as to a number and may be singular or plural in reference.

SCB has a strong predilection for impersonal constructions. Although many sentences have a subject in the direct case and a finite verb, transitive or intransitive, agreeing with it in person, many sentences have an invariable, third person ordinary verb form, the person affected in the genitive or, less often, objective case.

Examples:

> ami ciṭhi peechi.
> I received a letter.
> ram ciṭhi peeche.
> Ram received a letter.
> amar (ramer) khide peeche.
> I'm (Ram is) hungry ('of-me (of-Ram) hunger has-received')

Also, many sentences have an invariable third person ordinary verb with an indefinite agent in the locative-instrumental case (Ferguson, 1970, F13). Such sentences can usually be said also in the personal construction, i.e., subject in the direct case, but often the impersonal construction is more common and 'natural'. Examples:

> ami mach khaĭ.
> I eat fish.
> ram mach khaĕ.
> Ram eats fish.
> loke mach khaĕ.
> People eat fish.
> ('by-people fish eats')

The direct object in such sentences often has -*ke* if it is animate and definite.

   Finally, instead of a direct, personal 'I did thus-and-so' SCB may use a construction 'my doing thus-and-so took place' in which the verb is third person ordinary and the whole noun clause is the subject. Sometimes the basic meaning seems just the same, but in some cases there may be a shift in meaning.

> ami take dekhlam.
> I saw him.
> tar sɔŋge amar dækha holo.
> I saw him OR I met him.
> ('of-him with of-me seeing took-place')
> take amar dækha holo.
> I saw him. (=I really looked him over, I inspected him)

The phonological system of Bengali may be outlined in taxonomic phonemic terms as showing seven oral vowels /i e æ a o u/; seven nasal vowels; obstruents in five positions /p t ṭ c k/; four-way contrast throughout the obstruents, voiceless-unaspirated, voiceless-aspirated, voiced-unaspirated, voiced-aspirated /p ph b bh/; three nasals /m n ŋ/; three liquids /l r ṛ/; one fricative, the voiceless sibilant /s/ which is in most positions a palatal sibilant resembling English *sh*. Aspiration tends to fluctuate except in word-initial position, and there is a pervasive system of vowel alternation in verbs, of more limited application in the nouns. Stress tends to be phrase-initial but may be displaced by the emphatic suffix *-i* or under other circumstances. The lexicon consists of three major components which tend to exhibit somewhat different phonological alternations: (a) the core vocabulary of words descended from Old Indo-Aryan (*tadbhava*) and some of local origin (*deśī*), (b) Sanskrit loan words (*tatsamas*), and (c) foreign loanwords, chiefly Perso-Arabic and English.

4. USES OF 'ACHE'

The verb *ache* has full sets of forms in the present and past tense, but no other forms at all.[3] The forms of *ache* are regular in formation except that the initial *a-* of the stem is absent in the past:

			present	*past*
1			achi	chilam
2 i			achis	chili
2 o			acho	chile
3 o			ache	chilo
2 h	3	h	achen	chilen

The negative of the present tense forms is the invariable *neĭ* 'there is no, there are no'; 'am not, is not, are not'; the negative of the past is formed regularly by the addition of *-na*: *chilamna*, *chilina*, etc.

All other tenses are supplied by forms of *thaka* or *hɔŏa*. The verb *thaka* 'stay, dwell' may be regarded as the normal suppletion, but forms of *hɔŏa* 'become' are used whenever the meaning involves a change of state. For example, the future of *ache* is *thakbe* in the meaning 'will be, will continue to be', but in the meaning 'will be, will become, will come into being' the future is *hɔbe*. The present tense forms of *ache* are invariably replaced by those of *thaka* in what might be called 'subjunctive' clauses. These include conditional clauses with *jodi* 'if', purpose clauses with *jæno* or *jate* 'in order to', and relative clauses defining a class. These clauses are not marked by a special 'mood' of the Bengali verb, but they share the feature of having the negative marker placed *before* the verb.

The uses of *ache* fall into three syntactically and semantically distinct sets: existential uses (including locative and possessive expressions),[4] copulative

---

[3] A verbal noun *acha* is sometimes used by gramarians for their convenience (e.g. Page (1934), passim) but seems not to occur elsewhere.

[4] The set of uses labeled existential here is roughly coincident with Clark's Locationals (Clark, 1970), but the term 'existential' is used because her Possessive₂ is not included among *ache* constructions, some of the existential uses of *ache* do not seem to be locative in the sense she maintains, and it is possible to have a personal locative in existential uses as in sentence (24).

uses (with certain kinds of adjective complements), and auxiliary uses (suffixed to form verb tenses). All these uses share similarities in the ways *ache* is negated and is replaced by other verbs under certain conditions. Also, they all share a basic range of meaning: the existence of something or the existence of a state of affairs viewed as resulting from previous action. The three sets of uses differ in the particular areas of meaning they denote and in the degree to which *ache* may be omitted.

4.1. Existential uses. The verb *ache* occurs in a number of uses in which (a) there is a noun or pronoun subject, (b) *ache* means something like 'exists', 'is (somewhere)', 'is (in some state)', and (c) there is no noun or adjective complement. In addition to the simple existential uses, which include locative and possessive expressions, combinations of these, and other closely related uses, the following will be identified: verbal noun in *-ba* qualifying the subject, noun of modal value as subject, verbal noun in *-a* as subject, infinitive in *-te* as subject.

Simple existential. The verb *ache* occurs in clause-final position with an indefinite subject, in the meaning 'there is, there are, (there) exist(s)'. The clause may include an expression of place, a genitive of possession, or both. In this use the verb is third person ordinary. Examples of existential uses with indefinite subject:

(17)　boĭ ache.
　　　　Books exist. There's a book (somewhere). There are (some) books (somewhere).

(18)　pap o punno ache.
　　　　Evil and virtue exist.

(19)　ekhane ⎫
　　　　ṭebiler opɔre ⎬ boĭ ache.
　　　　bhetore ⎭

　　　　There are books ⎱ here.
　　　　(There is a book) ⎰ on the table.
　　　　　　　　　　　　　　 inside.

(20)　amar boĭ ache.
　　　　I have a book (some books).

(21)　ramer boĭ ache.
　　　　Ram has a book (some books).

(22)　amar baṛite boĭ ache.
　　　　I have a book (some books) at home.

Since the genitive in sentences such as (22) can refer either to the subject or the expression of place, there is a potential ambiguity which is only partly resolved by word order. Thus *baṛite amar boĭ ache* tends to mean 'My books are at home', while the order *amar baṛite boĭ ache* tends to mean 'I have some books at home', but in an appropriate context either order can have either meaning. Although this ambiguity is readily discerned by speakers of the language, an apparently similar potential ambiguity in sentences such as (20) seems not to exist within Bengali but to be an artifact of translation into English. That is, there seems to be no difference within Bengali between the English senses 'I have books' and 'My books exist'. Similarly a sentence with two identical genitives such as *amar baṛite amar boĭ ache* seems to have only one basic meaning in Bengali, not differentiating the possible English senses 'I have my books at (my) home' and 'My books are at (my) home'.

In addition to the use with indefinite subject, *ache* also occurs in existential and locative constructions with definite subjects, including proper names and pronouns. In this use the verb agrees with the subject in person and has appropriate respect grading. Possessive expressions with definite subjects (i.e., things possessed) do not take *ache*; the Bengali equivalents of sentences of the type 'The books are mine' or 'I have the books' belong with the zero copula constructions (cf. 5. below). Examples of existential uses with definite subject:

(23) boiṭi ṭebile ache.
      The book is on the table.
(24) se ki tomar sɔŋge neĭ?
      Isn't he with you?
(25) ram ekhane chilen.
      Ram was here.
(26) tini ki achen? – na, tini neĭ, kintu tãr bhaĭ achen.
      Is he here? – No, he isn't, but his brother is.
(27) tumi acho? – hæ̃ ami achi.
      Are you there (is it you)? – Yes, I'm here (it's me).
(28) ram ache.
      There's Ram.

In these sentences with definite subject the normal, unemphatic, non-expressive word order is Subj + Loc + Vb in contrast to the normal word order of Loc + Subj + Vb when the subject is indefinite. This is like the tendency to distinguish in Russian between *u menja kniga* 'I have a book' and *kniga u menja* 'The book is in my possession'; Clark (1970) gives a full discussion of this widespread tendency to put the definite subject toward the beginning in existential-locative-possessive sentences.

The subject of sentences of the type illustrated in (24)–(28) must be a movable person or thing. That is, one can say in SCB 'The table is (*ache*) over there' but not *'The house is (*ache*) over there' or *'Where is (*ache*) the tree?'. These starred sentences belong with zero copula expressions (5. below).

Sentences such as (26)–(28) without a locative expression are not clearly locative, since the meaning is not exactly that Ram, for instance, is in a certain place, but that he 'exists' in the sense that he is available or is to be considered. In making a list of possible candidates or invitees, for example, one could say *ram ache* 'Then there's Ram (as a possibility)'. The sentence *ami achi* is not translated exactly either by 'I'm here', which is too locative, or by 'It's me', which is simply identifying. In reply to the Bengali question *ke?* 'Who's there?' the most natural answer is *ami* alone (i.e., with zero copula). The sentence *ami achi* asserts something like 'I'm present,' 'I belong to the group', or 'I'm to be kept in mind'.

The simple existential sentences illustrated by (17)–(28) may be expanded by various kinds of modifiers of the subject, the expression of place, or the genitive of possession; in addition they may have expressions of time and other adverbial expressions. Some sample sentences will give an indication of the variety possible:

(29)   e klase soloți chele ache.
       There are sixteen boys in this class.
(30)   sonibare tomra kothaĕ chile?
       Where were you on Saturday?
(31)   tate sɔndeho neĭ.
       There's no doubt of it.
(32)   o ghɔre ki keu ache?
       Is there anyone in that room?
(33)   tar kɔthaĕ o tar kaje ḍher tɔphat ache.
       There's a big difference between his words and his deeds.

Verbal noun in -*ba*. One common type of expanded *ache* sentence has the genitive case of the verbal noun in -*ba* qualifying the subject. Typically the subject of the *ache* sentence functions at some level as the object of the verbal noun. Examples:

(34)   ajke apnar ɔnek kaj *korbar* ache ki?
       Do you have a lot of work to do today?
       ('Today of-you much work *of-doing* there-is?')
(35)   apnake amar ekți kɔtha *bolbar* ache.
       I've got something to tell you.
       ('To-you, of-me one word *of-telling* there-is.')

Sometimes the subject is a kind of dummy which is, in effect, in apposition with a noun clause containing the verbal noun. Here is an example with *kɔtha* 'word':

(36)   ebar casader kichu ṭaka *juṭbar kɔtha* ache.
         This time the farmers are likely to make some money.
         ('This-time of-the-farmers something money *of-obtaining word*
         there-is.')

Modal noun. Another common sentence type consists of an *ache* sentence
in which the subject noun has some kind of modal force, e.g., *dɔrkar*
'necessity'. In this kind of sentence there may be a subjective or an objective
genitive; for the objective use the objective case in *-ke* may occur instead
of the genitive, and this is especially likely if both nouns are present.
Examples:

(37)   tomar moton loker *dɔrkar*.
         It needs a man like you.
(38)   tomake *dɔrkar*.
         You're wanted.
(39)   take amader *dɔrkar* ache.
         We need him.

Some of these nouns take a subjective genitive and a noun in the locative-
instrumental case:

(40)   tar lekha-pɔṛaě *onurag* ache.
         He's fond of studying.
(41)   tar dhɔrme *srɔddha* neï.
         He has no respect for religion.

Additional examples of 'modal nouns' used with *ache* are: *sɔndeho* 'doubt'
(cf. (31) above), *bhɔě* 'fear', *apotti* 'objection'.

Verbal noun. Similar to the preceding use is the construction in which
the subject of *ache* is a verbal noun in *-a*. This construction occurs fairly
freely with any verb, especially transitive verbs of animate subject. The verbal
noun takes a subjective genitive; other elements such as direct object or
locative are in the form they would have in an independent sentence with
a finite verb. Examples:

(42)   amar e boiṭa *pɔṛa* ache.
         This book has been read by me.
         ('My this book reading there-is.')
(43)   amar tomake *jana* ache.
         You're well known to me.
         ('My you knowing there-is.')
(44)   amar take se kɔtha *bɔla* ache.
         I have told him that.
         ('My him that word telling there-is.')

This construction, like the copulative use of *ache* with participial complement (4.2 below), is sometimes equivalent to the English passive, but SCB has no grammatical category which corresponds well to the English passive, and this use of *ache* with the verbal noun in *-a* is only one of about a dozen constructions with non-finite verb forms and auxiliary verbs which coincide in some part with the passive (Svetovidova, 1964).

Infinitive. Finally, there is an existential use in which a noun clause containing an infinitive in *-te* serves as the subject of *ache*, with the modal value of permission. This occurs more often in questions or negatives than in declarative, affirmative sentences. Examples:

(45)   ta ki amader *korte* ache?
        Are we allowed *to do* that?
(46)   tomar ekhane *thakte* neĭ.
        You mustn't *stay* here.

Usually the genitive of possession of the *ache* sentence functions as the subject of the infinitive, but more complex constructions occur, e.g.:

(47)   tumi chaṛa amar apnar *bolte* keu neĭ.
        I have no ne but you *to call* my own.

The tendency to omit *ache* in existential uses is difficult to specify, but a number of observations can be made. The greatest likelihood of omission, other things being equal, seems to be in locative sentences with definite subjects and in modal sentences with words like *dɔrkar*. Other factors seem to be the avoidance of ambiguity and the degree to which the *ache* is 'exposed', i.e., in a position of emphasis or a position where it is required as a peg for something else in the sentence.[5] While it is perhaps most often the present tense which is omitted, the speakers of Bengali when asked to supply the missing verb will sometimes prefer another tense, most often the perfect *hoeche* or the future *hɔbe*. The most convenient test of existential use is to transpose the sentence to the present negative, which is invariably *neĭ*. Bengali speakers generally find this easy to do and can give a definite 'yes' or 'no' verdict. It must be noted on the one hand that many sentences resist omission of *ache*, i.e., speakers assert that they cannot imagine saying the sentence without *ache*, and on the other hand that informants tend to fluctuate in their judgments of the omissibility of *ache*, both inter-informant fluctuation as in Sableski (1965) and the same informant giving different judgments on different occasions.

[5] The nature of this variable rule is reminiscent of the rules for contraction in English (Labov, 1969); cf. also Ferguson (1971).

4.2. Copulative uses. The verb *ache* does not serve as a copula connecting nouns, but it frequently functions as a copula with certain adjectival complements. These complements are mostly participles, i.e., adjectives which are inflectional forms of verbs and exhibit some characteristics of verbs not shown by ordinary adjectives. There are, however, at least two non-verbal adjectives which occur as complements with *ache*.

The verb *ache* occurs with three kinds of participles as predicate complements. All these constructions denote a state reached by the action of the verb, with no emphasis on the action as such. SCB has a rich variety of constructions in this general semantic area, and the shades of meaning are often difficult to characterize. In this study only such constructions which involve a verb of 'being' will be treated, but occasionally references will be made to other constructions. Karpuškin (1964) gives a more extensive treatment of some of these constructions, with examples from Bengali literature.

Passive participle. The verb *ache* occurs with passive participles as predicate complements, both Sanskrit-loan participles in -*t*- and the Bengali form in -*a*. The construction with Sanskrit participles is more frequent in the literary language than in SCB, although *rohiache* (SCB *roeche*) is often used rather than *ache*. The Sanskrit participles used with *ache* in SCB are generally ones for which there is no direct colloquial equivalent. Examples:

(48)   janalaṭi *unmukto* ache.
        The window is open.
(49)   ṭebile boiṭa *rakha* ache.
        The book is lying on the table.
        ('On-table the-book kept there-is.')

Conjunctive. The verb *ache* also occurs with the conjunctive of intransitive verbs of bodily motion or bodily state. These verbs are generally inchoative, i.e., are to be translated 'sit down', 'fall asleep', 'stand up', and the like, and the construction with *ache* denotes the state 'is seated, asleep, standing up'. Example:

(50)   cheleṭi bose ache.
        The boy is seated (OR sitting down).

Examples of other such verbs: *dā̃ṛie ache* 'is standing', *ghumie ache* 'is asleep', *jege ache* 'is awake', *sue ache* 'is lying down', *poṛe ache* 'is lying fallen', *bĕce ache* 'is alive', *takie ache* and *cee ache* 'is staring',[6] *pete ache* 'is lying spread out', *lukie ache* 'is hidden'.

---

[6] The last verb is a good illustration of the semantic limitations of the class of verbs which are used in this construction: *cee* occurs in the meaning 'stare' but in its common meaning 'want' it does not occur in this use.

This use contrasts in meaning with the perfect tense of the verb described in 4.3 below, e.g., *boseche* 'he sat down, he has sat down' ≠ *bose ache* 'he is seated'. The perfect past (*bosechilo*) and the past tense of *ache* in this copulative construction (*bose chilo*) are ordinarily homophonous, but speakers of Bengali can discern the ambiguity and a distinction is usually made in writing by using a word space in the copula construction.

Verbs which are used in this conjunctive construction with *ache* also occur with *thaka* and *rɔǒa* in the same construction, particularly with the present tense of *thaka* and the perfect of *rɔǒa*. The meaning of *thake* is something like 'stay, keep on being', while that of *roeche* is very much the same as *ache*, possibly with a nuance of 'has been': *bose ache* 'he's seated', *bose thake* 'he stays seated', *bose roeche* 'he has been seated'.

Adjectives. The two adjectives *bhalo* and *thik* are used with *ache* and with zero copula with different but related meanings, as follows:

(51)   se bhalo ache.
         He is well (in good health).
(52)   se bhalo.
         He is good (in character or behavior).
(58)   ta thik ache.
         That's all right (OK, settled).
(54)   ta thik.
         That's right (correct, true).

Apparently no other non-participial adjectives are used with *ache*. The semantic analysis of sentences like (51) and (53) may not be clear, but at least they must be recognized as a copulative use of *ache*. It is worth noting that the word for 'good health' in Malayalam also exhibits different shades of meaning when used with the copula and with the existential verb, although there the difference seems to be between simply being well and being well with the implication of having recovered from illness (Asher (1968), p. 101). It may be that such words as 'good' and 'true' tend to play lead roles in the diachrony of linguistic systems of 'being' and should be studied for semantic shifts or mergers and splits in progress.

In all its copulative uses the negation of *ache* is *neĭ* and in conditional clauses *ache* is replaced by *thake*. The omission of *ache* in copulative uses is much less frequent than in existential uses. For example, in the existential use with the verbal noun in *-a* the *ache* is frequently omitted, but in the copulative use with the homophonous participle in *-a* the *ache* is very rarely omitted. In the copulative use with *bhalo* and *thik* the omission of *ache* would, of course, lead to ambiguity with the zero copula. The *ache* with *bhalo* in the meaning 'in good health' is, however, often omitted when the word *sorir* 'body' is used, as *tar sorir bhalo* (*ache*) 'His health is good.'

4.3. Auxiliary uses. By 'auxiliary uses' is meant those uses which primarily serve to carry such grammatical categories as tense and person within the verb phrase. An auxiliary which carries grammatical categories in this way may appear in various languages in very different forms, for example as a phonologically separate word or fused with the verb as a tense formant. In SCB the verb *ache* appears as a suffix in the formation of four tenses: it combines with the perfect conjunctive to form the perfect and perfect past tenses and it combines with a form of the verb stem to form the present and past continuous tenses (Ferguson (1964), Karpuškin (1964)).

Perfect tenses. The perfect and perfect past tenses are formed by suffixing respectively the present and past tenses of *ache* to the conjunctive. In this suffixation the initial *a*- of the stem is lost, and the aspiration is often dropped.

(55)

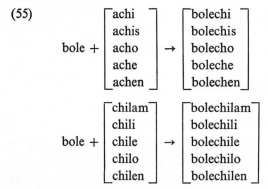

The meaning of the perfect tense tends to be resultative very much like the English perfect ('I have said') but it is more frequent in use than the English perfect and is often best translated by a simple past ('I said'). The perfect past is an 'anterior' tense which does not necessarily place the action before some other past action like the English past perfect ('I had said'); it is much more frequently used than the English tense. The Bengali simple past in -*l*- seems limited chiefly to reporting single events in a narrative context. The resultative meaning of the SCB perfect is not as clear as in the construction of conjunctive plus *ache* (4.1). This latter is, however limited to a small class of verbs, while the perfect tenses can be formed from any verb.

Although *ache* and *chilo* may seem to have lost their identity in the suffixation of the perfect tenses and one might be tempted to make no connection between the tense suffixes and the verb *ache* in a synchronic analysis, there are sufficient syntactic and semantic similarities to justify the recognition of lexical identity. The two most striking similarities are the

special form of negation and the replacement by periphrastic forms with
thaka in conditional clauses. All other tenses in SCB are negated by the
addition of -*na*, but these two tenses are negated by adding -*ni* to the corresponding form of the present tense. Thus the negatives of *boleche* and
bolechilo are not **bolechena* and **bolechilona* as might be expected, but
boleni, which serves as the negative for both tenses, neutralizing the tense
distinction. In the formal literary style the negative existential *neĭ* and the
perfect negative suffix -*ni* both have the form *naĭ*, which shows the relationship even more clearly.[7] In if-clauses the perfect tense is replaced by the
perfect conjunctive plus the present tense of *thaka*: *bole thaki, bole thakis*,
etc. The perfect past is not normally used in if-clauses. This periphrasis with
thake is formally identical with the use of *thaka* with the conjunctive mentioned in 4.1. That construction is, however, limited to a particular set of
verbs but is used in any kind of clause; this construction occurs with any
verb, but only in conditional clauses.

Continuous tenses. The present and past continuous tenses are formed by
suffixing respectively the present and past tenses of *ache* to a form of the
verb stem. The initial *a-* is lost throughout, and the aspiration is usually
dropped.

(56)

$$
\text{bole} + \begin{bmatrix} \text{achi} \\ \text{achis} \\ \text{acho} \\ \text{ache} \\ \text{achen} \end{bmatrix} \rightarrow \begin{bmatrix} \text{bolchi} \\ \text{bolchis} \\ \text{bolcho} \\ \text{bolche} \\ \text{bolchen} \end{bmatrix}
$$

$$
\text{bole} + \begin{bmatrix} \text{chilam} \\ \text{chili} \\ \text{chile} \\ \text{chilo} \\ \text{chilen} \end{bmatrix} \rightarrow \begin{bmatrix} \text{bolchilam} \\ \text{bolchili} \\ \text{bolchile} \\ \text{bolchilo} \\ \text{bolchilen} \end{bmatrix}
$$

It is not clear what form of the stem is involved. The literary *sadhu bhasa*
and some local dialects have the infinitive in -*te* (*boliteche*), other dialects
have the stem extension in -*i* which underlies the conjunctive and future
imperative (*boliche* or *boilche*). The SCB form is not unequivocally derivable
from either source, synchronically or diachronically. For discussions of the
issues, cf. Chatterji (1926), pp. 1019–27; Karpuškin (1964), pp. 103–4.

The meanings of the two tenses correspond fairly closely with English

---

[7] The historical development of the negative in -*ni* is of some interest since one would
expect the negative marker *neĭ* or its surrogate to be joined to the conjunctive, not the
present tense.

'he is saying' (including 'he has been saying') and 'he was saying.' The negatives are formed regularly by suffixing -na (*bolchena, bolchilona*). In its auxiliary uses *ache* is never omitted. The conjunctive, for example, is not used under particular conditions as the syntactic and semantic equivalent of the perfect tense.[8]

4.4. Position and omission of *ache*. Previous sections have reported that *ache* is most likely to be omitted in existential use, less likely in copulative use, and is not omitted at all in auxiliary uses. This pattern of omission seems to run counter to the observation (Ferguson, 1971) that verbs of 'being' tend to be omitted in copulative functions, so that some kind of explanatory hypothesis is needed. The following two 'universal tendencies' may be hazarded as hypotheses to be tested:

(Hyp. 1) An existential or copulative element tends to be omitted more often in a construction which involves a full predication such as a noun complement, a locative complement, or a clausal subject.

(Hyp. 2) A grammatical element is less likely to be omitted the greater the ambiguity which would result from its omission.

Clark (1970) notes the tendency for existential verbs with indefinite subject to precede their subject:

(Hyp. 3) Existential verbs of indefinite subjects tend toward clause-initial position.

None of the SCB sentences provided here as illustrations show this phenomenon. Further investigation would show, however, that instances of fronting of *ache* do occur, as in the beginning sentence of a story:

(57) æk chilo casa ar tar chilo æk chele.
      Once there was a farmer and he had a son.

It seems plausible that the 'universal tendency' here, familiar from the fronting of *there is* in English, meets greater resistance the more firmly established verb final order is in the language.

---

[8] Although auxiliary uses of verbs of 'being' seem generally less omissible in languages than existential and copulative uses, omission of auxiliary does occur, as in the Swedish omission of the auxiliary *ha(va)* 'have' in compound tenses in subordinate clauses, or the Persian tendency for the third person singular -*e* 'is' to drop out in colloquial speech in the perfect.

5. USES OF ∅

The zero copula is a grammatical element in SCB which occurs in a number of copulative uses. It is distinct from omission of *ache* in three respects: (1) no verb can be supplied to replace it in the normal verb position without change in basic meaning, (2) it is negated by the negative copula *nɔ-*, and (3) it is invariably present-tense or tenseless in meaning. Ferguson and Preston (1946) symbolized this zero copula by 'X' in their morpheme-by-morpheme representation of Bengali proverbs.

The negative copula *nɔ-* has a full set of forms in the present tense:

1		noĭ
2 i		nos
2 o		nɔŏ
3 o		nɔĕ
2 h	3 h	nɔn

In addition there is a conditional conjunctive *noile*, but this is not used as the conjunctive for the negation of the zero copula in conditional clauses (*na hole* is used, see below). The form *noile* always has the meaning 'if not' or 'otherwise' and introduces an alternative; it does not combine with other elements to form a clause except for the sequence *ta noile* 'if that's not so,' 'other than that'.

In 'subjunctive clauses' (cf. 4.1 above) the zero copula is replaced by the present tense of *hɔŏa*, and the negative copula *nɔ-* is replaced by *na hɔ-*, i.e., the negative marker *na* preceding a form of the present tense of *hɔŏa*. In a conditional clause without *jodi*, the conditional conjunctive *hole* occurs, and the negative is *na hole*. It may be noted here that *na hole* or *ta na hole* can apparently always be substituted for (*ta*) *noile*, but the reverse is not true.

Other tenses than the present of the zero copula are supplied by other verbs. In the past tense the existential *chilo* is regularly used unless change of state is indicated, in which case *holo* is supplied. Apart from the past tense, where the *chilo* forms are in effect shared by *ache* and ∅, forms of *hɔŏa* are the normal suppletion, but in instances where the meaning is 'continue to be' forms of *thaka* occur.

5.1. The zero copula is used in a full range of copulative constructions. Most commonly the subject is definite and the complement indefinite, but both may be indefinite in the generic use, and it is not rare to have both subject and complement definite. A set of examples, (58)–(66), selected for comparison with the illustrative sentences of Twi (Ellis and Boadi, 1969) gives some indication of the range. Possessive and modal constructions will be mentioned separately because of similarities to constructions with *ache*.

(58)   lokṭi kerani.
        The man is a clerk.
(59)   lokṭi dhoni.
        The man is wealthy.
(60)   se baŋali.
        He's a Bengaḷi.
(61)   era amar mee.
        These are my daughters.
        ('these of-me daughters Ø')
(62)   amra dəsjon.
        There are ten of us.
        ('we ten-person Ø')
(63)   gach gach.
        A tree is a tree.
(64)   aj budbar.
        Today is Wednesday.
(65)   gachṭa choṭo.
        The tree is small.
(66)   gachguli choṭo.
        The trees are small.

Possessive complement. Zero copula occurs with genitive complement in a construction very close semantically to *ache* with genitive. Sentences of the type 'The book is mine' are distinct from sentences of the type 'I have the book'; the former has zero copula in SCB, the latter *ache*. This contrast exists only with definite subject (thing possessed). Examples:

(67)   boiṭi amar.
        The book is mine.
(68)   boiṭi amar nəĕ.
        The book is not mine.
(69)   amar boiṭi ache.
        I have the book.
(70)   amar boiṭi neĭ.
        I don't have the book.

Modal adjective. The zero copula is regularly used with a verbal noun in -*a* as subject and an adjective of modal value as complement. This construction is semantically close to the use of modal nouns with *ache*. Examples:

(71)   tomar jaŏa ucit.
         You ought to go.
         ('your going proper')
(72)   tomar jaŏa ucit nŏĕ.
         You shouldn't go.

5.2. Pro-copula. By the term pro-copula is meant an expression whose primary function is non-copulative, used in place of zero in a copulative sentence. Many SCB sentences containing zero copula may have a pro-copula inserted without change of basic meaning. The pro-copula always occurs BETWEEN the subject and complement, not in the normal clause-final verb position. The forms of the pro-copula are present, past, or present continuous forms of *hŏŏa* (e.g., *hŏĕ, holo, hocce*). There is no difference in basic meaning among the three tenses, which in their use as pro-copula have a present tense or timeless value. In this use they may not be negated by the addition of *-na* as in their regular use as forms of *hŏŏa*, but in the negative are replaced by forms of the negative copula *nŏ-* in the clausefinal verb position. Examples:

(73)   cheleṭi chatro.
         The boy is a student.

(74)   cheleṭi $\left\{ \begin{array}{l} \text{hŏĕ} \\ \text{holo} \\ \text{hocce} \end{array} \right\}$ chatro.
         The boy is a student.

(75)   cheleṭi chatro nŏĕ.
         The boy isn't a student.

The basic meaning of (73) and the three alternatives of (74) is the same. The sentences with pro-copula may indicate emphasis, hesitation while searching for the right word for the complement, or other stylistic values. Interestingly enough the pro-copula may be inserted in the telegraphic style of newspaper headlines, one of the conditions under which the English copula may be omitted.

Without extensive sampling of actual usage it is difficult to characterize the connotations of the pro-copula and its variant tense forms. Informants differ in their judgments of the appropriateness of inserting the pro-copula, e.g., Sableski (1965) reported one informant who was willing to accept it in any zero copula sentence she submitted to him. On the basis of the data examined and the comments of informants, I would hazard the following generalization: There is a greater tendency to insert the pro-copula when the predicate complement is a noun than when it is an adjective or other predicate expression. Further, there seems to be a greater tendency to use the pro-copula in sentences which establish identity or equivalence rather than class membership or class inclusion. This latter preference includes formal definitions and mathematical equations.

It is worth noting that these preferred uses of the pro-copula also tend to be the preferred uses in which the copula is omitted in languages which have optional omission of the copula (Ferguson, 1971; Kiefer, 1968).[9] On the choice among the three tense possibilities, individual preference may be important, e.g., one informant may prefer *holo* in all cases, another *hocce*, but other determining factors are unclear.

The use of the pro-copula is of considerable linguistic interest since it seems to be an example of the development of an overt copula to replace zero. Perhaps we may assume two diachronic processes in a cycle. One begins with a fully overt copula, proceeds to optional omission of the copula, then obligatory omission of the copula, and finally full zero copula not lexically identifiable with any other copulative element. The other process begins with a zero copula, proceeds to the introduction of a pro-copula and ends with a fully overt obligatory copula.

Of particular interest is the position of the pro-copula between subject and complement. It is not clear on what evidence Benveniste (1950) made his assertion that there is always a pause in the position between subject and complement in *phrases nominales* without overt copula. It seems highly unlikely that there is always a pause, but there certainly are cases where such a pause can make the difference between an attributive construction and a copulative sentence. as in Chinese, omission of *shi* in sentences like *zhe (shi) shu* 'This is a book' where a distinct pause is made if the copula is omitted (Hashimoto, 1969, 84). In Semitic languages with zero copula which use a third person pronoun or demonstrative as a pro-copula, it is inserted between the subject and complement even though these may be VSO languages which normally have the non-present copulative verb in clause initial position. In descriptions of particular languages this phenomenon may be dealt with by appropriate ordering of the relevant transformations, as in Hetzron (1970) and Hayon (1970), but linguistic theory should offer some kind of explanatory principle. The phenomenon suggests that the following hypotheses deserve testing:

(Hyp. 4) When a language with a full copula begins to lose it, or when a language with a zero copula begins to develop one, the use in

---

[9] In Hungarian, according to Kiefer, some constructions require *van*, some obligatorily delete it, and a few allow optional omission. In this last instance the *van* when present is medial.

which the change is initiated is that of identity or equivalence with a noun complement.

(Hyp. 5) When a language with zero copula inserts a pro-copula it does so between the subject and complement regardless of the normal position of verbs in the language.

(Hyp. 6) In a language with optional omission of a copula (under the conditions of (Hyp. 4), there is a tendency for the optional copula to appear between the subject and complement regardless of its position in constructions where it may not be omitted.

5.3. Use of *na* as negative of Ø. In general, the negative copula *nɔ-* may be replaced in any use by the uninflected negative particle *na* in the same position. Thus, in principle, sentences (76a) and (76b) are equivalent in meaning.

(76a)   ram chatro nɔĕ.
(76b)   ram chatro na.
         Ram is not a student.

It is difficult to characterize the differing connotations of the two: neither seems more emphatic or more 'expressive', both may be used in written Bengali, and in prose or poetry, formal or informal style. The only observation which seems certain is that the use of *na* is less frequent than that of *nɔ-*, which seems to be the 'unmarked' or 'normal' negative copula.[10]

In this negative copula use, *na* is normally clause-final and is not, for example, put in medial position even if negating a pro-copula.

6. USES OF 'hɔŏa'

The verb *hɔŏa* is a high-frequency, 'basic' word in Bengali comparable to English *get* and as such has a wide range of uses with complex lexical restrictions and idiomatic expressions. Here we shall give attention to its absolute uses ('happen', 'turn out well', and modal values), its copulative uses with noun or adjective complement, its auxiliary uses as passivizer or intransitivizer in compound verbs, and several marginal uses in which a form of the verb has been lexicalized out as a particle of some kind. The verb

---

[10] In Ferguson (1966) it was hypothesized that *na* was used more often than *nɔ-* in addressing young children and was acquired earlier by children, because of its greater simplicity and its formal identity with the regular verbal negative *-na* and the general negative *na* used in answering yes-no questions, etc., but this has not been tested empirically.

hɔŏa has a full set of forms for all tenses and is negated regularly. Table I gives a second-person ordinary synopsis of the verb.

TABLE I

Synopsis of *hɔŏa*, 2nd person ordinary

	Affirmative	Negative
Present	*hɔŏ*	*hɔona*
Past	*hole*	*holena*
Future	*hɔbe*	*hɔbena*
Conditional	*hote*	*hotena*
Perfect	*hoecho*	*hɔoni*
Perfect past	*hoechile*	
Present imperative	*hɔŏ*	*hoĕona*
Future imperative	*hoĕo*	
Verbal noun	*hɔŏa*	*na hɔŏa*
Infinitive	*hote*	*na hote*
Conjunctive	*hoe*	*na hoe*
Conditional conjunctive	*hole*	*na hole*

6.1. Absolute uses. The verb *hɔŏa* occurs as an intransitive verb, without predicate complement, in the meaning 'happen, take place.' It can also take a genitive or adjective complement, with the meaning 'happen to':

(77) ki holo? ki hoeche?
What happened? What (has) happened?

(78) dækho okhane ki hocce.
Look what's happening over there!

(79) ɔmabossar rattirei kali puja hɔĕ, na?
The Kali Puja takes place on the night of the new moon, doesn't it?

(80) tomar ki hoeche?
What (has) happened to you?

It also may have the value 'can happen,' 'can properly happen,' 'turn out well.' The verb *cɔla* 'go, walk, be in motion' is also used in this sense and may often be exchanged for *hɔŏa*. Examples:

(81) se sɔŋge na ele hotona.
It wouldn't have done for him to come along.
('he along not if-come it-would-not-go-well')

(82) ami } na gele nɔĕ
amar }
It won't do for me not to go.

This occurs most commonly in the negative, after the conditional conjunctive. The negative of the present tense in this sense is usually *nɔĕ* instead of the expected *hɔena*.

Verbal noun in *-a*. The verb *hɔǒa* is used with the verbal noun in *-a* as the subject. This construction is similar in semantic value to the English passive (cf. the use of *ache* with participial complements in 4.2 above), but it is used just as freely with intransitive verbs as with transitives. The construction emphasizes the action and de-emphasizes the agent.

In addition to *hɔǒa*, the verbs *jaǒa* 'go, proceed' and *cɔla* 'go, be in motion' are used with the verbal noun in approximately the same sense, and *jaǒa* seems to be the most frequently used of the three (Bykova, 1960; Svetovidova, 1964). Examples:

(83)   tar sɔŋge amar ækbaro dækha hɔeni.
         I haven't seen him even once.
         ('his with my once-even seeing hasn't-happened')
(84)   rajkonne bone rekhe asa holo.
         She left the princess in the forest and came.
         ('princess in-forest having-left coming happened')

Often *hɔǒa* refers to a change of state and can be translated 'come to be', 'become.'

(85)   aj bɔro mɔja hoeche.
         Today there's a great joke.
         (i.e., a joke has come about)
(86)   sealer khub dukkho holo.
         The jackal grew very sad.
         ('jackal's great sadness became')
(87)   sondhe hoe elo.
         Evening came on.
         ('evening having-become came')

For sentences like (86) the most natural English equivalent has an adjective complement for the Bengali noun subject.

Another common meaning of *hɔǒa* is 'pass, go by' with units of time as the subject:

(88)   tin mas holo.
         Three months passed.

Infinitive in *-te*. One of the common uses of *hɔǒa* is with a noun clause subject containing the infinitive in *-te*. The English equivalent of this use is 'must,' 'has to,' negative 'must not.' The subject of the infinitive may be either genitive or objective. The verb hɔŏa is most frequently in the future tense in this construction, but examples can be found of all tenses, although apparently not imperatives.

Examples:

(89)   tomar aste aste kɔtha bolte hɔbe.
        You'll have to speak slowly.

(90)   bæsto hote hɔbena.
        You mustn't get flustered.

(91)   tar strike sɔŋge kore ante hoeche.
        He has had to bring his wife along.

(92)   sastrer kɔtha sɔb somɔĕ mante hɔĕ, kæmon?
        One should always obey the Scripture, shouldn't one?

(93)   amar ekhuni srirampure jete hocce.
        I have to go to Srirampur immediately.

(94)   tomar e bɔndobɔsto korte hole, age ekṭu bisram korte hɔbe.
        If you have to make these arrangements, you must take a little rest first.

6.2. Copulative uses. The verb hɔŏa is the normal Bengali expression for the general meaning 'become, turn into, get to be' with noun or adjective complement. As such it is used in all tenses and persons, affirmative and negative. The suppletive functions of hɔŏa given in Sections 3 and 4 above, are simply instances of this basic use of hɔŏa and – with the possible exception of suppletion for zero copula in conditional clauses – are in no way syntactically and semantically special if the verb hɔŏa is taken as the basis of description. Their suppletive nature is only valid from the other side, i.e., from the transformational relations obtaining between certain clause types with ache or zero and certain clause types with hɔŏa. To put it in other words, the notion of 'becoming' in Bengali is expressed simply and regularly; it is the notion of 'being,' including both existence and static identity, class inclusion, and the like, which is lexically and morphologically anomalous. Examples of copulative sentences with hɔŏa in the sense of 'become':

Although sentences with noun complement occur such as:

(95)   ram chatro holo.
        Ram became a student.

the common type of 'become' sentence is with adjective complement:

(96)   tãti gorib hoe pɔrlo.
        The weaver became poor.

(97)   casa buṛo holo.
        The farmer became old.

(98)   raja bɔṛoi khusi holen.
        The king became very happy.

Sanskrit participles in -t- occur with hɔŏa in a construction which is probably
the nearest Bengali equivalent to the English passive. This construction is,
however, generally limited to the literary *sadhu bhasa*, and other passival
constructions are used in SCB.

One limited copulative use of hɔŏa deserves special mention because it is
so close to the value of the zero copula. The verb hɔŏa is used to mean 'turns
out to be', 'has the role of', 'is' in expressing degrees of kinship and similar
relationships. In this use the hɔŏa appears in the usual clause-final position,
but is negated by nɔ̆ rather than hɔena.

(99)   ram tar nati hɔ̆.
        Ram is his grandson.

6.3. Auxiliary use. The verb hɔŏa combines with preverbs of various kinds
to constitute compound verbs. The compound verbs with hɔŏa are typically
intransitive, and often there is a transitive counterpart with kɔra 'do'. Thus,
with *ses* 'end' one may have *ses hɔŏa* 'to finish (intr.), 'come to an end' and
ses kɔra 'to finish (tr.)', 'bring to an end'. Other examples are *sthir hɔŏa* 'get
decided', *sthir kɔra* 'decide', *bod hɔŏa* 'seem', *bod kɔra* 'understand'. Sometimes the transitivity relationship does not hold, as in *ɔsuk hɔŏa* and *ɔsuk
kɔra* both 'be sick'.

6.4. Marginal uses. Several forms of hɔŏa have become specialized in
idiomatic, non-verbal uses and have almost become completely lexicalized
as independent words, although in each instance some trace of syntactic-
semantic relationship with the verb remains.

The conjunctive *hoe* is used with nouns as a postposition, with the semantic
value of 'by the way of, via'. This postposition is similar in origin to *die*
'by means of, along', *nie* 'about, concerning', and *dhore* 'during, for', which
are the conjunctives of *deŏa* 'give', *neŏa* 'take', and *dhɔra* 'catch'. Although
most postpositions in SCB are noun-derived and take a preceding noun in
the genitive, these verb-derived postpositions take the absolute case of the
noun, except that with *die* a definite, animate noun or pronoun takes the
objective ending -*ke*. Cf. the use of *theke* 7.3 below. Examples:

(100)   amra ḍhaka hoe kolkata jabo.
        We're going to Calcutta via Dacca.

(101)   se jɔkhom hoe more gæche.
        He has died of ('by way of') his wounds.

Similarly the past tense form *holo* 'passed (of time)', the conditional conjunctive *holo* (*hoile*), and the infinitive *hote* (*hoite*) are used more or less as
postpositions, with meanings 'ago', 'in the case of', and 'from' respectively,
but the first two of these may be regarded as purely verbal uses, and the
third is not common in SCB although frequent in the literary style and in
local dialects.

SCB has a variety of equivalents for English *or* (e.g., *kimba, ba, othoba,
ki, na*). Some of these may be used in series as correlatives of the *either ...
or ...* type (e.g., *ki ... ki ...*), but there is also a common equivalent of
'either ... or ...' derived from *hɔŏa*: *hɔ̆ ... nɔ̆ ....* Here *nɔ̆* rather than
hɔena serves as the negative counterpart of *hɔ̆*, as in the uses of *hɔŏa* meaning
'goes well' and 'is (related as)'. Example:

(102)   hɔ̆ ami jabo nɔ̆ tumi jabe.
        Either I'll go or you'll go.

The ordinary way to express 'not X and not Y' or 'neither X nor Y' in SCB is
to connect two negative clauses with a conjunction such as *ar* 'and' or *-o* 'also',
sometimes with the addition of the particle *to* in the first clause. There is also
a special 'expressive' way which uses no conjunction, puts the negated verb
at the head of each clause, and inverts the order of verb and negative
particle, i.e., instead of forming the negative in the usual way by suffixing
the negative *-na*, the *na* precedes the verb in both clauses. When this expressive means is used with clauses requiring zero copula or *ache*, the
negative forms are *na hɔ̆* and *na ache* respectively, serving as inversions of
nɔ̆ and *neĭ*. Examples:

(103)   na jabo ami na jabe tumi.
        Neither you nor I will go!
(104)   amar okhane gele, na hɔ̆ pɔṛasuna, na hɔ̆ bærano.
        If I go there I won't get either studying done or going around.
(105)   sekhane na ache ghɔr-dɔr, na ache kichu.
        There aren't any houses and the like there, not anything at all.
(106)   na hɔ̆ phɔsol, na ache æk phɔ̃ṭa jɔl.
        No crops grow and there's not a drop of water.

6.5. Omission of *hɔŏa*. Many copulative sentences without overt copula may
be regarded as having a form of *hɔŏa* omitted, since the speaker of SCB when
asked to supply the missing element will supply a form of *hɔŏa*. Generally,

however, the form which is supplied is either the pro-copula described above in 5.2 or it is a tense other than the present (e.g., *hoeche, holo, hɔbe*). In the latter case transposition of the sentence to a present-tense or timeless value shows that the sentence is either one with *ache* omitted or is an instance of zero copula. Accordingly, it seems, in spite of the evidence of suppliable forms of *hɔŏa*, that *hɔŏa* as such in absolute, copulative or auxiliary uses is rarely omitted.

7. USES OF 'THAKA'

The verb *thaka* has a full set of forms, with only one slight irregularity: the third person ordinary present imperative has a short form *thak* in free variation with the regular *thakuk*. The basic range of meaning is 'stay, continue to be' and it is used in this meaning in all tenses and non-finite forms. The verb *thaka* has copulative uses only insofar as it supplies missing forms of *ache* or is used in constructions alternating with *ache* where its meaning of continuing or being in a state for a period of time is added to the basic copulative function (cf. 4.2 above).

It also occurs as a suppletive form of *ache* in auxiliary uses, and is used in auxiliary functions not closely related to *ache* with the infinitive *-te* and with the conjunctive. Finally, the conjunctive *theke* is used as a postposition.

7.1. Absolute uses. The verb *thaka* is used in a full range of uses in the sense 'stay (in a place)', 'reside'. Examples:

(107) bhojpure ramlal bole æk tãti thakto.
       A weaver by the name of Ramlal used to live in Bhojpur.

(108) ækhon rajkonne bhablen ar gacher bhetore na theke ebare ækṭa
       mosto baṛi toiri kore thakte hɔbe.
       Now the princess thought that instead of staying in the tree she
       ought to build a big house right away and live in it.

(109) tumi jekhane thakbe amio sekhane thakbo.
       I'll stay wherever you stay.

7.2. Suppletive uses. The verb *thaka* supplies tenses of *ache* except present and simple past, and it takes the place of *ache* in 'subjunctive' constructions. This suppletion holds for all uses of *ache*, existential, copulative, and auxiliary. In the tense suppletion, which is commonest in the future tense, it is not completely clear that *thaka* has other than its basic lexical meaning (cf. the situation with *hɔŏa*, 5), but in the subjunctive suppletion *thaka* seems to have no trace of its lexical meaning. In those few constructions where an auxiliary use of *thaka* coincides with suppletion of *ache* there is ambiguity. For example, *se jodi bose thake* may mean either 'if he has sat down' (subjunctive suppletion for *boseche*) or 'if he stays seated' (auxiliary use of conjunctive verb *thaka*).

(110)   jar dhɔn thake take bɔṛomanus bɔle.
        A person who has wealth is called a rich man.
(111)   se jodi sekhane thake ta hole take bolbo.
        If he is there, I'll tell him.
(112)   se jodi ese thake...
        If he has come...

7.3. Non-suppletive auxiliary uses. The verb *thaka* occurs in constructions with the infinitive in *-te*, with the value of continuous action. Some grammarians (Chatterji, 1926; Page, 1934) regard the combination of *-te* with the future of *thaka* as a future continuous tense analogous to the present or past continuous tenses. Bykova (1960) points out that other forms of *thaka* including also non-finite forms occur in this construction and *thaka* seems to have its basic lexical meaning of 'keep on doing'. Example:

(113)   se sunbena, kɔtha bolte thakbe.
        He won't listen, he'll keep on talking.

The verb *thaka* also occurs in combination with the conjunctive, with the value of repeated, customary action. The commonest tenses of *thaka* in this construction are the present, future, and conditional and the first two of these or all three are sometimes regarded as separate tenses, with the same objections made by Bykova. Here the meaning seems to be somewhat farther from the basic lexical meaning of *thaka*; for example, conjunctive plus future of *thaka* often has the form of 'may have been, must have been, probably was'. Examples:

(114)   ami roj sekhane gie thake.
        I go there every day.
(115)   e deser lokera bhat khee thake.
        The people of this country eat rice.
(116)   tumi e kɔtha sune thakbe.
        You must have heard this.

7.4. Marginal uses. The conjunctive *theke* has become lexicalized as a postposition meaning 'from,' but even in its postpositional uses it can sometimes be understood as 'having stayed' and hence still retains its lexical identity with *thaka*. The preceding noun may be in the locative, as might be expected from the original construction ('having stayed in...') or in the direct case, as with other deverbal postpositions (cf. *hoe* 6.4 above), or in the genitive, as with most SCB postpositions. Example:

(117)   se $\left\{\begin{array}{l} \text{ghɔr} \\ \text{ghɔre} \\ \text{ghɔrer} \end{array}\right\}$ theke eseche.

He came from the room.

8. SUMMARY

Forms. SCB has a set of present-tense and past-tense forms of an existential verb (*ache*, etc., *chilo*, etc.), a systematic zero copula (∅) which is present-tense or timeless in function, an invariable present-tense negative existential verb (*neĭ*), and a set of present-tense forms of a negative copula (*nɔĕ*, etc.). The regularly negated past-tense forms of the existential verb serve as past negative for both the existential verb and the zero copula. The existential verb in reduced form also serves as a tense/aspect formant for two perfect tenses (present and past) and two continuous tenses (present and past).

These grammatical elements are highly defective in that they lack most of the tense forms and non-finite forms characteristic of SCB verbs. In effect they intrude on a number of regular, fully inflected 'sister verbs'[11] which support them by supplying their lacking forms. The sister verbs include *hɔŏa* 'be, become, happen', *thaka* 'stay, live in a place', *rɔŏa* 'be, stay', *pɔṛa* 'fall, happen', *jaŏa* 'go, happen', *cɔla* 'go, go well'. Of these, *hɔŏa* and *thaka* are of particular importance since they regularly replace the present tense of *ache* and ∅ in certain kinds of subordinate clauses ('subjunctive clauses') and *thaka* replaces *ache* in the 'subjunctive' use of the present perfect tense. In the present-tense and past-tense uses, *ache*, ∅, and their negatives are not synonymous with the corresponding forms of any of the sister verbs. Sometimes in other tenses the sister verbs are clearly ambiguous, having both the existential or copulative meaning and their own lexical meaning.

Uses. Existential, locative, and possessive clause types in SCB generally have *ache* ('books exist', 'there are some books on the table', 'I have some books'). There are two notable exceptions: possessive clauses with definite subject, i.e., thing possessed, ('the book is mine') and locative clauses with definite subject referring to an immovable object ('the tree is over there'); these have zero copula.

---

[11] This term is taken from traditional Arabic grammar, which speaks of *kāna* 'be' and 'her sisters' which are copulative verbs meaning 'be, become, be regarded as' and the like.

Copulative clauses with subject and complement (present or deleted) in SCB generally have zero copula ('Ram is a student', 'the weaver is poor'). Exceptions are the use of *ache* with participial adjectives in several constructions and with the adjectives *bhalo* 'good' and *ṭhik* 'right' which then have the meanings 'well (in health)' and 'all right (agreed)'.

All the sister verbs have auxiliary uses in constructions with nonfinite forms of other verbs, but only *ache* is clearly a tense formant. Some uses of *ache* with verbal noun as subject or participle as complement could also be regarded as auxiliary uses.

Both *ache* and ∅ participate in modal constructions, the modal value being represented by a noun subject with *ache* (e.g., *dɔrkar* 'necessity') and by an adjective complement with ∅ (e.g., *ucit* 'proper'). Also, both *ache* and *hɔǒa* have modal value in constructions with an infinitival subject clause (e.g., *jete ache?* 'is one permitted to go'; *jete hɔě?* 'must one (usually) go?').

Omission. The existential verb and some tense forms of *hɔǒa* are optionally omitted in certain constructions, but these cases are distinct from occurrences of the zero copula since the omitted form may be supplied without change in basic meaning and the negative is different from that of the zero copula.

A pro-copula, consisting usually of a simple past tense or present continuous form of *hɔǒa*, may be inserted in a zero copula sentence between the subject and the complement; it has present-tense or timeless copulative function. This differs from regular use of *hɔǒa* in such a sentence since the pro-copula does not have the lexical meaning of *hɔǒa*, occurs in medial instead of the normal clause-final position of the verb, and must be negated by the negative copula rather than the regular negative of *hɔǒa*.

9. LANGUAGE UNIVERSALS AND A NOTE ON AMHARIC

Greenberg (1966) suggested a typology of languages based on the co-occurrence of certain features of order and some related phenomena and hinted at diachronic processes which could lead to the alternative types. In this section verbs of 'being' will be examined in the light of the Greenberg suggestions, using Bengali as the point of focus.

Bengali is an example of a common language type, Greenberg's 'rigid III', which includes such languages as Japanese, Turkish, and Amharic.[12] These

---

[12] Greenberg did not include Amharic in the same Basic Order Type (#23, p. 109) as Turkish, Japanese, and Bengali because he classified it as predominantly postpositional. In fact it has both prepositions and postpositions and seems closer to a predominance of the latter. This is discussed below. Polotsky (1960) discusses common characteristics of Amharic and Turkish from a similar point of view.

languages are characterized by the following features and complexes:[13]

1. SOV order. The verb is sentence-final in the normal word order of declarative sentences. Any auxiliary verb follows the main verb.

2. Suffixes. The language is exclusively or nearly exclusively suffixing, uses predominantly postpositions rather than prepositions and has a case system marked by noun suffixes.

3. Interrogative markers. Questions words ('what', 'where', etc.) are non-initial and any general sentence-interrogative particle comes at the very end of the sentence, after the verb.

4. Modifiers precede their head. Subordinate clauses (including relative expressions) precede the main clause, genitives and adjectives precede their noun, and adverbs (by virtue of 1 above) precede their verb.

5. Comparison marker on standard noun. Comparisons take the form 'X-than Y good is' where Y is better than X and the morpheme 'than' is a marker referring to the standard X.

In addition to these features, which are all explicit or implied in Greenberg's discussion, several others may be noted:

6. Conjunctive verb form. There is a frequently-used, non-final verb form, a 'conjunctive', with the semantic value 'having done such-and-such' or 'do (did) such-and-such and...' which appears in subordinate clauses.

7. Compound verbs. In addition to simple verbs there are compound verbs including such types as (a) noun-like or interjection-like preverbs plus colorless auxiliary verbs such as 'do, give, say,' and (b) conjunctive as preverb plus colorless auxiliary. These syntactic combinations may be productive constructions of consistent semantic value, highly restricted idiomatic compounds, or simple lexical co-occurrences.

8. Sequences of events of the 'go, do, and return' type appear as 'having done, return' rather than 'go and do' as in English and many other verb-medial languages.

9. Optional plural. Expression of plural in the noun is optional and is normally absent in nouns when they are used in construction with numerals.

It is unlikely that all these features are independent, and Greenberg has proposed implicational universals connecting some of them, but for our purposes here it is enough to point out that they characterize a number of languages which are genetically unrelated and have no strong diffusional relationship. Other features could doubtless be added to this list, some of

---

[13] These features are based on Greenberg's point of view, but include features and relationships he has not made explicit. In some cases he may not agree with my extensions. Whatever merits the general approach has are due to Greenberg; errors of application are mine. The primary contributions of this section are intended to lie in the treatment of verbs of 'being' and the specific comparison between Bengali and Amharic.

them predictable from those already listed, others harder to understand. For example, from the fact that subordinate clauses precede, it might be predicted that quotations would precede the quoting verb. Also, from the presence of conjunctive verb forms, one might predict a tendency to use the conjunctive of a verb 'to say' as a quotation-ending particle. In fact, Bengali, Amharic, Turkish, and Japanese all have quotations before the quoting verb, and Bengali and Amharic use the conjunctive form of 'to say' as a quoting particle. What seems less predictable, given the present state of semantic theory, is that all four languages have uses of clauses with quotation-ending markers which are extensions from pure quotation to the expression of intention or purpose.

Some languages with full SOV characteristics, such as Turkish and Japanese, seem to have had this structure for long periods of time, although the details may have changed and parts of the structure may have formed and re-formed several times in recorded history. If Turkish and Japanese are regarded as ultimately related, this structure may, in fact, be attributed to the period of proto-Altaic. In other languages, however, such as Bengali and Amharic, documentation of earlier stages of the language shows that it was not always of this type. In the case of Amharic the shift has been attributed to the influence of Cushitic languages on the neighboring Ethio-Semitic, and this seems very likely although it raises the question of the typological characteristics of proto-Afroasiatic. The Bengali shift has also been attributed to outside or substratal influence, but the facts seem much less clear.

On the basis of historical shifts of the type shown by Bengali and Amharic, whatever their external or internal causes may have been, it seems at least possible to assume that languages may move toward and away from such well-defined types, with various parts of their structure moving at somewhat different speeds and in different patterns depending at least in part on the details of the grammar of the particular language.

For example, it seems likely that the change from a VSO language with prepositions, adjective after its noun, etc., to a language of the Bengali type begins with the shift of the verb, and the shift of the prepositions and adjectives may be stretched out over succeeding centuries. Ethio-Semitic languages furnish a good example of this. Classical Ethiopic, like Arabic and other Semitic languages, was a verb-initial, prepositional language in which adjectives followed their nouns. Modern Amharic, Tigrinya, and Tigre have all become verb-final languages and seem to be moving toward the full SOV type under discussion. Tigre still has only prepositions, Tigrinya has prepositions which are used simultaneously with postpositions, and Amharic has predominantly these preposition-postposition combinations of which the preposition part is frequently dropped in colloquial speech. Thus, it would seem that on this point as on others Amharic has moved furthest from its ancestral form, Tigrinya less so, and Tigre even a little less.

If it can be assumed that there are regularities in the way clusters of features change in the kind of global typological shifting which we are dealing with here, it is worth examining the verbs of 'being' in several languages to see whether they constitute a block of features which move in some patterned way within the shift. Even a very superficial examination of the verbs of 'being' in Bengali and Amharic shows a striking congruence of features. Table II lists twelve features of the verbs of 'being' complex which are structurally identical or nearly so in the two languages. Features 9 and 10 are quite parallel and features 11 and 12 are similarly parallel, so that these might be counted as one each, but the others are not obviously interrelated, so that there seem to be at least ten features in the two languages which are highly congruent. Since there is no genetic or diffusional relationship involved (and the morphemes do not in fact show striking similarity in phonetic shape), this must be attributed to universal properties of languages or at least be explained as a convergence related to the general shifting to the full SOV type, conditioned by other features of the grammatical structure similar in the two languages.

Beginning with the first two common features, it can simply be acknowledged that the lexical separation of existential and copulative functions along with the lexical identification of indefinite-subject and definite-subject existential functions constitutes a common pattern among the world's languages. Table III gives examples of four of the five logical possibilities; Bengali and Amharic are of type AAB. This pattern does not seem to correlate with the basic word order typology, but once this pattern is present other features may follow from it. For example the following 'universal tendency' may be hazarded as a hypothesis. (In the following hypotheses the abbreviations Ex, Cop, and Aux will be used for lexical items with existential, copulative, or auxiliary function, and illustrative examples will generally be selected from other studies in the series.)

(Hyp. 7) If an Ex or Cop is grammatically unique, i.e., lacks criterial features of any major word class in the language, it will tend to have a grammatically unique negative, i.e., the negative will not be formed the way other negatives in the language are formed.

For example, the Mundari Ex-Cop *menaq* is grammatically unique and it has a unique fused negative Ex-Cop *bangaq* ($\leftarrow ka + menaq$) (Langendoen, 1967).
Another 'universal tendency' would account for feature 5 of the table:

(Hyp. 8) If Ex and Cop are lexically separate in the present tense, they tend to share a single past tense.

Classical Armenian offers an example of this tendency: present Ex *goy*, present Cop *ē*, past Ex+Cop *lini* (Coiġneallaiġ, 1968).

(Hyp. 9) The negative of past tense forms of Ex and/or Cop tends to be more regular in formation than the present-tense negative.

TABLE II

Comparison of verbs of 'being' in Bengali and Amharic

	Bengali	Amharic
1. present tense existential verb, inflected for person (incl. locative and possessive uses)	*ache*	*allä*
2. present tense copula [a]	∅	*näw*
3. present tense negative existential verb, irregularly formed [b]	*neĭ*	*yälläm*
4. present tense negative copula, irregularly formed, inflected for person	*nɔĕ*	*aydälläm*
5. common copula/existential past tense, inflected for person	*chilo*	*näbbärä*
6. common past tense negative, regularly formed, inflected for person	*chilona* (*chilo* + *-na*)	*alnäbbäräm* (*näbbärä* + *al...m*)
7. other tenses of copula (incl. imperative and infinitive) suppleted by regular forms of verb 'to become'	*hɔoa*	*honä*
8. other tenses of existential verb (incl. imperative and infinitive) suppleted by regular forms of verb 'to stay, dwell'	*thaka*	*norä*
9. present tense of existential verb suffixed to conjunctive, yielding a 'perfect' tense (resultative)	*koreche* (*kore* 'having done' + [a]*che*)	*säbroall* (*säbro* 'having broken' + *all*[*ä*])
10. common past tense suffixed to conjunctive, yielding an 'anterior' tense (emphatic past and past perfect)	*korechilo*	*säbro näbbär*
11. present tense of existential verb suffixed to verbs, yielding a present continuous tense [c]	*korche*	*yisäbrall*
12. common past tense suffixed to verbs, yielding a past contibous tense	*korchilo*	*yisäbir näbbär*

[a] Amharic *näw* is a unique set of forms, inflected for (subject) person by object suffixes' not regular verb endings.

[b] Bengali *neĭ* is invariable, Amharic *yälläm* is inflected.

[c] Bengali present continuous contrasts with general present; Amharic serves also as general present in main clauses.

TABLE III

Examples of types of lexical identification in verbs of 'being'

	Existential-locative with indefinite subject	Existential-locative with definite subject	Copula with noun-complement
AAA Hungarian	van	van	van
AAB Twi	wɔ	wɔ	yɛ
ABB German	es gibt	ist	ist
ABA?			
ABC Spanish	hay	está	es

Mundari illustrates this tendency: the copula *menaq* with its unique negative *bangaq* has a suppletive past tense *tai* with regular negation. A very striking instance of the tendencies identified in (Hyp. 8) and (Hyp. 9) is Bilen (Palmer, 1965). The facts are summarized in Table IV.

TABLE IV

Verbs of 'being' in Bilen

	Existential		Copulative
Present	hambɐkʷ		gən OR ʔakkɛ́ʷ
Present negative	ʔəllá		ʔɐxlá
Past		sɐŋɛ́kʷ	
Past negative		sɐŋɛ́la	

NOTE: Both 'həmbɐkʷ' and 'ʔakɐkʷ' are past in form but present in meaning, 'gən' is a unique uninflected verb, 'ʔəllá' is a unique negative verb.

The Bilen system differs from that of Amharic and Bengali in a number of respects, e.g., it is almost the mirror image in terms of suppletion since it is the present existential and copulative forms ('həmbɐkʷ' and 'ʔakɛ́kʷ') which are from the regular verbs 'to stay' and 'to happen' respectively, while it is the non-present forms which are from 'wanna' 'to be' (Ex)' and 'sɐŋna' 'to be (Cop).'[14]

[14] It must be noted that Bilen is spoken in the Ethiopian language area (Ferguson, 1970b) and its similarity with Amharic may be related to the long-continued interaction between Cushitic and Ethio-Semitic languages in that area.

In many languages there is formal complementation between verbs of 'being' and semantically related sister verbs. For example, a verb 'to become' often supplies forms lacking in a defective verb 'to be,' as with Hungarian *lesz* 'become,' which supplies the infinitive, gerund, past conditional, and imperative of *van* 'be' and is ambiguous in these forms (e.g. *legyen* 'let him be' and 'let him become'). Thoroughgoing semantic analysis might yield a number of universal tendencies or implicational universals in this kind of complementation, but even without such analysis one universal tendency may be hypothesized to account for the agreements in points 7 and 8.

> (Hyp. 10) If Ex and Cop are lexically separate, and they are in a suppletive relation with verbs meaning 'become' and 'stay,' then 'become' will be related to Cop and 'stay' to Ex.

One of the common auxiliary functions of verbs of 'being' is the formation of tenses[15] with the semantic value of emphasis on present state, either perfect tenses in which the present state results from past action or continuous tenses in which the present state is characterized as an ongoing process. In either case the tense contrasts with simple present and past tenses, and in some languages it may be ambiguously perfect and present continuous (e.g. Japanese *site iru*). As a partial explanation of the Bengali and Amharic similarities in this kind of tense formation (points 9–12), the following more specific universal tendency is hypothetical.

> (Hyp. 11) In an SOV language with Ex and Cop lexically separate, the Ex tends to be used as an auxiliary combining with the conjunctive to form 'present state' tenses of perfect or present continuous value; as such it tends to change from an independent following auxiliary to a tense-forming suffix.

This process is similar in effect to the well-known processes: (a) development of perfect tenses in languages which have a verb 'to have' by combining a past participle with 'have' or 'be' (e.g. German *hat getan, ist gegangen*), and (b) development of continuous tenses by combining a present participle with 'be' or a definite-subject Ex (e.g. English *is doing*, Spanish *está haciendo*). In languages whose history is known in some detail it may be possible to document this process as a recurrent diachronic phenomenon, i.e., when the tense formant begins to lose lexical identity with its source it is added again

---

[15] "Tense" is used in these paragraphs as a cover term for tense and aspect, although the difference between these two categories may be of importance in particular languages and may even have some kind of universal semantic validity. For the purpose of (Hyp. 11) the reference is to a formally definable set of verb forms with the semantic values indicated, regardless of the exact tense/aspect system of the language.

as an auxiliary, repeating the process. This has apparently happened in Japanese (Sansom (1928), 175–9 and 209–12), and the current use of *bose ache* in Bengali (4.2) seems to be a recurrence of the process examplified by *boseche* (4.3).

Thus, all the similarities between Bengali and Amharic verbs of 'being' listed in Table II are seen to be related to general processes. It may turn out that the hypotheses presented here are wrong in detail, need much qualification, or should be related to other general principles than those suggested, but even if they are eventually disconfirmed empirically or rejected on theoretical grounds, the line of reasoning seems promising, and more detailed study of a larger number of languages should yield some satisfying universals of diachronic processes in the lexical expression of 'being.'

BIBLIOGRAPHY

Asher, R. E.: 1968, 'Existential, Possessive, Locative and Copulative Sentences in Malayalam', in Verhaar, Part. 2, 88–111.

Bach, Emmon.: 1967, '*Have* and *be* in English Syntax', *Lg.* **43**, 426–35.

Beneviste, Emile: 1950, 'La phrase nominale', *BSL* **46**, 19–36.

Beneviste, Emile: 1960, '"Être" et "avoir" dans leurs fonctions linguistiques', *BSL* **55**, 113–34.

Bykova, E. M.: *Podležaščee i skazuemoe v sovremennom bengal'skom jazyke*, Izdatel'stvo Vostočnoj Literatury, Moscow.

Bykova, E. M. (ed.): 1964, *Voprosy grammatiki bengal'skogo jazyka*, Izdatel'stvo Nauka, Moscow.

Chatterji, Suhas: 1962, 'A Study of the Relationship between Literary and Colloquial Bengali', University of Chicago dissertation.

Chatterji, Suniti Kumar: 1926, *The Origin and Development of the Bengal Language*, 2 vols, Calcutta University Press, Calcutta.

Chowdhury, Munier: 1960, 'The Language Problem in East Pakistan', in Ferguson and Gumperz, pp. 64–78.

Čižikova, Kseniya L. and Ferguson, Charles A.: 1969, 'Bibliographic Review of Bengali Studies. Current Trends in Linguistics 5, Linguistics in *South Asia*', ed. by Thomas A. Sebeok, 85–98. Mouton, The Hague.

Clark, Eve Vivienne: 1970, 'Locationals: a Study of the Relations between 'Existential', 'Locative', and 'Possessive' Constructions', *WPLU* 3, L1–L37.

Coignealliġ, M. Ó.: 1968, 'On Verbs of Being in Classical Armenian', in Verhaar, Part 3, 44–52.

Dimock, Edward C.: 1960, 'Literary and Colloquial Bengali', in Ferguson and Gumperz, 43–63.

Ellis, Jeffrey and Brodi, Laurence: 1969, '"To be" in Twi', in Verhaar, Part 4, 1–71.

Ferguson, Charles A.: 1963, 'Clause Negation in Bengali', Seattle. (Multilithed.)

Ferguson, Charles A.: 1964, 'The Basic Grammatical Categories of Bengali', in *Proceedings of the Ninth International Congress of Linguists* (ed. by H. Lunt), Mouton, The Hague.

Ferguson, Charles A.: 1966, 'Linguistic Theory as Behavioral Theory', in *Brain Function III*, (ed. by E. C. Carterette), 249–61, University of California Press, Berkeley and Los Angeles.

Ferguson, Charles A.: 1970a, 'Grammatical Categories in Data Collection', *WPLU* **4**, F1–F14.

Ferguson, Charles A.: 1970b, 'The Ethiopian Language Area', *Journal of Ethiopian Studies* **8**, 67–80.

Ferguson, Charles A.: 1971, 'Absence of Copula and the Notion of Simplicity in Normal Speech, Baby Talk, Foreign Talk, and Pidgins', in *Pidginization and Creolization* (ed. by D. Hymes), Cambridge University Press, Cambridge.

Ferguson, Charles A. and Chowdhury, Munier: 1960, 'The Phonemes of Bengali', *Lg.* **36**, 22–59.

Ferguson, Charles A. and Preston, W. D.: 1946, '107 Bengali Proverbs', *JAF* **59**, 365–86.

Ghosh, Samir: 1962, 'Negation in Bengali', University of Chicago, South Asian Languages Program. (Dittoed.)

Greenberg, Joseph H.: 1970, 'On the "Language of Observation" in Linguistics', *WPLU* **4**, G1–G15.

Harris, Zellig S.: 1942, 'Morpheme Alternants in Linguistic Analysis', *Lg.* **18**, 169–80.

Hashimoto, Anne Yue: 1969, 'The Verb "to be" in Modern Chinese', in Verhaar, Part 4, 72–111.

Hayon, Yehiel: 1970, 'Having and Being in Modern Hebrew', Paper read at Middle East Studies Association annual meeting, Columbus, Ohio.

Hetzron, Robert: 1970, 'Nonverbal Sentences and Degrees of Definiteness in Hungarian', *Lg.* **46**, 899–927.

Kachru, Yamuna: 1968, 'The Copula in Hindi', in Verhaar, Part 2, 35–58.

Karpuškin, B. M.: 1964, 'Sočetanie soveršennogo deepričastija s glagolami bytija stanovlenie složnyx vremennyx form glagola v bengal'skom jazyke', in Bykova 1964, 96–105.

Kiefer, Ferenc: 1968, 'A Transformational Approach to the Verb Van "to be" in Hungarian', in Verhaar, Part 3, 53–85.

Labov, William: 1969, 'Contraction, Deletion and Inherent Variability of the English Copula', *Lg.* **45**, 715–62.

Langendoen, D. Terence: 1967, 'The Copula in Mundari', in Verhaar, Part 1, 75–100.

Page, W. Sutton: 1934, *An Introduction to Colloquial Bengali*, Heffer, Cambridge.

Palmer, F. R.: 1965, 'Bilin "to be" and "to have"', *African Language Studies* **6** 101–11.

Polotzky, H. J.: 1960, 'Syntaxe amharique et syntaxe turcque', in *Atti del convegno internazionale di studi etiopici*. Accademia Nazionale dei Lincei, Rome.

Ray, Punya Sloka: 1966, *Bengali Language Handbook*, Center for Applied Linguistics, Washington.

Sableski, Julia: 1965, 'Equational Clauses in Bengali', *Lg.* **41**, 439–46.

Sansom, George: 1928, *An Historical Grammar of Japanese*, Clarendon Press, Oxford.

Svetovidova, I. A.: 1964, 'Ob izmenenii sposobov peredači značenii v bengal'skom jazyke', in Bykova 1964, 131–52.

Turner, Ralph L.: 1936, 'Sanskrit *a-kṣeti* and Pali *acchati* in Modern Indo-Aryan', *ESOAS* **8**, 795–812.

Verhaar, John W. M.: 1967–70, *The Verb 'be' and its Synonyms*, Parts 1–4, Reidel, Dordrecht–Holland.

PAUL J. HOPPER

VERBLESS STATIVE SENTENCES IN INDONESIAN

1. INTRODUCTION

1.1. Indonesian (*Bahasa Indonesia*) is a variety of Malay spoken as second language by some 125 million people in the Indonesian Republic. As the national language (*bahasa kebangsaan*) of the Republic since the founding of the nation in 1945, it is the language used for all official purposes, and in the newspapers, radio broadcasts and all other matters of national communication. It is also generally used between people of different ethnic backgrounds (there are some 200 ethnic and linguistic groups in Indonesia). Indonesian is also the language of education and of formal contacts between Indonesians of the same linguistic background. Indonesian is presently taught in the schools from the third grade on, and will eventually be extended to all grades. The local and regional languages are thus being relegated to informal and strictly local matters, where, however, there is little likelihood that they will be entirely replaced.

1.2. Malay, which forms the basis of Indonesian, is spoken natively by some 7 million people in Eastern Sumatra and the Riau Islands, as well as by the 8 million Malays of the neighboring countries of Malaysia and Singapore. Although Indonesian is sometimes held (especially by Indonesians) to be an advanced form of Malay which has significantly diverged from the original language, this is true only in terms of the social situations in which Malay and Indonesian are characteristically used. In fact, an energetic program of modernization is rapidly bringing Malay forward to the same level as Indonesian, and official Malay, problems of racial politics aside, is no less versatile than official Indonesian.

1.2.1. A form of Malay has been used as a *lingua franca* along the coastal areas of the Peninsula and the Archipelago from very early times.[1] Inscriptions in what, despite some disagreement among scholars, appears to be a language close to the ancestor of Modern Malay have been found in Sumatra and Java, and date from the early seventh century onward, the flourishing period of the Śrivijaya empire. Malay appears to have established

---

[1] Cf. A. Teeuw, 'The History of the Malay Language: A Preliminary Survey', *Bijdragen tot de Taal-, Land- en Volkenkunde van Nederlandsch-Indië*, **115**, 2 (1959), 138–56.

Verhaar (ed.), The Verb 'Be' and its Synonyms 5, 115–152. All Rights Reserved.
Copyright © 1972 by D. Reidel Publishing Company, Dordrecht-Holland.

itself as a language of culture and polite intercourse by the fourteenth century. It became a literary language in the courts of Johore and the Riau Archipelago, and remained an important means of communication throughout insular South-East Asia during the difficult period of colonialism.

The Japanese occupation of the Indonesian islands 1942–45 provided, as it turned out, the principal impetus and opportunity for the establishment of *Bahasa Indonesia*. The Dutch, who had expanded their empire in the Indies during the nineteenth century, had never attempted to impose their language on the natives, and the Japanese had little trouble in eliminating it. Malay, or Indonesian, as it had become known since the nineteen-twenties, was already marked as the national language by the growing independence movement, and was aided in its spread by the Japanese who used it as a language of administration. The Indonesian language flourished. It was carefully nurtured by official encouragement into a language which could accommodate every facet of twentieth-century life. Today, Indonesian stands almost unique as an achievement of language planning in a multilingual nation with a colonial history. Takdir Alisjabana, an Indonesian intellectual who was closely concerned with the modern development of the language, says of it: "This rapid growth of the Indonesian language is undoubtedly one of the most, perhaps the most, spectacular linguistic phenomena of our age." [2]

1.3. The artificial background of Indonesian, its modern history as a language almost deliberately created, its earlier history as a pidgin and creole, bear directly on one of the principal difficulties of the present study. Indonesian is, in a sense, no one's language at the same time that it is everyone's. Its lexicon is drawn from a multitude of sources, including local languages such as Javanese and Sundanese, and extraneous languages (Sanskrit, Arabic, Dutch, English). Its syntax is greatly influenced at the more formal levels of usage by the syntax of Western languages, while at the lower levels it tends to become highly simplified into a narrow-range pidgin known as Bazaar Malay (*Pasar Melayu*). To exclude foreign constructions in dealing with a language like Indonesian is a precarious procedure, for if taken to extremes it would remove from consideration well-established patterns which are consistently felt as 'native'. Yet most of what is interesting in Indonesian syntax for Western linguists lies, of course, in the areas of the language least touched by Western influences. In practice, isolating these areas is an impossible task, one whose goal is indeed probably not even valid. Informants are hopelessly inconsistent, accepting one day

---

[2] Takdir Alisjabana, *Indonesian Language and Literature*. New Haven, Yale University, South-East Asia Studies, 1962 (Cultural Report Series No. 11), p. 23.

what they reject the next, often prejudiced by the norms of Western grammar, on other occasions almost snobbishly relegating an offered sentence to the category of Bazaar Malay. Written normative grammars remain to be developed. The everyday usage of the newspapers and other official and semi-official documents is not a reliable guide, since it is precisely here that Western influence is greatest. Even native speakers of Malay show a similar insecurity in distinguishing 'true' Malay from Western patterns of language, finding themselves unable to reconcile the conflict between the every-day language of the kampong from the official variety taught in the schools.

It might then be asked what an examination of Indonesian can contribute to a cross-linguistic investigation such as that undertaken in the present series? The answer is that even Malay with a heavy Western adstratum is in many ways a uniquely suitable language for this kind of study. To a large extent the original topic system which it shares with other languages of the Austronesian group has remained intact, and since, as I shall show, the syntax and semantics of *have-* and *be*-like verbs is intimately bound up with questions of focus and topic, the Indonesian equivalents of these sentences show an almost unique transparency. The almost total absence of tense, number, gender and case morphemes enables the syntactic transformations involved in verb-less and other sentences to be stated with a minimum of distraction by redundant formatives. Indonesian is, in fact, in some ways what might be called a 'primitive' language; not, of course, in any evaluative sense, either of the language or of the people who use it, but in the sense that underlying linguistic relationships are reflected with a relatively high degree of directness in surface structures. This directness is especially evident in verb-less sentences.

1.4. The Indonesian sentences used in this study are drawn from my own knowledge of the language checked with the usage of Mr Tjakra Tanuat-madja, Assistant in Indonesian at Washington University. Mr Tjakra's reactions and hesitations, as well as his verbal responses to certain utterances when these called for a judgment concerning the 'genuineness' of a particular construction, have formed a valuable part of the data. Examples have also been drawn from standard works on Indonesian grammar, in particular A. A. Fokker's *Inleiding tot de Studie van de Indonesische Syntaxis* (Gronin-gen, Djakarta, J. B. Wolters, 1951), and Slametmuljana's *Kaidah Bahasa Indonesia*, Volume II (3rd edition, Djakarta, 1960). In addition, I have occasionally consulted Miss Tan Suan-Neo, a 'Straits Chinese' (one of a group of Malay-speaking Chinese from the Johore Straits settlements) with regard to facts about Peninsular Malay. Of course, neither Mr Tjakra nor

Miss Tan are in any way accountable for the use I have made of the data; their friendly cooperation is gratefully acknowledged.[3]

1.5. A strictly phonological presentation of the data has not been attempted, since phonology does not enter into this study. All examples are therefore given in the standard Indonesian orthography in use at the present time. The phonemes are listed as follows, together with their graphemic symbols:

Obstruents

Phonemic Symbol	Orthographic Symbols
/p/	p
/b/	b
/t/	t
/d/	d
/c/	tj
/j/	dj
/s/	s
/k/	k
/g/	g

Non-obstruent Consonants

/m/	m
/n/	n
/ñ/	nj
/ŋ/	ng
/y/	j, i
/w/	w, u
/h/	h
/r/	r
/l/	l

(Phonetic notes: Voiceless stops are unaspirated. /t/, /d/, /n/ are dentals or alveolars, although for some speakers only /t/ is dental; /c/, /j/ are alveo-palatal affricates for some speakers, alveolar affricates for others. /k/, /g/ have velar and post-velar allophones, and /k/ is a glottal stop word-finally. The high glides /y/ and /w/ are spelled *i* and *u* after vowel-symbols.)

[3] Thanks are also due to Anthony Bruck, Marshall Durbin and Don Vesper, who have clarified my thinking on a number of points. Extensive written comments on an earlier version of this paper were sent to me by Alan Stevens, and for these, too, I am very grateful. Not all of these comments have been incorporated into the present version, however, and no responsibility for any of the mistaken notions which remain rests with anyone but myself.

Vowels

/i/	i
/e/	é
/a/	a
/u/	u
/o/	o
/ə/	e

(/e/ ranges from high-mid to low-mid, but these distinctions, although possibly phonemic, are not reflected in the orthography. In actual orthographic practice, /e/ and /ə/ are not differentiated, but the acute accent to mark the front vowel will be used in this study. The 'diphthongs' /ay/, /aw/ (*ai, au*) are pronounced [ɛ] and [ɔ] by most speakers.)

2. THE VERB 'BE': SOME GENERAL CONSIDERATIONS

2.1. A cross-linguistic investigation of *be-* and *have*-like verbs gives rise to a number of significant questions which recur in language after language, and which must be resolved by reference both to individual languages and to universals. Some of the more important questions which must be confronted are:

a. Are *be-* and *have*-like verbs introduced by transformations as surface-structure formatives, or are they present as lexical items, perhaps as a subcategory of Verb?

b. How are the relationships of identity, class membership and class inclusion realized in particular languages?

c. What is the deep-structural relationship between equative (copular) and attributive verbs such as *be* and possessive verbs or structures such as *have*?

d. What is the status of 'existential' verbs?

e. In sentences involving the *be/have* relationship, how are syntax and semantics affected by the distribution of topic and focus over the constituents of the sentence?

Although there are several other problematical aspects, most of the discussion in the present monograph will be concerned with the above questions from the point of view of Indonesian. In this Section, I will make some general comments on *have/be* from the point of view of English. It should be remembered that English is suitable as a starting-point only because it is the native language of the author, as well as of several other contributors to the series, and is the language in which all the other monographs have been written. In other respects, English is perhaps less useful, it is indeed almost idiosyncratic in its insistence on two fully conjugated verbs of 'having' and 'being'.

2.2. The framework which I shall adopt in the analysis of *be/have* both for the discussion of English and for the main body of the work is a modification of that presented in Emmon Bach's article '*Have* and *Be* in English Syntax', *Language* **43**, 2.1 (1967), 462–85. This article is a treatment within the paradigm of transformational grammar. Bach proposes that the two surface verbs *have* and *be* are not present as deep-structural entities, as had been proposed by Chomsky[4] and generally assumed by other linguists working within this paradigm, but must be introduced as formatives in transformations. The result of this proposal is to make the category of Verb optional, and to eliminate the Copula altogether, yielding a class of *verb-less sentences* into which the 'verbs' *have* and *be* can be predicted. The rule assumed for the generation of such verb-less sentences is then:

$$VP \rightarrow \left\{ \begin{array}{l} \text{Predicate} \\ \text{NP} \end{array} \right\}$$

Be- and *have*-insertion rules operate specifically on strings not containing a V-sequence, in such a way that the formative-verb *have* is eventually added if NP is chosen, and *be* if Predicate is chosen. The possible expansions of Predicate are:

$$\text{Predicate} \rightarrow \left\{ \begin{array}{l} \text{NP} \\ \text{(Degree) Adjective} \\ \text{Time} \\ \text{Place} \end{array} \right\}$$

In verb-less sentences in which a second NP predicates something of the subject-NP, then, there will be a *be*-relationship, and where the second NP is non-predicative, i.e. where there is simply one NP juxtaposed in the same sentence with another NP, there will be a *have*-relationship. The *be*-relationship is, in other words, an attributive relationship.

2.3. The term 'attributive relationship' in fact covers not one, but a variety of relationships. In a given language, the question of whether a copular verb is introduced transformationally or is directly generated by the rules of the base depends on whether these different relationships, if expressed by different surface copular verbs, are predictable in some way (perhaps from feature-contents of the subject and predicate), or are not so predictable.

---

[4] N. Chomsky, *Aspects of the Theory of Syntax*, Cambridge, MIT Press, 1965, p. 107.

For English, it seems that the copula is predictable, since all attributive relationships are subsumed under the single category of 'being'. This is the position taken by Bach, who points out[5] that in the following three sentences (among others) the relationship is already adequately specified by the features of the NP's (such as *definite, specific, generic*):

1.	McX is a cat.	(class-membership)
2.	Armadillos are mammals.	(class-inclusion)
3.	John is the armadillo...	(identity)

Any ambiguities which occur can be accounted for as a superficial convergence of different underlying componential structures in a way familiar from syntax and phonology. Thus the sentence

4.   The giraffe is a vertebrate.

may be an example of either class-membership or class-inclusion, depending on whether the first NP is specific or generic. It will need much empirical investigation to discover whether these relationships are invariably predictable or not, from a universal viewpoint, but at this point there appears to be no convincing evidence that a copular verb such as exists in the Western European languages contributes to the meaning of a sentence.

2.4. The close relationship between the two English surface verbs *have* and *be* has been understood for some time.[6] The evidence points to a close similarity between verb-less sentences having a locative Noun Phrase as their predicate, and those having the same NP as their subject. The exact locative relationship in such sentences is not specified if the locative is subject; it may be near-ness:

5.   The house has a garden.

on-ness:

6.   The house has a roof.

in-ness:

7.   The house has a bathroom.

---

[5] *Op. cit.* p. 477.

[6] Recent discussions are found in several of the articles in the present series, and in E. Benveniste, '"Être" et "avoir" dans leurs fonctions linguistiques', *BSL* **55** (1960), reprinted in E. Benveniste, *Problèmes de Linguistique Générale*, Paris, Gallimard, 1966, pp. 187–207; J. Lyons, 'A Note on Possessive, Existential and Locative Sentences', *FL* 3 (1967), 390–6; C. Fillmore, 'The Case for Case', in: E. Bach and R. Harms (ed.), *Universals in Linguistic Theory*, New York, Holt, Rinehart and Winston, 1968, pp. 1–88; M. and M. Durbin, 'The First rule in a Universal Grammar', *Lingua* 23 (1969), 109–26; I. Lehiste, '"Being" and "Having" in Estonian', *FL* 5 (1969), 324–41 (reprinted this Volume, pp. 207–24).

and so on. With human subjects, surface *have* signals a more inherent relationship in which the complement somehow interests the subject. Here, the attempt to paraphrase the many different relationships which are involved is itself limited by the difficulty of defining such terms as 'pertinence', 'possession', 'ownership', 'availability', etc., in any but a single-language context, and the problems raised in attempting to assign a unitary meaning to *have*-like verbs are not solved by replacing these verbs with a list of substitutes which happen to exist in a particular language. Bach's solution to this problem rests in the assumption that the number of relationships expressible by *have* is identical with the number of relationships inherent in two juxtaposed noun phrases such that the second is not a predicate of the first.[7]

The suspicion remains, however, that the distinction between attributive and non-attributive nouns is itself resolved at some higher level. Bach's assumption does not seem to account satisfactorily for the rather evident relationship between sentences such as

8a.   The house has a roof.
8b.   The roof is on the house.

which differ only in the definiteness of the NP's, nor for the fact that 8a and 8b are in a kind of complementary distribution as compared with the non-sentences:

9a.   *A house has the roof
9b.   *A roof is on the house

(although no doubt some situation could be contrived which would render this last sentence grammatical). There is furthermore a class of sentences in English represented by:

10.   The house has a roof on it.

and also the well-known pair:

11a.   The book is mine.
11b.   I have a book.

beside

12a.   *A book is mine
12b.   ?I have the book

(where the first NP does not have focal stress). It is, of course, possible to

---

[7] Bach, 1967, p. 477.

impose restraints on the distribution of topical and other features over the sentence, but it would be better, if possible, to account for this distribution in a natural way. I shall take up this question again at a later point.

2.5. *Topicalization in Verbless Sentences*

2.5.1. In the communicative situation in which ordinary language is used, some of what is communicated is material already inherent in the linguistic or material content context of the discourse, and some is truly informative, or new information. The number of transformations which depend on this distinction is quite large, and the specific rules involved vary widely from language to language. In English, there is a tendency for new items to be placed toward the end of the sentence, and to receive sentence-stress, while old constituents, including the *topic* of the sentence, tend to be unstressed. The topic frequently appears as the subject of the verb in surface structure. Old constituents may be pronominalized or even deleted. An item which is old and which is the topic, i.e. that of which new information is predicated, will here be referred to as the *primary topic*. The primary topic is part of the presupposition of the sentence.

An item which is new in a discourse can be topicalized in its sentence by introducing it first with sentence-stress and then, under some circumstances, taking it up later in the sentence as a pronoun. This kind of topic will be referred to here as the *secondary topic*. In English, secondary topics often appear as the complements of expressions such as *with respect to, as regards, as for*, etc. An example would be:

15.   As for Sukarno, I think the people loved him.

The effect of this construction is to permit two items of new information in the sentence by converting one of them into a topic which is from that point on, so to speak, presupposed. The mechanism by which this transformation is accomplished is not clear, but I shall assume here that a noun phrase which is (somehow) marked with the feature (topic 2) is copied in front of the subject noun phrase and its second occurrence is pronominalized. Topic nouns in English are normally definite, and the definite article functions, among other uses, as a topic marker. Although indefinite nouns *may* be found in the topic position, they are often either emphatic (focussed) nouns which are not topics, pronounced with focal stress, as in:

14.   *A student* wishes to see you.

or are generic:

15.   An automobile is a dangerous weapon.

The question of topicalization and focus both in general and with respect to English, has much wider implications than can be dealt with in any but a minimal way in this paper.[8]

2.5.2. With respect to the *have/be* constructions in English, topicalization is of primary importance. Pairs of sentences such as those adduced above (8a, 8b; 11a, 11b) differ semantically only in the assignment of topic to one or the other noun phrase. The surface subject of both *have* and *be* is always a topic; the indefinite article is found only if the subject is generic:

16.   A giraffe has a long neck.

Furthermore in sentences like 10 above:

10.   The house has a roof on it.

there is a strong resemblance to such topicalized constructions as 13, in which a relic pronoun is left by a forward shifted topic.

Consideration of the relationship between topicalization and the presence of *have* versus *be* leads to the conclusion that the *be/have*-insertion rules operate on strings that are identical at some prior point in the derivation except in the assignment of the feature (topic 1). In fact, the subject of *have* appears to be simply an underlying predicate locative which has been topicalized in such a way as to yield a string which fits the structural description of the have-insertion rule.

2.6.1. This assumption involves, of course, regarding human subjects of *have* as also being in some sense 'locative'. It may be that possession, ownership, etc. are in fact locative relationships in some sense of the word, or that the term locative itself must be replaced by some more general term of which true spatial and temporal expressions are special cases, perhaps distinguished by the presence of a preposition. Yet the term locative is not too far-fetched to describe the *have*-relationship (locatives and genitives are

---

[8] A predictive framework for the treatment of topicalization which seems to hold promise is the theory of *presuppositions* currently being developed in the U.S.A.; this work, which is still in its initial stages, is to be found mostly in the papers of the 4th, 5th and 6th meeting of the Chicago Linguistic Society (1968, 1969, 1970). Another model incorporating topicalization as old and new information is put forward by W. Chafe, *Meaning and the Structure of Language*, University of Chicago Press, 1970 (to appear). British linguists have also studied the phenomenon, cf. especially M. A. K. Halliday, 'Notes on Transitivity and Theme in English', *JL* 3, 1 (1967), 37–81; 3, 2 (1967), 199–244; 4, 2 (1968), 179–215. The pioneers in this area have been the Prague School syntacticians, whose work is being continued in Czechoslovakia by Jan Firbas and others, cf. the articles on syntax in the *Travaux Linguistiques de Prague*, the *Prague Studies in Mathematical Linguistics*, and the *Brno Studies in English*.

indistinguishable in some Indo-European languages, for example, cf. Latin *Romae*, the Hindi *mujh-kee paas* construction, etc.). The surface-verb *have* in its stative sense[9] still requires a large store of contextual, cultural and other information to be interpreted semantically, of course. Among the possibilities are:

16. The Andersons have a Mercedes.   (Ownership)
17. Macy's have some fine necklaces.   (Availability to another)
18. Dr Hogitall had the pepper, the mustard and the salt.
                                        (Proximity to subject)

and so on. The surface interpretation of such sentences involves a large amount of familiarity with social conventions concerning ownership as opposed to casual and temporary occupation, identification of proper names, the function of stores as distributors of goods, etc., but the 'verb' *have* itself plays no role in the interpretation. Rather, the relationship between the two Noun Phrases must be indicated by features attached to the Noun Phrases themselves. The ambiguity involved in the relationships expressed by *have* in 16, 17 and 18 above is identical to that already observed in sentences 5, 6 and 7:

5. The house has a garden.
6. The house has a roof.
7. The house has a bathroom.

Indeed, 16–18 above can be paraphrased with the 'possessed noun' as topic and a preposition or preposition-substitute in the 'possessing noun':

19. The Mercedes is the Andersons'.
20. The necklaces are available in Macy's.
21. The pepper ... was near Dr Hogitall.

It is, in fact, a general characteristic of *have* that it serves, among other things, to neutralize a particular locative relationship which, if the locative is not topicalized, will be realized by prepositions and other means (such as the genitive /s/).

2.6.2. A specific kind of relationship which has been much discussed is that of *inalienable possession*. Without attempting to review the rather extensive literature on this subject, I will present a brief treatment within the framework just discussed.

---

[9] The use of *have* as a non-stative pro-verb, e.g. in *John is having a cup of coffee*, will not be considered in this paper.

The sentence

22.   That man has only four fingers.

is ambiguous, given a particular context, depending on whether the body-parts are attached to the body or not. In the former case, the relationship between the two nouns is one of inalienable possession. In many languages the difference between the two types of possession is marked syntactically or morphemically in some way; in English, for example, the surface-adjective *missing* in such sentences as

23.   I have a missing tooth.

is allowed to precede the noun only when the noun is inalienably possessed.[10]

In order for an object to be inalienably possessed, it must in some way be inherent to the possessor, that is, the possession of the object must be thought of as an attribute inseparable from the possessor. I will here assume that possessed Nouns, i.e. nouns which are the subjects of predicate possessive locatives, are marked with the feature [±inherent] with respect to the locative NP. This procedure does not, of course, exhaust the discussion of inalienable possession, since no explanation is offered of the origin of this feature. For the present purpose, it is simply assumed to be marked in every possessed noun, and the presence or absence of inherent-ness, i.e. the + or − value of the feature [inherent], conditions the application of certain transformational rules having to do with alienable versus inalienable possession.

2.7. *'Existential' Verbs*

Verbs and verbal expressions purporting to assert the 'existence' of a person or thing have played an important role in the Western philosophical tradition,[11] as is seen in the centuries-long debates over sentences such as

24.   God exists.
25.   There is a god.
26.   I think, therefore I am.
27.   Before Abraham was, I am.
28.   There are such things as mermaids.

Without entering into ontological and other speculations, we can reduce statements of being and existence linguistically to assertions predicating a

[10] This example from C. Fillmore, 1968, p. 63.
[11] Cf. A. C. Graham, '"Being" in Linguistics and Philosophy: A Preliminary Inquiry', *FL* 1 (1965), 223–231 (and this Volume, pp. 225–33).

locative, perhaps indefinite, of a subject Noun Phrase.[12] For example, in

29.   Unicorns knit in Ruritania.

it is possible to object that there are unicorns in Ruritania, but that they do not knit, whereas in

30.   Unicorns exist in Ruritania.

it is scarcely possible to claim that there are unicorns in Ruritania but that they do not exist. Entirely parallel observations can be made about the corresponding sentences in which the locative is left unexpressed, i.e. 'Unicorns exist/Unicorns knit'. Existence, then, as has been recognized for some two hundred years, is not itself a predicate. The English verb *exist* appears as a partially suppletive replacement of *be* in locative sentences where i. the locative, being indefinite, is deleted, or ii. the subject is non-topical. Consequently the following strings are not grammatical:

31.   *The unicorns exist in Ruritania.
32.   *The unicorns are.
33.   *Unicorns are.
34.   *Unicorns are in Ruritania.

The further consequence that strings such as 26 and 27 above are 'un-grammatical' is unavoidable; presumably the fairly uniform interpretation which they receive in Western philosophy stems from analogies to the verb *exist*.[13] The whole question of counterparts of *exist* versus *be* in non-Western languages appears to be of only peripheral interest except from a purely contrastive point of view or from the point of view of comparative metaphysics.

2.8. *Conclusion of Section 2*

The preceding discussion of the have/be relationship in English syntax and semantics has not been intended to be exhaustive, but rather I have attempted to single out aspects of the question which are applicable to Indonesian. In this concluding part, I will hazard some rules which might be used as the basis for an account of verbless stative sentences in both English and Indonesian. These rules cannot, of course, stand without extensive modification as even a sub-set of those which would be necessary for a more inclusive syntactic description of either language, but they will suffice as a provisional

---

[12] This is also the view of J. Lyons, 1967.
[13] For a fuller discussion, cf. A. C. Graham, 1965, and also the same author's contribution to the present series, Vol. I: '"Being" in Classical Chinese', 1967.

framework within which the grammar of verbless sentences can be displayed.

1.   S   → NP Predicate

2.   Predicate → $\begin{Bmatrix} NP \\ Loc \\ Adj \end{Bmatrix}$

3.   Loc   → (Preposition) NP

4.   NP   → $\begin{Bmatrix} Pronoun \\ N(S) \\ Indefinite \end{Bmatrix}$

The transformational rules are considered to be language-specific, and those required to generate Indonesian sentences from the above rules will be discussed in the next Section. I further make no mention here of so-called 'syntactic' features such as [animate], nor of non-inherent features such as [demonstrative], [proximate], etc., which are of course no less problematical in Indonesian than in any other language. Finally, I avoid the question of the mechanism by which features of topic are to be assigned to nodes. Instead, the attributes (topic 1), (topic 2) and (focus) are placed parenthetically beside the nodes concerned, and are assumed to derive in some unknown way from the total discourse situation. The problem with formalizing topic assignment is that the attribute of topic is not restricted to nouns or other categories alone, but may be spread over a configuration of nodes, especially the noun phrase. Theoretically this spreading could be accomplished by a process of copying the feature of the head noun over adjacent constituents, but this solution is not only in practice impossible to state explicitly, it also seems counter-intuitive.

3. INDONESIAN EQUIVALENTS OF 'HAVE' AND 'BE'

3.1. Verbless sentences in Indonesian may be either stative or non-stative. The non-stative kind of sentence is represented by directional expressions such as:

1.   Pak Supomo ini ke Djogjakarta
                    here to
        'Mr Supomo here is off to Djogjakarta'

There is no real reason to separate this type of sentence from the stative kind in which the so-called *be/have* is expressed. Indeed English sentences making use of the structure *be off to* (as in the rendering of 1 above) suggest that a neutral verb of motion should also be predicted by rule rather than introduced into the base, presumably when the predicate is a directional complement.[14] The phenomenon found in several languages of a verb of motion being 'understood' when a modal auxiliary is present would support such an analysis. In the remainder of this paper, however, I shall not be concerned with non-stative sentences of this kind.

3.2. *Copular Equations*

3.2.1. Copular Equations involving two Noun Phrases have an underlying phrase-marker:

(1)

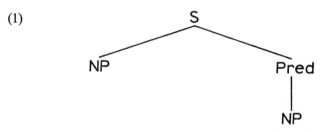

Except for the circumstances discussed below (3.2.2), no overt formative is introduced to separate the two noun phrases. The three basic relationships of class membership, class inclusion and identity are thus not distinguished by the "verb"; but the presence of the definite marker *-nja* on a predicate noun will always indicate the identity relationship.[15] Definiteness on a topic noun which is subject is generally shown by the weak demonstratives *ini* and *itu*. The following sentences exemplify these relationships:

2.   Orang itu tukang kebunnja
       man   that gardener   def.
       'That man is the gardener'

3.   Pohon ini pohon njiur
       tree   this   coconut
       'This tree is a coconut tree'

4.   Orang Belanda orang Eropah
                    Dutch
       'The Dutch are Europeans'

Itu also marks generic nouns. The syntax of the enclitic *-nja* will be discussed

---

[14] This has already been proposed informally by R. Binnick, "On the nature of the 'Lexical Item'", *Papers from the 4th Regional Meeting*, Chicago Linguistic Society, 1968, esp. p. 9, fn. 2.
[15] An alternative re-statement would be that definiteness, or perhaps definite articles, might be some kind of trace left by referential indices attached to nouns.

later; it is used to mark definite nouns not in the topic position, and as the third person possessor.[16]

The predicate noun, and indeed any predicate constituent, may be focused. A focused element is fronted and is spoken with an intonation which distinguishes it from the topic-subject, in that the element with focus has high intonation and the element which is a topic in the subject position has low and rising intonation. A focused constituent may further have the particle *-lah* attached to it. The following rule is posited to state these facts:

T1.   SD: [NP   [X   Y   Z   ]   ]
                       (Focus) Pred S
                 1   2   3   4

         SC: ⇒ 3 (+*lah*) 1   2   4

The ordering of this rule with respect to other transformations will be discussed later. If the focused element is a noun, sentences such as 5 will result:

5.   Orang itu-lah tukang kebun kami
                                        our
          '*That man* is our gardener'

3.2.2. In response, perhaps, to the increasing complexity of life and the adaptation of the language to the expression of technological and other new concepts, overt copula markers are coming into increasing use in Indonesian. Although the use of these markers is undoubtedly often conditioned by equivalent copular verbs in Dutch and English, languages with which most writers of the formal written language are familiar, they have no morphological resemblance to verbs, and are to be analyzed as predicate markers in sentences where complexity might obscure the break between subject and predicate. Presumably the written language, in which no intonational cue to the subject-predicate division is available, is largely responsible for the spread of these markers. A typical example of one of these markers, *ialah*, is in the following sentence:

6.   Djawab jang saja dapat dari X pada waktu itu ialah bahwa
          answer rel. I   receive from at that time   that
          barang-barang itu benar-benar kepunjaan Y
          items   truly   property
          'The answer which I received from X at that time was that those
          items were indeed the property of Y'[17]

---

[16] In many varieties of Indonesian, however, *-nja* is generalized as a definite marker on all definite nouns not having a demonstrative or possessive pronoun, including those in the subject position. Some Indonesians consider this usage to be a contamination from the regional languages, especially Javanese and Sundanese.

[17] Example from Sutomo Tjokronegoro, *Tjukupkah Saudara membina Bahasa Kesatuan Kita?* Bandung, Djakarta, P.T. Eresco, 1968, p. 95.

The use of *ialah* is common when the subject or predicate constituent contains a relative clause, as in the above sentence.

A second frequently encountered 'copula' is *adalah*, which appears to be interchangeable with *ialah*:

7.   Dia adalah seorang saudagar kaja raja
      he   class.   merchant rich
      'He is a rich merchant'

In the discussion of *ialah* and *adalah*, the question arises whether they are to be considered as morphologically complex or not. The particle *-lah* was presented above as a focusing or emphatic particle. *Ia* is a singular topic pronoun of the third person, while *ada* is an 'existential' verb meaning roughly 'there is'; a more extended discussion of *ada* will be undertaken below. Although in the intuition of the native speaker of Indonesian these two formatives, *ialah* and *adalah*, are not analyzed into morphemic components, their use can probably be related to a general characteristic of the Indonesian language, that extended or complex subjects are avoided and are replaced instead with topic-comment structures by the process of 'secondary topicalization'. By such an analysis, the *ia* morpheme in *ialah* would be the relic pronoun left by a forward-shifted topic. The *ada* of *adalah* would have to be analyzed in surface structure as an initial constituent in a sentence which is itself the predicate of a topic, i.e. as *Topic + S*, but in which no formative corresponding to the topic was present. (In English, sentences of this kind also exist, but they are probably all exclamatory, e.g. *Alexander – there was a great general!*) In both cases, the problems of analysis are considerable. In what follows, I assume that both *adalah* and *ialah* are morphemically simple.

The rules posited for the insertion of copular formatives will now be given. They are 'stylistic' rules, that is to say, they operate optionally on strings corresponding to the structural description provided certain contextual conditions of style are present. Their ordering is late, but can be shown to precede the rule of secondary topicalization.

T2a   SD: NP NP_{Pred}
              1   2

      SC: 2 $\overset{\text{opt}}{\Rightarrow}$ ialah + 2   where 1 or 2 dominates S

  b   SD: (same as 2a)

      SC: 2 $\overset{\text{opt}}{\Rightarrow} \begin{Bmatrix} \text{ialah} \\ \text{adalah} \end{Bmatrix} + 2$

Some speakers apparently hesitate to use *ialah* when the two nouns are not identical. For these speakers, *ia-lah* may still be experienced as a focused definite pronoun. Its use as a copula would then be restricted to the joining of nouns with identity of reference, in a way analogous, perhaps, to the Classical Chinese particle *chi* discussed by A. C. Graham.[18]

3.3. *Adjectival Attributes*

Simple adjectival attributes are derived from phrase-markers such as (2):

(2)
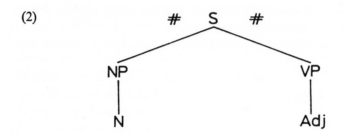

which directly generate sentences such as:

7.   Bunga itu mérah
       flower   red
       'That flower is red'

etc. There is no copula-like formative. More complex kinds of adjectival attributes will be discussed in the sub-section on embedding, below (3.6).

3.4. *Locative Predicates*

The general class of predicates subsumed under the heading of locatives includes locatives with an explicit preposition or prepositional complex, and locatives which are prepositionless noun-phrases.

Prepositional complexes in Indonesian are composed of a class of inherently locative nouns meaning 'upper surface', 'lower surface', 'side', 'face', etc., preceded by the prime preposition *di*.[19] The inherently locative noun is omitted when the relationship is already adequately specified by the context. For the purposes of the present discussion, prepositional complexes will be regarded as unanalyzed wholes, i.e. *di dalam rumah* 'in the house' and *di rumah* 'at home' are regarded equally as having a single preposition.

[18] *Op. cit.*, p. 11.
[19] I will depart here from the official orthographic practice of writing *di* as one word with a following non-proper noun.

The transformations which operate on locative predicates depend on the assignment of the feature [±topic] to the subject or predicate Noun Phrase. The simplest kind of sentence is that in which the subject NP is also the topic, and a spatial relationship is indicated by a preposition, e.g.:

10.   Rumah saja di Djakarta
       house I   in
       'My house is in Djakarta'
11.   Andjing itu di bawah médja
       dog   beneath table
       'The dog is under the table'

As with adjectival predicates, the derivation of these sentences raises few problems:

(3)

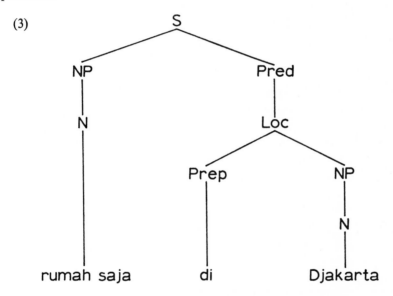

3.4.1. The distribution of new and old information in 'unmarked' locative sentences such as 10 and 11 is such that the subject is old and the predicate locative new. A different construction is used when this distribution is altered. This construction is illustrated in the following three sentences:

12.   Pondok itu di kaki bukit
       hut   at foot hill
       'The hut is at the foot of a hill'
13.   Ada pondok di kaki bukit itu
       'There is a hut at the foot of the hill'

14.   Di kaki bukit itu ada pondok
         'At the foot of the hill there is a hut'

In 13, the subject is new and the predicate locative old. In 14, the situation is the same, but the locative has undergone primary topicalization. In both sentences, a formative *ada* is added before the NP which is the underlying subject. The rule which accomplishes this is ordered so as to precede the rule of primary topicalization:

T3   SD: NP   Locative
             1   2

        SC: 1 ⇒ *ada* + 1   (where 1 is not (topic))

The formative *ada* is the closest parallel which exists in Indonesian to a *be-* or *have*-like verb. It has many functions, some of which will now be examined in order to illustrate its nature.

3.4.2. *Functions of Ada*

3.4.2.1. *Ada*, being a formative introduced by rule rather than a morpheme, has no semantic content of itself, but derives its meaning from context. Because its most typical use is with locative expressions as described above, it is usually rendered in English as "to be present, to exist, to be (in a place)". It is the equivalent in Indonesian to an 'existential verb', a function illustrated by such sentences as:

15.   Ada hantu
               spirits
         'There are spirits'
16.   Ada hantu di sawah itu
                        field
         'There are spirits in that field'
17.   Hantu itu ada
         'Spirits exist; there are such things as spirits'
18.   Tuhan ada
         God
         'God exists'

Of these uses of *ada*, 16 is already accounted for by T3, which predicts the presence of *ada* when a locative is predicated of a non-topical noun phrase. 15 is also to be considered as a case of rule T3, in which, however, the Locative is extended as Indefinite:

(4)

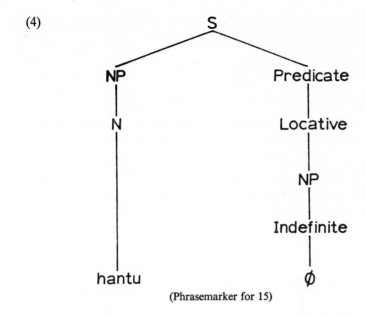

(Phrasemarker for 15)

The other two sentences reveal what is apparently a predicative use of *ada*, that in which the subject is a topic. Yet, as we have seen from the discussion in Section 2 (2.7), existence is not itself a predicate, but rather the attribution of an unexpressed locative to a topic noun, an affirmation that a noun denoting a thing or event known or presupposed by speaker and hearer is present at some undetermined place. The purely existential use of *ada* still does not require the introduction of *ada* in the lexicon. It can be introduced by a modification of rule T3, which remains the same but has the further condition:

Condition: *Either 1 is not a topic, or 2 dominates Indefinite*

A further justification for this modification to rule T3 is that for some speakers at least *ada* may be used in the 'neutral' locative type of sentence in which the subject is old and the locative predicate new, e.g.:

19.   Andjing itu ada di bawah médja
        dog   under table
        'The dog is under the table'

For these speakers, the restriction that the locative must be indefinite if the subject is a topic has been removed, and the entire condition is thus taken out of the rule.

3.4.2.2. In the *Inleiding tot de Studie van de Indonesische Syntaxis*, Fokker discusses other uses of *ada*, all of which, it seems, are derivable from the 'existential' sense discussed above. One of these is the *durative aspect*,[20] of which the following is an example:

20.   Ishak ada menulis buku
      write   book
    'Ishak is (in the process of) writing a book'

In this kind of sentence, *ada*, if it is to be associated with the existential use of *ada*, as I assume it is, has the force of *is now present*. Thus presence in an unspecified place at the time of the utterance is being predicated of the entire event expressed by the sentence, and the formative *ada* is inserted before the sentence. (The subject noun, of course, later undergoes primary topicalization and is fronted.) The underlying phrase-marker for 20 is then:

(5)

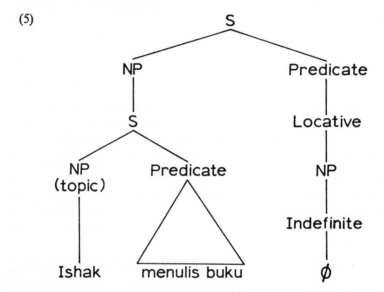

In sentences of this kind, *ada* is spoken with normal or low intonation.

In 20 it will be noticed that the subject noun phrase of the lower S is a topic and is old, while the predicate is new. There is a further type of sentence containing *ada* with a similar underlying structure but in which both subject and predicate are old, and in which *ada* has high or emphatic (focal) intonation, e.g.:

21.   Saja *ada* menerima surat tuan
    I   receive   letter your
    'I *did* receive your letter'

[20] Cf. A. A. Fokker, *Inleiding tot de Studie van de Indonesische Syntaxis*, Groningen, Djakarta, J. B. Wolters, 1951, pp. 48–52.

This type of sentence differs from 21 in that the whole of the lower sentence is presupposed or old, rather than just the predicate. In this case the attribute (topic) is assigned to the entire lower node S, and what is predicated of the topic is the truth or real existence of the proposition. *Ada* in this use functions as the negation of the negation, having the sense 'it is the case that, it is true that'. The same sense is seen in the common question type with *ada* and the interrogative particle *kah*:

22.   *Adakah* tuan menerima surat saja?
       'Have you received my letter?'

3.4.2.3. The use of *ada* in constructions denoting possession will be discussed in the following paragraphs.

3.5. *Expressions of Possession in Indonesian*

3.5.1. In formal written Indonesian, a complex verb has come into general use which corresponds to most uses of English *have* in the sense of *own* or *possess*. This verb is *mempunjai*. It is suspect from the point of view of its morphology of being a relatively recent word in the language. The prefix *meng-* which forms the first morphemic component is normally associated with active verbs, such as *memukul* (*pukul*) 'to beat', *menari* (*tari*) 'to dance', under conditions of topicalization such that the subject is topic and no part of the sentence has a special focus. (There are, however, non-active verbs which also take *meng-*, so that the presence of this prefix is not of itself anomalous.) The phonology of *mempunjai* displays a suspension of morphophonemic rules of prefixation: after the homorganic nasal, /t/, /k/, /p/ and /s/ (the voiceless obstruents excluding /c/) should disappear, e.g. *pukul*/ *memukul*. The function of *mempunjai* is so close to that of the Western European verbs of having as to be clearly modeled on these verbs. It appears to offer no fresh insights into the *have* and *be* relationship, and I shall therefore leave this particular expression of possession aside.

3.5.2. The root of *mempunjai* is *punja*, a noun which is in fact morphemically complex, and consists of (*em*)*pu* and *-nja*. The root *empu*, which is now no longer found in its pure root form, originally meant 'control (over); authority (over); master'. An object-nominalized form with the superfix *per-an* occurs as *perempuan* 'woman; one who is under authority'.[21]

Possessive constructions involving *punja* in its 'correct' use have the thing possessed as topic, e.g.

---

[21] Speakers of Indonesian may still be conscious of the root. It seems that the female emancipation movement in Indonesia, particularly during the last two decades, is bringing about its replacement by the more neutral word *wanita*, a borrowing from Portuguese.

23.   Rumah itu saja punja
       house   I
       'That house is mine'

24.   Keréta jang besar itu punja seorang Tiong Hoa
       car   big   class.   Chinese
       'That big car belongs to a Chinese'

In paradigm examples of this kind, the order of elements is: 1. Thing possessed, 2. *punja*, 3. Possessor, unless the possessor is a pronoun as in 22, or a proper name, when it may be focused. The derivation from an intermediate phrase-marker with the structure

(6)

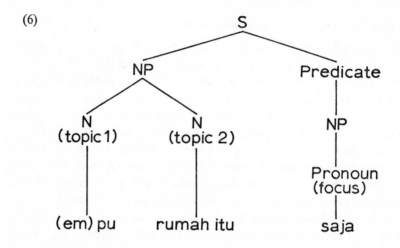

proceeds by means of rules of primary and secondary topicalization, which will be discussed in detail when complementizing constructions are presented (3.8). Informally, the rule of secondary topicalization fronts a noun or noun phrase marked (topic 2) and leaves in its place a 'relic' pronoun, in this case -*nja*. The resulting string is of the type 'That house, I (am) its owner'.

There can be no doubt, however, that *punja* is losing, or has already lost its original connection with the root (*em*)*pu*, and in all varieties of Malay, including Indonesian, is analyzed as the colloquial equivalent of *mempunjai*. An older informant remembers a Malay teacher in his youth who insisted on the pronunciation *empunja* and prescribed the usage represented by sentences 22 and 23 above, but the rule is scarcely observed in the spoken language, and is often broken in the written language also. Like *mempunjai*, *punja* serves as a general equivalent of Western *have*-like verbs, and also as a kind of 'genitive case' marker; this latter usage, for example, is common in the poetry of Chairil Anwar:

> Dalam sunji malam ganggang menari
> Menurut beta punja tifa
> follow   I   drum

> 'In the night-time quiet seaweed dances
> To the sound of my drum' [22]

Both constructions, but especially the last, are sometimes disapproved of by purists, or are identified with Bazaar Malay, the pidgin which is the inter-racial contact language for casual transactions in the three Malay-speaking countries; yet they are becoming increasingly mobile, and will presumably be accepted by normative grammars. [23]

3.5.3. Another way of expressing possession in Indonesian involves *ada*, the same formative as that discussed in 3.4.2. This use of *ada* is illustrated in such sentences as:

25.   Ia ada anak banjak
       he   child many
       'He has many children'

26.   Kami mémang ada rokok   "Kréték"
       we   indeed   cigarette
       'Certainly we have "*Kretek*" cigarettes'

27.   Saja ada sebuah rumah
       I   class. house
       'I have a house'

Ada in this sense is said to bear the same resemblance to *punja* as *have* does to *own* in English, although probably few speakers really make the distinction. [24] The relationship between the two noun phrases is such that the topic has the surface predicate noun phrase 'at his disposal': it exists with respect to the topic. The topic is thus an underlying predicate locative, and this analysis is confirmed not only by the use of *ada*, but by the occurrence of

---

[22] Cited from *The Complete Poetry and Prose of Chairil Anwar*. Edited and translated by Burton Raffel. Albany, State University of New York Press, 1969, p. 99: 'Tjerita buat Dien Tamaela'.

[23] Slametmuljana (*Kaidah Bahasa Indonesia*, 2nd Edition, vol. II: Djakarta, 1960, p. 62) suggests that acceptance of the usage saja punja rumah = rumah saja 'my house' is slower in Standard Malay than in Bahasa Indonesia.

[24] R. Ross MacDonald and Soenjono Darwidjojo, *A Student's Reference Grammar of Modern Formal Indonesian*. Washington, Georgetown University Press, 1967, p. 251.

sentences in which the locative is made explicit by the use of a preposition, e.g.:

28.   Ada pada-ku seékor kambing Benggala
                          class. goat
          'I have a Bengalese goat' [25]

(where *pada* is a preposition with the sense of 'to, with respect to', and *-ku* is the enclitic form of the first person pronoun). Such sentences are found mainly in the literary language. It should also be pointed out that the possessive use of *ada* without a preposition (as in 25) is not considered acceptable by all speakers.

3.6. *Noun Phrase Complements*

3.6.1. We now come to the question of noun phrases consisting of a head noun and a complementary sentence. In structures of this kind, some noun phrase in the complement sentence which is identical to the head noun is fronted and then either deleted or replaced with the relative pronoun *jang*, as in the following two examples:

29.   Kami tinggal di rumah jang besar itu
                      live   house   big
          'We live in that *big* house'
30.   Kami tinggal di rumah besar itu
          'We live in that big house'

For many speakers the distinction between the type with *jang* and the type without *jang* is one of restrictive versus non-restrictive clauses, but this distinction is being erased; with a few exceptions (which would unnecessarily complicate the analysis), the presence or absence of *jang* in this kind of sentence is relegated to the undefined realm of 'style'.

Simple sentences like 29 and 30 are generated by the following rules:

T4   SD: $[_N \ [_X \ NP \ Y] \ ]$
                  1   2   3   4 $^{S \ NP}$ (where 1 = 3)
        SC: $\overbrace{1 \ 2 \ 3} \ 4 \Rightarrow \overbrace{1 \ 3 \ 2} \ 4$

This rule, which will later be modified, accomplishes the fronting of the NP in the complement sentence. A second rule optionally (?) either deletes this

---

[25] This example from Slametmuljana, *op. cit.* p. 86.

NP or replaces it with the relative *jang*:

T5   SD: [N [NP X]]
                          S   NP
                1   2   3

          SC: $2 \Rightarrow \begin{Bmatrix} \emptyset \\ jang \end{Bmatrix}$

3.6.2. Since the predicate of a verbless sentence can be an adjective, a locative expression or a noun phrase, we would expect to find surface structures in which all of these predicates appear as the complements of nouns. This is in fact true, but there are restrictions in the case of the noun phrase predicate. The various types of predicates will be discussed in turn, together with the transformations involved with them.

3.6.2.1. Rule T5 already accounts for noun phrases qualified by an adjective, such as

          pohon jang tinggi itu
          tree   tall   that
          'that tall tree'

and so on. A slight complication exists in that when more than one adjective modifies the same noun, *jang* may only appear before the second adjective, e.g.:

          bunga jang mérah itu
          flower   red
          'that red flower'
          bunga mérah jang ketjil itu
                                small
          'that small red flower'

Further adjectives must be joined by the general coordinator *dan* 'and':

          bunga indah jang mérah dan ketjil itu
                lovely
          'That lovely, small red flower'

The introduction of *jang* and *dan* into noun phrases of this type is probably best regarded as taking place in surface structures of the form Noun-Adjective-Adjective..., rather than at the same time as T5.

3.6.2.2. Locatives consisting of a preposition and a noun phrase are similarly produced, as for example the sentence:

31.   pohon jang di halaman itu pohon pisang
           tree   garden   banana
           'The tree in the garden is a banana-tree'

which has an underlying phrase-marker:

(7)

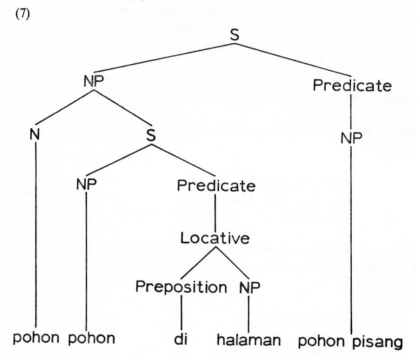

Sentence 31 is produced from this phrase-marker directly through rule T5.

3.6.2.3. *Possessive Locatives*

The syntax of simple possessive locatives is no different from that of other types of locative: the subject NP is deleted, leaving two nouns in juxtaposition, the first of which is the object possessed and the second the possessor. Representatives of this type are:

        daun pohon
        leaf tree
        'the leaves of the tree'
        pandjang daun pohon
        'the length of the leaves of the tree'

etc. It might be pointed out here, incidentally, that an analysis of the possessive relationship in which the possessor rather than the object possessed is the underlying predicate permits the genitive modifier to be produced by the same rule as other modifiers. As an illustration, the underlying phrase-marker of 32:

32.   Pandjang daun pohon itu dua meter
                                two
       'the length of that tree's leaves is two meters'

       is given.

(8)

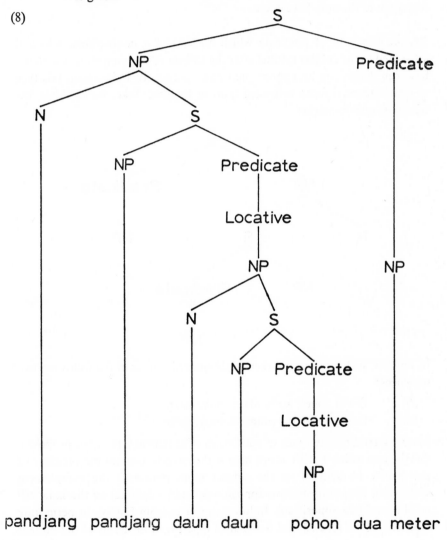

pandjang pandjang daun daun   pohon dua meter

As it stands, T5 will permit the generation of ungrammatical noun-phrase strings such as:

*daun jang pohon

Noun phrases of this kind are blocked by a constraint which prevents *jang* from appearing between nouns which are immediately dominated by the same NP; this constraint does not constitute an argument against regarding the possessing noun as an underlying predicate, since such a constraint is needed in any case, cf. 3.6.2.4 below. The application of T5 to phrase-markers such as (8) is cyclic, that is, it applies to the lowest occurrence of S first, then to the next-lowest, etc.

3.6.2.4. The kind of predicate which consists of a noun phrase which is attributed to the subject results, after the subject of the complement sentence has been deleted, in an appositional noun phrase. In Indonesian, this type of complement is more restricted than in English. Take, for example, the following phrase-marker:

(9)

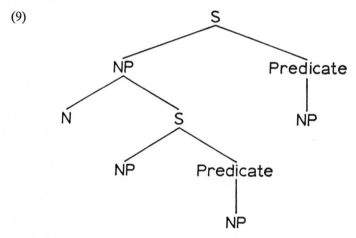

In English, such a phrase-marker might underlie either of the following two sentences:

33.   David Jones, a plumber, spoke next.
34.   David Jones the plumber spoke next.

Several alternative analyses of such pairs of sentences have been proposed, but the one which I shall adopt here is that which assumes the presence of the feature [+definite] on the subject noun phrase of the complement sentence in 33 (non-restrictive apposition), and [−definite] on the same NP in 34 (restrictive apposition). Indonesian differs from English in permitting sentences of the type 33, but not that of type 34; in the terms of the present analysis, it can be said that Indonesian requires identity of all features in the two NP's involved in T5, whereas in English they may differ in the feature of definiteness. Thus 35 is accepted:

35.   Sutjipto, seorang tukang batu, sudah mengakui kedjahatan itu
              class.   bricklayer   asp. confess   crime
       'Sutjipto, a bricklayer, has confessed to the crime'

But the restrictive appositional noun phrase has to be placed into a separate sentence:

36.   Seorang anak sudah mengakui kedjahatan itu. Anak itu adik
       class.   child   confess   crime   ( )
       Sutjipto.
       'A child who was the younger brother of Sutjipto has confessed
       to the crime' (*adik* = younger sibling)

There is an apparent exception to this restriction on embedding in what may be called 'strict apposition'. In strict apposition, the first noun is either a title or a generic term of which the second noun is an instance:

       Pulau Bali '(the island of) Bali'
       Kota Bandung '(the city of) Bandung'
       Saudara Sumitro 'Mr Sumitro'
       Pohon njiur 'coconut tree'

Since the construction is of limited productivity, expressions of this kind are probably best dealt with not as apposition (i.e. complementation of copular sentences) but under the heading of classifiers, an area which will not be considered in the present article. Classifiers are formatives which are predictable in terms of the semantic composition of the nouns to which they are attached.

The derived constituent structure of appositional noun phrase constructions will be of the form:

(10)

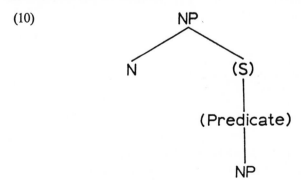

where the nodes in parentheses are considered to be 'pruned'. Hence in surface structure the two nouns (head noun and appositional noun) are immediately dominated by the same NP, the constraint which blocks the presence of *jang* between the two nouns (cf. 3.6.2.3 above) will operate, and noun phrases of the kind

> *Sutjipto jang seorang tukang batu

will not be generated.

3.6.3. *Topicalization in Complement Sentences*

Thus far, all the examples of complementation which have been presented have been ones in which the topic noun was already in the subject position, and no movements have been necessary in order to provide the correct input strings to rule T5. I will now consider the analysis of sentences in which some noun other than the subject is marked as topic. I will distinguish between *primary* and *secondary topicalization* (cf. 2.5.1 above).

Primary topicalization shifts a constituent tagged with the marker (Topic 1) to the front of the sentence, and, in the case of transitive verbs having direct object as topic, puts the verb into a 'passive' form. A detailed discussion of this rule is beyond the scope of the present article, but the following pair of sentences illustrates the difference between a sentence in which the subject is primary topic (37) and one in which the object is primary topic (38):

37.   Ali membuka pintu
          open   door
          'Ali opens the door'
38.   Pintu dibuka Ali
          'The door is opened by Ali'

There is in Indonesian another type of topicalization which I shall refer to as secondary topicalization. The effect of secondary topicalization is to shift a 'new' constituent marked as (Topic 2) to the front of the sentence and leave in its place a pronoun. This type of construction is especially common when the topicalized noun is part of the complement of a head noun. For example from 32 above:

32.   Pandjang daun pohon itu dua meter
          'The length of the leaves of that tree is two meters'

the constituent *daun pohon itu* may be extracted as a secondary topic to yield:

39.   Daun pohon itu, pandjang-nja dua meter
          'The leaves of that tree, their length is two meters'

(where -*nja* is the third person singular enclitic pronoun). The following rule is posited in the first stage of this process:

T6   SD: [X   NP   Y]
                   (Topic 2)   S
              1   2   3

        SC: 1 2 3 ⇒ 2 1 2 3

This rule does not immediately generate strings underlying sentences like 39, since the pronoun is not introduced at this stage. Instead, the topic NP is copied at the head of the sentence, and pronominalization takes place by a later rule; T6 carries the condition that it applies only once to any given NP. The reason for delaying pronominalization is that it can be exploited further to account for 'relic' pronouns left by the operation of a modified form of rule T4, which fronts NP's later to be replaced by *jang*. Consider the following sentence:

40.   Kami melihat pohon jang daun-nja pandjang-nja dua meter
         we   see   tree   leaf   length   two
         'We saw trees whose leaves were two meters in length'

In order to account for this type of sentence, rule T4 must be changed. This rule is in any case too general, in that it fails to account for the fact that in Indonesian a noun phrase cannot be directly taken out of the predicate to be relativized, i.e. there are no sentences corresponding to English 'the man whom the dog bit', etc. The input string to rule T5, in other words, must already have the noun phrase to be relativized as a constituent of the subject or as a topic. The following version of rule T4 is offered to display this situation:

T7   SD: N   [[X   NP   Y]   Z]
                             NP   S
              1   2   3   4   5

        SC: 1 2 3 4 5 ⇒ 1 3 2 3 4 5
                                Condition: 1=3, and 2≠null

The repetition of a noun phrase within the same S, then, has at least two possible sources, T6 and T7.

The second occurrence of the noun phrase is now replaced by the pronoun *ia*, under the condition that both of the identical noun phrases are dominated by the same S, and no instances of 'interior' S are present:

T8   SD: [NP   X   NP   Y]
                               S
              1   2   3   4   (1=3)

        SC: 1 2 3 4 ⇒ 1 2+*ia* 4

(11)

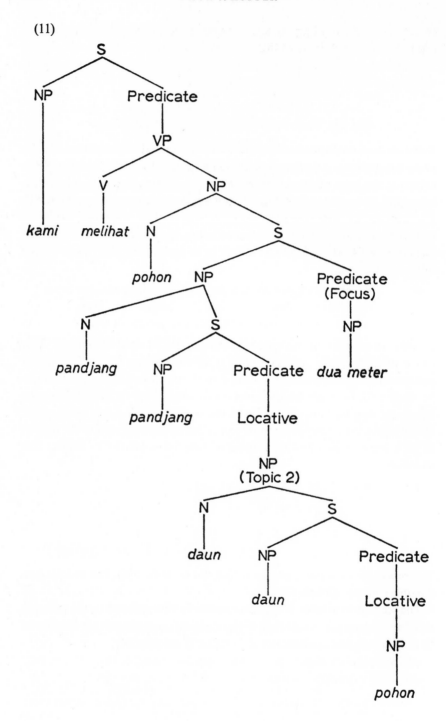

The pronoun *ia* will be replaced by its enclitic form *-nja* if the variable X is a formative, i.e. when X is not null.

The predicate of the relative sentence may undergo focusing by rule T1, and if this rule is applied to sentence 40, the result will be:

41.   Kami melihat pohon jang daun-nja dua meter pandjang-nja
        'We saw trees whose leaves were *two meters* in length'

As an example of the rules just presented, and as an illustration especially of the ordering relations between these rules, a full derivation of this sentence will now be given, beginning with the initial phrase-marker (see (11)). No transformations affecting primary topics being necessary, the first rule which applies is the cyclical deletion of identical nouns by T5. The structure of the noun phrase in the highest predicate after the application of T5 is, after the 'pruning' of higher nodes:

(12)

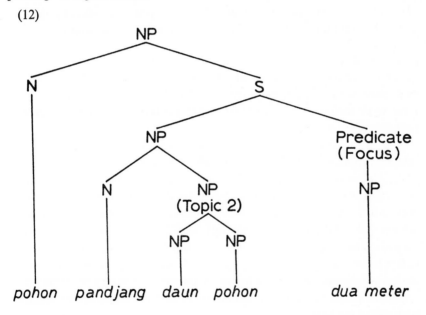

The predicate is now focused by T1, yielding a phrase-marker (represented now for convenience by the labeled bracketing convention):

[pohon   [dua meter   [pandjang daun pohon]   ]   ]
         (Focus)   (Topic 2)   NP S NP

Secondary topicalization (T6) now operates, fronting the NP marked with (Topic 2) and leaving behind it a copy:

[pohon   [daun pohon   dua meter   pandjang daun pohon]   ]
                                                       S   NP

After secondary topicalization, T8 applies, replacing the second occurrence of the constituent *daun pohon* with *ia* (written here in its alternate form -*nja*):

[pohon [daun pohon dua meter pandjang-nja]]
                                                      S   NP

The interior noun *pohon* which is identical to the exterior head noun is now fronted by T7, leaving its copy:

[pohon [pohon daun pohon dua meter pandjang-nja]]
                                                          S   NP

Rules T8 (*ia*-replacement) and T5 (*jang*-replacement) now apply to the string in order to produce the surface sentence. The successive outputs are as follows:

[pohon [pohon daun-nja dua meter pandjang-nja]]
[pohon jang   daun-nja dua meter pandjang-nja]

With respect to the ordering of rules, *jang*-replacement (T5) is a 'last-cycle' rule, i.e. it operates only after all cyclical rules have been applied, and only one lower S remains, namely that one which immediately dominates the noun to be replaced. T5 is, in other words, the last rule of those which have been discussed to apply.

One further observation must be made concerning the introduction of the relative pronoun *jang*. Rule T5 has been formulated in such a way as to make the presence of *jang* optional. Yet there are structures (such as that consisting of a head noun and an appositional noun) in which *jang* may not appear (cf. 3.6.2.3 and 3.6.2.4 above), and others, an example of which is sentence 41, whose derivation has just been given, where *jang* may not be omitted. These and other facts about Indonesian indicate that *jang* should in fact be introduced obligatorily by rule T5, and deleted either optionally or obligatorily under certain conditions. A full account of this situation would require a somewhat more ambitious study of Indonesian syntax than has been aimed for here.

3.8. *Complementation of Predicate Locatives*

The embedding of sentences in which the pronominalized constituent is the simple subject of the embedded sentence is straightforward; in the case of predicate locative sentences, the subject is simply deleted or replaced by *jang*, cf. 3.6.2.2 above. It is also possible, however, to have a locative noun phrase which is identical to the head noun, the subject of which is new. In sentences of the type:

42.   Rumah jang ada pohon di muka-nja...
           house   tree   face
           'The house which has trees in front of it'

rule T3 has operated on an underlying string:

[rumah [pohon [di muka   rumah]]   ]
                         (Topic 2) Loc S   NP

to produce:

[rumah [ada+pohon [di muka   rumah]]   ]
                             (Topic 2) Loc S   NP

and T6 (Secondary Topicalization) duplicates the topic NP at the front of
the sentence:

[rumah [rumah ada+pohon [di-muka   rumah]]   ]
                                       Loc S   NP

Pronominalization (T8) and relativization (T5) now apply to produce
successively:

[rumah [rumah ada+pohon [di muka-nja]]]
[rumah [jang   ada+pohon [di muka-nja]]]

This type of sentence is possible in Indonesian, but a difficulty arises when
the preposition is not compound, as in *di muka* 'opposite, in front of', but
simple, especially if it is the prime stative preposition *di*. There appears to
be no completely accepted alternative to the ungrammatical type:

         *halaman di jang ada pohon
          garden   tree
          'the garden in which there are trees'

Various ways out of the difficulty are used in practice, such as the Western-
influenced *dimana* 'where? (interrogative)', or the colloquial Malay usage of
tempat 'place' as a substitute for **di jang* or **jang...di-nja*.[26]

3.9. *Conclusions*

I have attempted in this section to make a few observations on verbless
stative sentences in Indonesian and provisionally suggest and formalize some
of the rules which appear to be involved. It would be premature to present
'conclusions' in the sense of significant generalizations from evidence when
clearly so much more substantive and theoretical work remains to be done,

---

[26] *Tempat* is perhaps more widely accepted than I have suggested here; cf. A. A. Fokker,
op. cit. p. 169.

but a few comments can be made with regard to universals and to Indonesian in particular.

The centrality of the concepts of topic and focus is apparent in verbless sentences, and this is true presumably of other types of sentence also. But these are notions which require considerable refinement. There is much about the origins and mechanisms of topicalization which I do not understand, yet which seems to play an important role in the *have/be* relationship, and in an account of existential verbs. I strongly suspect that many of the phenomena which I have been discussing are bound up with presuppositions, and will not be elucidated until the theory of presuppositions and the way in which it is to be incorporated into a grammatical theory have much advanced beyond their present state of confusion.

Several linguists have pointed to the close relationship between the expression of 'being' and 'possession', and E. Bach in particular has incorporated these observations into a formal syntactic account. In this paper, I have placed the set of phenomena into a slightly wider framework which I have called 'verbless stative sentences', and have attempted to explore Bach's proposal in its applications to an Austronesian language with a history of interaction with Western languages. This framework has been essentially a syntactic one. Yet semantic considerations have persistently threatened to dominate the account and to push it perhaps in the direction of a 'case grammar'; I have consciously tried to avoid this direction, but the problems of dealing with semantic aspects such as topic and focus, social factors such as speaker variation, bilingualism, etc., and even political moments inherent in nationalist movements, modernization and many other trends all appear to be involved in a complete account of the language and take it beyond the narrow concern of syntax.

Washington University, St. Louis

PERI BHASKARARAO

ON THE SYNTAX OF TELUGU EXISTENTIAL
AND COPULATIVE PREDICATIONS*

I. INTRODUCTION

Telugu, with its thirty-seven million speakers, is the second most widely spoken language of India. Its position in the Dravidian family of languages is unique in two ways: it is the major Dravidian language, and it is included in the South-Dravidian sub-family as well as the Central-Dravidian sub-family (Krishnamurti, 1961, p. 272).

Three works on Telugu grammar are worth mentioning. Arden's (1927) *A Progressive Grammar of the Telugu Language* (first published in 1873) in spite of its shortcomings as a traditional grammar with its conventional treatment and, to some extent, its approach of reading English grammar into Telugu, stands as the only traditional grammar with an authentic treatment of Telugu syntax which is "assisted by copious examples and exercises". The chapter 'On The Telugu Equivalents to the Verb to Be' (pp. 145–72) includes a good description of the nature of the equivalents of the verb *to be* in Telugu. Written as a basic course, Krishnamurti and Sivananda Sarma's (1968) *A Basic Course in Modern Telugu* contains a thorough analysis of the language in light of modern descriptive methodology. Sivaramamurthi's (1968) *Telugu Grammar* is a good descriptive analysis of the modern literary language which includes phonemics, morphemics, graphemics and a comparison of modern literary language with classical literary and colloquial languages.

A grammar of the equivalents of the verb 'to be' in Telugu is attempted in the present essay. The author being a native speaker of a coastal dialect of Telugu has freely utilized material from his own memory and other informants.

The transformational-generative model of the grammar proposed by Noam Chomsky in his *Aspects of the Theory of Syntax* (1965) is followed in this analysis.

* The research reported in this essay was made possible by a Fellowship at the Centre of Advanced Study in Linguistics, University of Poona at Deccan College, Poona.
   I am thankful to Professors A. M. Ghatage and Ashok R. Kelkar of the University of Poona and Professor P. H. Mattews of the University of Reading for their valuable comments and criticisms over the preliminary drafts of this essay. My thanks are due to Mr. Robert Berdan, Mr. Peter Hook, Mr. T. D. Francis, Mr. Ramesh K. Shrivastav Miss Susie Andres and Mr. John Anderson who helped me in improving this essay.

The scope of this essay is limited to the treatment of the equivalents of the verb 'to be' in Telugu as a main verb. It will be noted that in the following treatment the verb 'to be' is separated from the other verbs in the immediate expansion of the Predicate Phrase for clarity.

II. OUTLINE GRAMMAR

The main aim being the exposition of the syntactic nature of the equivalents of the verb 'to be', an outline grammar of Telugu is formulated in the following pages. Necessary and partially justified Phrase-structure rules and sub-categorizations and some important transformations constitute the outline grammar. No separate Morphophonemic sub-component is formulated but a rough representation of some morphophonemic rules is given wherever necessary. Although the rules are numbered for convenience of reference they are unordered.

The initial symbol S (Sentence) is expanded into:

   1)   S→NP   Pr.P   (NEG)

a Noun Phrase (NP) followed by a Predicate Phrase (Pr.P) which is followed by an optional Negative element (NEG). Whenever the optional NEG is selected, a transformation is triggered giving rise to negative sentences.

1. *Predicate Phrase*

The expansion of Pr.P results in

$$2) \qquad \text{Pr.P} \rightarrow \begin{Bmatrix} \text{BP} \\ \text{(Loc.P)} \quad \text{(TP)} \quad \text{VP} \end{Bmatrix} \text{TE}$$

a Verb 'Be' Phrase (BP) or a Verb Phrase (VP) preceded by an optional Time Phrase (TP) which may be preceded optionally by a Locative Phrase (Loc.P). A Tense element (TE) follows the BP or VP. This expansion sets the BP as a distinct phrase from VP.

VP is further expanded as:

   3)   VP→(P.P)   (P.P)   (Adv.P)   (S)   V

a Verb (V) preceded optionally by an S, an optional Adverbial Phrase (Adv.P) and two optional Post-positional Phrases (P.P). The introduction of S as an optional element preceding V accounts for some surface Adv.Ps derived from underlying sentences as will be seen later.

Depending on the selection of one, two or no P.Ps in the pre-verbal position in a VP, the verbs are classified as: Object-verbs, Double-object

verbs and Non-object verbs respectively. The following sentences exemplify
the above classification:

(1)   *si:ta a:lo:cistu:ndi*
      Sita   thinking
      'Sita is thinking'

(2)   *ra:ma:ra:v kontadu:ram   nadice:ḍu*
      Ramarao   some distance walked
      'Ramarao walked for some distance'

(3)   *uyy:la u:gindi*
      cradle swung
      'The cradle swung'

The above sentences stand as examples for non-object verbs and sentences (4)–(6) for object-verbs:

(4)   *ne:nu annam tinna:nu*
      I   food ate
      'I ate food'

(5)   *si:ta:ko:kacilakalu te:neni ta:gutunna:y*
           butterflies   honey drinking
      'The butterflies are drinking honey'

(6)   *ne:nu pustakam ra:stunna:nu*
      I   book   writing
      'I am writing a book'

The following are examples for double-object verbs:

(7)   *mo:han na:ku pustaka:nni icce:ḍu*
      Mohan me to book   gave
      'Mohan gave me a book'

(8)   *si:ta va:ḍiki i:ma:ṭa   ceppindi*
      Sita him to this word   told
      'Sita told this word to him'

P.P is expanded into:

   4)   P.P→NP+Po.P

an NP followed by a Post-position (Po.P). This Po.P when it follows an NP
dominating an N denoting an inanimate being is optionally deleted on the
surface structure and hence besides (6) and (8), (6') and (8') also are acceptable.

(6')   *ne:nu pustakam-ni ra:stunna:nu*
       'I am writing a book'

(8')   *si:ta va:ḍiki i:ma:ṭani ceppindi*
       'Sita told this word to him'

BP is further expanded as:

$$5) \quad BP \rightarrow \left\{ (TP) \quad \left(\left\{ \begin{matrix} Loc.P \\ Nom \end{matrix} \right\} \right) \atop NP \right\} Be$$

a Verb 'Be' (Be) preceded by a TP or a Loc.P or a Nominal (Nom) or an NP or nothing. Either the Loc.P or the Nom that precede the Be may further be preceded by an optional TP. Individual readings of the BP expansion are given in the following pages.

Expansion of Loc.P gives rise to:

$$6) \quad Loc.P \rightarrow \left\{ \begin{matrix} NP \\ DEM \end{matrix} \right\} \ LPo.P$$

an NP or a Demonstrative (DEM) followed by a Locative Postposition (LPo.P). A DEM may be marked for the features Proximate or Remote as:

$$7) \quad [+DEM] \rightarrow \begin{bmatrix} +DEM \\ \pm Proximate \end{bmatrix}$$

The following sentences stand as examples for the above Loc.P expansion:

(9)   *mo:han mancam-mi:da paḍukunna:ḍu*
        Mohan cot   on sleeping
        'Mohan is sleeping on a cot'

(10)   *pillaḍu a-k-kaḍa a:ḍukuṇṭunna:ḍu*
        child that at   playing
        'The child is playing there'

(11)   *pustakam i-k-kaḍa peṭṭu*
        book   this at keep
        'Keep the book here'

It was noted that the LPo.P *kaḍa* 'at' as in (10) and (11) occurs only after a DEM but not an NP. Similarly a DEM can take only the LPo.P *kaḍa* 'at' but not any other LPo.P. In another nonstandard speech this LPo.P is seen following an NP as in (12).

(12)   *satteyya iṇṭi-kaḍa unna:ḍu*
        Satteyya home at is
        'Satteyya is at home'

Some other LPo.Ps that can follow an NP dominated by a Loc.P are: *kinda* 'below', *payna* 'above', *lo:pala* 'inside', *bayṭa* 'outside', *venaka* 'behind', *mundu* 'in front', *edurukuṇḍa:* 'opposite', *cuṭṭu:* 'around', *pakkana* 'by the side', *tarva:ta* 'after' etc.

TP is further expanded as:

8) $TP \rightarrow \left\{ \begin{array}{c} \text{T-Word} \\ \left\{ \begin{array}{cc} \text{NUM} & \text{T-Unit} \\ \text{DEM} \end{array} \right\} \quad \text{TPo.P} \end{array} \right\}$

a Time-Word (T-Word) or a Time-Unit (T-Unit) preceded by a NUM and followed by a Time Post-position (TPo.P) or a DEM followed by a TPo.P. The following sentences stand as examples:

(13)   *mo: han ninna   vacce: ḍu*
        Mohan yesterday came
        'Mohan came yesterday'
(14)   *nuvvu oka-gaṇṭa-lo: veḷipocce: y*
        you   one hour in comeback
        'Come back in an hour'
(15)   *pa: ṭham i-p-puḍu undi*
        lesson   this at is
        'There is a lecture now'

ninna 'yesterday' in (13) is a T-Word. Some other examples of T-Word are *monna* 'day before yesterday', *re:pu* 'tomorrow', *elluṇḍi* 'day after tomorrow', *niruḍu* 'last year' etc. *gaṇṭa* 'hour' in (14) is a T-Unit and other examples of T-Unit are *nimaṣam* 'minute', *gaḍiya* 'second', *ro:ju* 'day', *nela* 'month' etc. Some of the TPo.Ps are homophonous with LPo.Ps. Some more examples of TPo.Ps are *tarva: ta* 'after', *mundu* 'before', *se:pu* 'for' etc. It may be noted that the TPo.P *puḍu* occurs only after a DEM. This restriction gives us only two types of DEM+LPo.P type of TPs, viz., *a-p-puḍu* 'then' and *i-p-puḍu* 'now'.

The TE obtained from the expansion of the Pr.P is, for the present purpose, subcategorized as Future or non-Future.

9) $[+\text{TE}] \rightarrow \begin{bmatrix} +\text{TE} \\ \pm\text{Future} \end{bmatrix}$

The following sentences exemplify this distinction:

(16)   *ne:nu ninna   vacc-e: -nu*
        I   yesterday came
        'I came yesterday'
(17)   *ne:nu ippuḍu vacc-e: -nu*
        I   now   came
        'I came now'

(18)   *ne:nu re:pu vas-ta:-nu*
         I   tomorrow will come
         'I will come tomorrow'

2. *Noun Phrase*

NP is expanded further into:

10) $\text{NP} \rightarrow (S) \left(\left\{ \begin{matrix} \text{DET} \\ \text{NUM} \end{matrix} \right\} \right) N$

a Noun (N) preceded by an optional Determiner (DET) or a NUM. An S may precede these optional elements optionally. It may be noted that no provision for any Modifier is made in the NP. It is proposed to derive all the Modifiers from modifier complements of underlying sentences. A DET is never a Demonstrative. It may be recalled that a DEM is included in the expansion of Loc.P and TP. Further analysis shows that the Demonstrative+N type of NPs are only surface structure NPs which should be derived from underlying Loc.P or TP complemented existential sentences.

A Noun is further subcategorized as:

11)   [+N] $\rightarrow \begin{bmatrix} +N \\ \pm \text{Adjective} \end{bmatrix}$

    [+Adjective] $\rightarrow [\pm \text{Psychosomatic}]$[1]

    [−Adjective] $\rightarrow [\pm \text{IIIrd Person}]$

    [+IIIrd Person] $\rightarrow [\pm \text{Singular}]$

    [+Singular] $\rightarrow [\pm \text{Human Masculine}]$

    [−Human Masculine]$\rightarrow [\pm \text{Psychosomatic}]$

    [−Singular] $\rightarrow [\pm \text{Human}]$

    [−IIIrd Person] $\rightarrow [\pm \text{Ist Person}] [\pm \text{Singular}]$

                                                [$\pm$ Masculine]

3. *Subject Agreement*

In Telugu verbs 'carry' a subject agreement element that carries the α features corresponding to the α features of the N dominated by the subject NP. Generally, except in copulative constructions, the SA element is added by a transformation in the post-verbal position immediately adjoining the TE. The following SA introduction rule is posited. Some other SA introduction rules are formulated for copulative constructions as will be found in the treatment of copulative predications.

---

[1] Langendoen (1967, p. 51) used the term 'Psychosomatic' to denote a certain subset of verbs which denote a bodily or mental activity in Mundari.

12)   x $\begin{bmatrix} +N \\ \alpha \text{ III Person} \end{bmatrix}$ y   V   TE   z →

　　　1   2   3   4   5   6

→x $\begin{bmatrix} +N \\ \alpha \text{ III Person} \end{bmatrix}$ y   V   TE $\begin{bmatrix} +SA \\ \alpha \text{ III Person} \end{bmatrix}$ z

　　　1   2   3   4   5   x   6

where x, y, z are cover symbols and

z ≯ NEG   when   TE → [− Future]

The specification of z ≯ NEG when TE → [− Future] is made in view of the absence of an SA element in Negative sentences where the tense is marked for [− Future]. This rule introduces SA element into 'positive non-future' sentences and 'positive or negative future' sentences. Observe the following examples:

(19)   *ne: nu paṇḍu tinna: -nu*
　　　I   fruit   ate   *SA*
　　　'I ate a fruit'

(20)   *ne: nu paṇḍu tiṇṭa: -nu*
　　　I   fruit   will   *SA*
　　　　　　　　　eat
　　　'I will eat a fruit'

(21)   *ne: nu paṇḍu tina-nu*
　　　I   fruit   will   *SA*
　　　　　　　　　not eat
　　　'I will not eat a fruit'

(22)   *ne: nu paṇḍu tina-le: du*
　　　I   fruit   ate   not
　　　'I did not eat a fruit'

Sentence (19) is in positive and the tense is [− Future]. Sentences (20) and (21) are in [+ Future]. (20) is positive whereas (21) is negative. Sentence (22) has tense marked for [− Future] and is in negative with no SA.

4. Pre-nominal Modification

Nouns may be modified by transforms of embedded sentences. It may be recalled that a provision is made for an S to be dominated by an NP in the NP expansion. Whenever this optional S is selected a set of transformations are triggered to give rise to the prenominal modifiers in Telugu. The set of transformations mainly consist of relative clause formation and its reduction. Observe the following sentences:

(23)   *ra:ma:ra:v cadivina pustakam ne:nu ra:se:nu*
      Ramarao read   book   I   wrote
      'I wrote the book which Ramarao has read'

(24)   *ninna   vaccina ra:ma:ra:v iva:ḷa ku:ḍa: vacce:ḍu*
      yesterday came Ramarao today   also   came
      'Ramarao who came yesterday came today also'

The N *pustakam* 'book' in (23) is dominated by an NP containing the Modifier on the surface structure, *ra:ma:ra:v cadivina*, which should be derived from an embedded sentence like (25):

(25)   *ra:ma:ra:v oka pustakam cadive:ḍu*
      Ramarao a   book   read
      'Ramarao read a book'

A relative clause is formed from (25) by the application of the following transformation:

13) $X-x\ N_1\ N_2\ y\ V\ z-N_2\ Y \rightarrow X-e{:}\ N_2\ N_1\ V\ o{:}\ a{:}\ N_2\ Y$

where X, Y are cover symbols for the matrix sentence. N_2 is the N dominated by NP of the matrix sentence. x, y, z are cover symbols of the embedded sentence. *e:, o:, a:* are relative markers; *e:* roughly corresponds to the relative-*which* of English relative clauses and *o:* and *a:* correspond to *that* of English relative clauses. The relative clause resulting from (25) by the application of this rule looks like:

(25′)   *e:*   *pustakam ra:ma:ra:v cadive:ḍu o: a: pustakam*
      which book   Ramarao read   that book

Further reduction of the relative clause is formulated in the following rule:

14) $X-e{:}\ N_2\ N_1\ V\ o{:}\ a{:}\ N_2\ Y \rightarrow X-V'\ N_2\ Y$

where V′ is the relative participle of V of the embedded sentence. This transformation deletes all the relative markers and Ns to the left of the V. The reduced relative clause formed from (25′) will be of the form:

(25″)   *ra:ma:ra:v cadivina pustakam*
      Ramarao read   book
      'The book which Ramarao read'

which is seen to be embedded in (23).

5. *Objectival and Subjectival Relativization*

A brief examination of these two types of relativization will be useful for the analysis of relativization as applied to existential constructions later. In Telugu, either the subject NP or the object NP of a transitive sentence can be relativized. Thus, from (25), in addition to the reduced relative clause (25″), we have (25a) also:

(25a)   *pustakam cadivina ra:ma:ra:v*
       book   read   Ramarao
      'Ramarao who read the book'

as embedded in sentence (26):

(26)   *pustakam cadivina ra:ma:ra:v ma: tammuḍu*
      book   read   Ramarao my brother
      'Ramarao who read the book is my brother'

Subject relativization needs a change in the referential index of the Ns of embedded sentence. The following rule:

15) $X - x\ N_1\ N_2\ y\ V\ z - N_1\ Y \rightarrow X - e:\ N_1\ N_2\ V\ o:\ a:\ N_1\ Y$

will account for the formation of the relative clause (25′a):

(25′a)   *e:*   *ra:ma:ra:v pustakam cadive:ḍu o: a: ra:ma:ra:v*
      which Ramarao book   read   that Ramarao

which is further reduced by the rule:

16) $X - e:\ N_1\ N_2\ V\ o:\ a:\ N_1\ Y \rightarrow X - V'\ N_1\ Y$

The result is (25a) and is embedded in (26).

III. VERB 'BE' PHRASE

The following readings of rule 5) are possible:

    a) BP→Be
    b) BP→Loc.P Be
    c) BP→TP Be
    d) BP→Nom Be
    e) BP→TP Loc.P Be
    f) BP→TP Nom Be
    g) BP→NP Be

The Telugu equivalent of 'to be' enters into two types of predications, viz., existential as in the readings a) to f) and copulative as in the reading

g). This distinction in the syntactic function of the verb necessitates the
following subcategorization:

$$17) \quad [+\text{Be}] \rightarrow \begin{bmatrix} +\text{Be} \\ \pm\text{Existential} \end{bmatrix}$$

where $[-\text{Existential}] = [+\text{Copulative}]$.

Be is expanded as:

$$18) \quad \text{Be} \rightarrow (ga\text{:}) \quad \text{B}$$

a verb root (B) preceded optionally by a *ga:* element (*ga:*).[2] This expansion
of Be gives rise to a further distinction in the existential predications, viz.,
attributive constructions and non-attributive constructions. Attributive
constructions are those in which the constituent Be dominates a *ga:* followed
by a B, whereas non-attributive constructions do not contain a *ga:* element
as a constituent of the constituent Be. Readings a), b), c) and e) are non-
attributive and are further distinguished as absolute existential (reading a))
temporal existential (c)) and locative existential (b) and e)). Readings d) and
f) denote the attributive existential constructions.

   In the following pages each type of predication is discussed separately
under appropriate major heads.

1. EXISTENTIAL PREDICATIONS

A. *Absolute Existential Constructions*

In Telugu, there are sentences which denote absolute existence of abstract
entities like God, Truth, Law etc., where the N denoting these entities
functions as the subject and the constituent Be does not have a complement.
The following sentences serve as examples for Absolute existential predications:

   (27)   *de:muḍu unna:ḍu*
          God   is
          'God exists'
   (28)   *dharmam undi*
          Law   is
          'Law exists'
   (29)   *satyam undi*
          Truth is
          'Truth exists'

_____

[2] Arden (1927, p. 154) treats this *ga:* as an adverbalizer. Present analysis includes *ga:*
as a part of Be rather than a constituent of the complement that precedes the verb. This
analysis is motivated by the further analysis of psychosomatic sentences.

B. *Temporal Existential Constructions*

As shown by the reading c), a BP may be constituted by a Be complemented by a TP. The following sentences may be observed:

(30) *baḍi   iva:ḷa undi*
school today is
'There is school today'

(31) *a:fi:su reṇḍugantala-ki undi*
office   two hours   at is
'Office is at two'

(32) *pa:ṭham re:pu uṇṭundi*
lesson   tomorrow will be
'There will be a lecture tomorrow'

It may be noted that the N that constitutes these sentences denotes an
abstract phenomenon which is often connected with an event, happening
or ongoing. Thus in the sentence (30) above, *baḍi* 'school' does not signify
'school' as a concrete element but as an abstract entity and so also the other
nouns which can occur in this position like *a:fi:su* 'office', *ko:rṭu* 'court (of
law)', *pa:ṭham* 'lesson/lecture' and *sinima:* 'cinema' etc.

C. *Locative Existential Constructions*

A Loc.P may complement the Be (as obtained from the readings b) and e)).
The following sentences exemplify the point:

(33) *mo:han iṇṭi-lo: unna:ḍu*
Mohan home in is
'Mohan is at home'

(34) *ma:illu   koṇḍa-kinda undi*
my house hill below   is
'My house is at the foot of the hill'

(35) *pustakam ṭe:bilu-mi:da undi*
book   table on   is
'The book is on the table'

(36) *ra:ma:ra:v i-k-kaḍa unna:ḍu*
Ramarao this at   is
'Ramarao is here'

(37) *si:ta a-k-kaḍa undi*
Sita that at   is
'Sita is there'

A Po.P that follows an N in constituting a Loc.P may either denote
'possession' or 'location'. Both locative constructions and possessive con-

structions, constructions where the complement of the constituent Be is a
Loc.P with a Po.P denoting 'possession' show identical constituent strains
and undergo the same types of transformations. A possessive construction
cannot be treated as a transform of a corresponding construction with a
Loc.P complement or vice versa. The following sentences make the point
clear:

(38) *ḍabbu na:-daggara undi*
      money me at   is
      'I have money'
(39) *ḍabbu na:-ku undi*
      money me to is
      'I have money'

Sentence (38) means 'I have some money with me (now)', whereas the
meaning of sentence (39) is that 'I have money (I am rich)'. The distinction
is more explicit in the following set of sentences:

(40) *pennu va:ḍi-daggara undi*
      pen   him at   is
      'He has a pen'
(41) *pennu va:ḍi-ki undi*
      pen   him to is
      'He has a pen'

Sentence (40) as distinct from sentence (41) means that 'He has a pen
with him, which may not necessarily belong to him', whereas sentence (41)
means that 'He has a pen which belongs to him (by owner-owned relation)'.

In this treatment, two types of 'Possession' are grouped together as 'Possession', which may be termed as 'Inalienable possession' for simplicity, but
with an extension of the definition of 'inalienability'. Any 'intimate possession' showing some 'intimacy' between the possessor and the possessed also
is grouped under the extended term inalienable possession in this essay.
Thus the type of possession denoted in sentences (39) and (41) and the
constituent and constitute type of relation as expressed in sentences (42) and
(43) also come under this definition of inalienability.

(42) *ka:ḷḷu kurci:-ki unna:y*
      legs   chair to are
      'The chair has legs'
(43) *kommalu ceṭṭu-ki unna:y*
      branches tree to are
      'The tree has branches'

Thus, for instance, sentences (44) and (45) are acceptable whereas (46) and (47) are unacceptable:

(44)   *reṇḍu kaḷḷu na:-ku unna:y*
       two eyes me to are
       'I have two eyes'

(45)   *iddaru pillalu   na:-ku unna:ru*
       two   children me to are
       'I have two children'

(46)   **reṇḍu kaḷḷu na:-daggara unna:y*
       two   eyes me with   are
       'I have two eyes with me'

(47)   **iddaru pillalu   na:-daggara unna:ru*
       two   children me with   are
       'I have two children with me'

A Loc.P denoting possession cannot dominate a DEM when the other constituent is a Po.P denoting possession. That is why (48) is not acceptable, whereas (36) is:

(48)   **ra:ma:ra:v i-ku unna:ḍu*
       Ramarao   this to is

A Loc.P is optionally deleted in sentences like:

(49)   *mi:-na:nnaga:ru iṇṭi-lo: unna:ra: ?*[3]
       your father   home in is
       'Is your father at home?'

(50)   *ni:-pennu ni:-daggara unda:?*
       your pen you with   is
       'Have you got your pen with you?'

giving rise to (49') and (50') respectively with no difference in meaning:

(49') *mi:-na:nnaga:ru unna:ra: ?*

(50') *ni:-pennu unda: ?*

A Loc. P may optionally be permuted with the constituent subject NP.

---

[3] It may be noted that this type of deletion is possible in non-interrogative sentences also, though only interrogative sentences are given as examples in the above analysis. Thus, *ma:-na:nnaga:ru unna:ru* 'My father is there (at home)' is a possible answer to the question implied in sentence (49) or (49').

Note, however, that the deletion of a Loc.P is not always applicable as in the sentence *pustakam unda:?* 'Is there a book?' which cannot be derived from a sentence like *pustakam ṭe:bilu mi:da unda:?* 'Is there a book on the table?'. Several other semantic features at a level higher than the phrase level are implied and thus restrict the applicability of this transformation.

Thus sentences (38)–(41) have as their counterparts (38')–(41') respectively:

(38')   *na:-daggara ḍabbu undi*
(39')   *na:-ku ḍabbu undi*
(40')   *va: ḍi-daggara pennu undi*
(41')   *va: ḍi-ki pennu undi*

As evident from the reading e) an optional TP may precede the constituent Loc. P. The following sentences serve as examples:

(51)   *ra: ma: ra: v ippuḍu inṭi-lo: unna: ḍu*
        Ramarao   now   home in   is
        'Ramarao is at home now'
(52)   *ḍabbu iva:ḷa na:-ku undi*
        money today me to   is
        'I have money today'

There are certain restrictions on the selection of the TP in pre-Loc.P position and occurrence of the TE as a constituent of the Pr.P. Thus, (51) and (52) are acceptable whereas (53) and (54) are not:

(53)   **ra: ma: ra: v re: pu inṭi-lo: unna: ḍu*
        'Ramarao is at home tomorrow'
(54)   **na: ku ninna ḍabbu unṭundi*
        'I will have money yesterday'

D. *Attributive Existential Constructions*

The Nom that is obtained from the readings d) and f) of BP expansion can further be expanded as:

19)   Nom $\rightarrow$ (S) $\begin{bmatrix} +\text{N} \\ +\text{Adjective} \end{bmatrix}$

as an S optionally preceding an N with the features $\begin{bmatrix} +\text{N} \\ +\text{Adjective} \end{bmatrix}$.

It should be noted that the *ga:* element that results from the expansion of Be as an optional element occurs only when a Nom complements the Be. Thus, treating *ga:* as a complex symbol, following the convention, the following category may be produced:

$$[+ga:, \quad +(\text{TP}) \quad \text{Nom} \quad \text{B} \quad \underline{\qquad}]$$

In view of these restrictions, the BP expansion rule may be restated by combining the readings d) and f) together as:

5a)   BP $\rightarrow$ (TP)   (S) $\begin{bmatrix} +\text{N} \\ +\text{Adjective} \end{bmatrix}$ *ga:*   B

The following sentences may be observed as examples for this type of construction:

(55)   *ne:nu poḍugu ga: unna:nu*
       I   tall   am
       'I am tall'

(56)   *mo:han nalupu ga: unna:ḍu*
       Mohan dark   is
       'Mohan is dark'

(57)   *si:ta andam ga: undi*
       Sita   beautiful is
       'Sita is beautiful'

(58)   *a:pillaḍu muddu ga: unna:ḍu*
       that boy   cute   is
       'That boy is cute'

Arden (1927, p. 154) has pointed out in his grammar that the *-ga:* element functions as an adverbalizer. This is true with non-verb 'Be' sentences in Telugu, where the *-ga:* is added to an adjective or a noun to give rise to the corresponding adverbials. But in the case of verb 'Be' constructions, the *ga:* element is never 'suffixed' to the preceding 'adjectival' (treated as Nom in this essay, it constitutes the Be). This analysis has motivation drawn from the transformations applicable to psychosomatic sentences as will be seen in the discussion that follows.

The difference between *ga:* as an adverbalizer and as a constituent of Be is evident from the following sentences:

(59)   *mo:han nannu gaṭṭi-ga: koṭṭe:ḍu*
       Mohan me   hard   hit
       'Mohan has hit me hard'

(60)   *ma:miḍika:ya gaṭṭi ga: undi*
       mango fruit   hard   is
       'The mango fruit is hard'

The Phrase-marker for the attributive constructions is shown in diagram (I), whereas the Phrase-marker for sentences like (60) is represented in diagram (II).

i. *Gerundival and Cognate Noun Phrases.* An NP derived from an underlying sentence by gerundivalization or cognate noun formation may function as the subject in an attributive construction. The following examples may be noted:

(61)   *saro:ja ka:runaḍapaḍam jo:ru ga: undi*
       Saroja car driving   fast   is
       'Saroja drove her car fast'

(I)

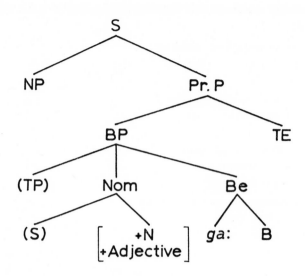

(II)

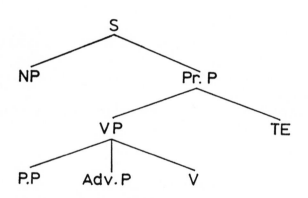

(62) *mi:ru ra:vaḍam ba:gu ga: undi*
      you   coming   good   is
      'It is good that you have come'

(63) *a: abba:yi pa:ṭa ba:gu ga: undi*
      that boy   song   good   is
      'The song sung by that boy is good'

(64) *saro:ja   navvu andam ga: undi*
      Saroja's smile beautiful is
      'Saroja's smile is beautiful'

(65) *na: ra:ta   ba:gu ga: undi*
      my handwriting good   is
      'My handwriting is good'

The tree-diagram (III) represents the deep-structure of the sentence (61).

(III)

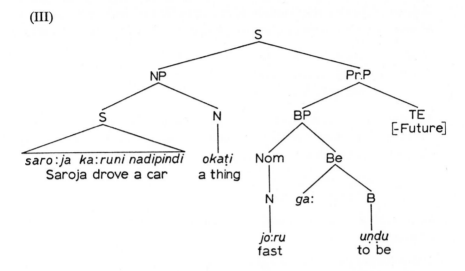

A gerundivalization transformation applied on the embedded sentence deletes the constituent Po.P, deletes the constituent TE and adds a gerundival marker to the V. Another transformation replaces the constituent N of the matrix sentence by the gerundival phrase giving rise to sentence (61).

Sentences (63)–(64) contain a cognate noun as the subject. A cognate noun in Telugu is derived from an underlying sentence with an intransitive verb. Thus, the sentence (64) will have a deep-structure represented as in the tree diagram (IV).

(IV)

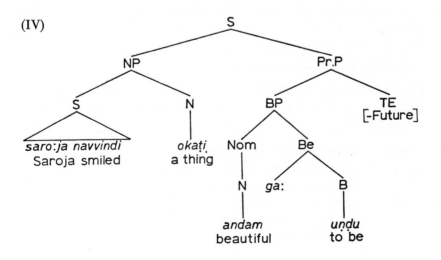

A transformation applied to the embedded sentence will copy down a noun cognate to the intransitive verb to function as an object of the matrix sentence. A further relativization of the embedded sentence gives rise to a relative clause which may further be reduced to a reduced relative clause as:

(66)   *saro:ja navvina navvu*
        Saroja smiled   smile
        'The smile Saroja smiled'

A further transformation brings out the modifier+N type of compound from this reduced relative clause by deleting the constituent relative participle *navvina* to result in:

(66')   *saro:ja navvu*
         'The smile of Saroja'

which replaces the constituent N of the matrix sentence giving rise to sentence (64).

ii. *Conditional Phrase.* An embedded sentence may undergo a transformation resulting in a conditional phrase as in sentences (67) and (68).

(67)   *mi:ru a:pani ce:ste: ba:gu ga: uṇṭundi*
        you   that work do if good   will be
        'It will be good if you do that work'
(68)   *ne:nu va:ḍiki ḍabbu icce:ste: marya:da ga: uṇṭundi*
        I   him to money give if   dignity   will be
        'It will be of some dignity if I give the money to him'

The tree-diagram (V) represents the deep-structure of sentence (68).

A transformation attaches *te:*, the conditional marker, to the verb of the embedded sentence and deletes the TE of the embedded sentence. The constituent N of the matrix sentence will be replaced by the formulated conditional phrase to give rise to sentence (68).

iii. *Derivation of some Adv.Ps.* Some Adv.Ps on the surface structure in Telugu can be derived from underlying sentences as made explicit in the sentences (69)–(71).

(69)   *ṭailaru na: cokka: poḍugga: kuṭṭe:ḍu*
        tailor   my shirt   long   stitched
        'The tailor made my shirt long'
(70)   *ra:ma:ra:v va:ci:ni ba:gu ce:se:ḍu*
        Ramarao   watch   good did
        'Ramarao repaired the watch'

(71)   *mallayya peraḍuni subhramga: tuḍice:ḍu*
        Mallayya backyard cleanly   swept
        'Mallayya swept the backyard clean'

(V)

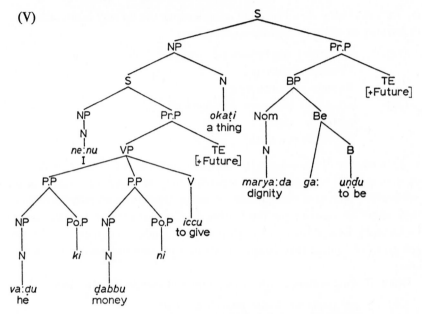

The deep-structure of the sentence (69) may be represented as in the tree-diagram (VI).

(VI)

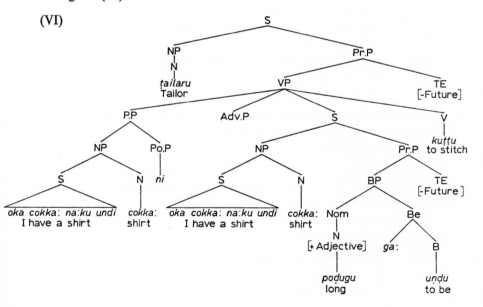

The embedded sentence of the VP, i.e. the sentence immediately dominated by the VP node of the matrix sentence, gives rise to the Adv.P on the surface structure.

iv. *Role Sentences.* The Nom that complements the Be may denote the 'role' of the subject as in the following examples:

(72)   *ra:ma:ra:v me:ne:jaru ga: unna:ḍu*
     Ramarao   manager   is
     'Ramarao is a manager'

(73)   *subba:ra:v guma:sta: ga: unna:ḍu*
     Subbarao   clerk   is
     'Subbarao is a clerk'

v. *Comparative Constructions.* In Telugu a comparative construction consists of an embedded sentence. The comparison may be either for 'degree' or for 'similarity', and so a comparator, which is transformationally introduced may either be marked for the feature [+Comparison] or for the feature [+Degree]. Except for this transformationally added comparator, the two sub-types of comparative constructions do not show any constituent difference.

The following sentences serve as examples of comparison for degree:

(74)   *sya:mala na:-kaṇṭe poḍugu ga: undi*
     Syamala me than   tall   is
     'Syamala is taller than I'

(75)   *i:-paṇḍu   a:-paṇḍu-kanna: ti:pi ga: undi*
     this fruit   that fruit than   sweet   is
     'This fruit is sweeter than that fruit'

(76)   *va:ḍu andari-kanna: huṣa:ru ga: unna:ḍu*
     that man all than   active   is
     'He is more active than all the others'

Tree-diagram (VII) represents the deep-structure of comparative constructions, taking sentence (74) as an example.

The comparativization transformation applied to the above sentence deletes the constituent Pr.P of the embedded sentence and introduces the comparator *kaṇṭe/kanna* to be attached to the constituent NP of the embedded sentence.

The following are examples for comparative constructions denoting comparison for similarity:

(77)   *ne:nu villu-la:ga poḍugu ga: unna:nu*
     I   bow as   tall   am
     'I am as tall as a bow'

(VII)

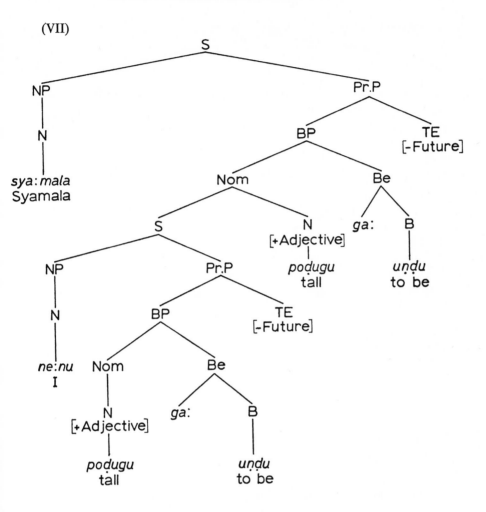

(78)   *a:me naḍumu simham naḍumu-la:ga sannam ga: undi*
       her waist lion   waist   as   slender is
       'Her waist is as slender as that of a lion.'

The deep-structure of these sentences is represented in diagram (VIII).

The comparativization transformation applied to the above structure deletes the constituent Pr.P of the embedded sentence and introduces the comparator *la:ga* which is marked for the feature [+Similarity] to be attached to the constituent NP of the embedded sentence.

vi. *Psychosomatic sentences.* A Nom constituted by an N marked for the feature $\begin{bmatrix} +\text{Adjective} \\ +\text{Psychosomatic} \end{bmatrix}$ may complement a verb Be in an attributive

(VIII)

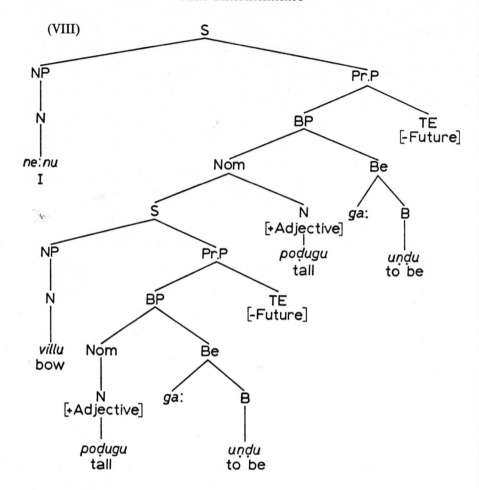

construction as may be observed in the following sentences:

(79)   *va:-ḍu   ko:pam ga: unna:ḍu*
       that man angry   is
       'He is angry'

(80)   *saro:ja huṣa:ru ga: undi*
       Saroja active   is
       'Saroja is active'

(81)   *mu:rti a:nandam ga: unna:ḍu*
       Murty pleasant   is
       'Murty is pleasant'

(82)   *si:ta sarada: ga: undi*
       Sita happy   is
       'Sita is happy'

(a) Nom Complementation. A Nom as expanded previously may contain a sentence under its immediate domination, provided the N that constitues the constituent Nom is marked for the features $\begin{bmatrix} +\text{Adjective} \\ +\text{Psychosomatic} \end{bmatrix}$.   The following sentences exemplify the point:

(83)   *va:ḍu   ne:nu vacce:nu ani ko:pam ga: unna:ḍu*
         that man I   came   angry   is
         'He is angry because I came'

(84)   *saro:ja tanu pari:tṣa   pe:sayindi ka:batti huṣa:ru ga: undi*
         Saroja she examination passed   hence active   is
         'Saroja is active because she passed her examination'

(85)   *mu:rti pillalu   ba:ga: caduvutunna:ru ani a:nandam ga: unna:ḍu*
         Murty children well   reading   happy   is
         'Murty is happy because his children are studying well'

Tree-diagram (IX) makes the deep-structure of this construction type explicit.

(IX)

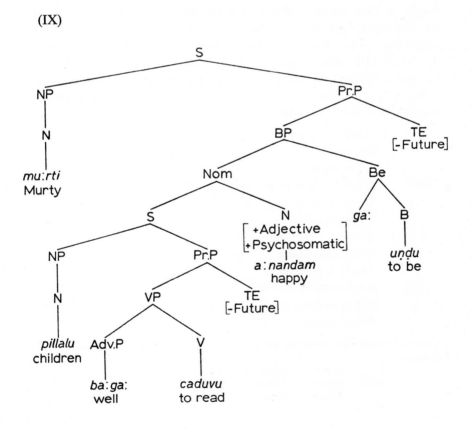

The complementizer *ani* is introduced by a transformation into a position following the embedded sentence.

A TP may optionally precede the Nom to give rise to sentences like:

(86)   *va:ḍu iva:ḷa   ko:pam ga: unna:ḍu*
        that man today angry   is
        'He is angry today'

(87)   *si:ta ninna   sarada:ga: undi*
        Sita   yesterday happy   was
        'Sita was happy yesterday'

(88)   *saro:ja re:pu   huṣa:ru ga: uṇṭundi*
        Saroja tomorrow active   will be
        'Saroja will be active tomorrow'

(b) Subject-less Sentences. In Telugu there is a particular set of sentences referred to as subject-less sentences, with the verb used impersonally. (Arden, 1927, p. 155.) On the surface it looks as if the subject of the sentence is 'missing' in this construction. A confusion of this sort arises because of the misbracketing of the constituents as 'subject' and 'complement'. Semantically, in these sentences also we can recognize a 'possessed quality' and its 'possessor'. Syntactically the form that denotes the 'possessor' constitutes the Loc.P as an NP. By accepting the point that the element *ga:* is an adverbial suffix as Arden (1927, p. 154) did, one has to submit that the nouns denoting the psychosomatic phenomena are adverbalized by the addition of this element. This is the type of misbracketing[4] that makes one perceive that sentences like:

(79′)   *va:ḍiki ko:pam ga: undi*
        him to angry   is
        'He is angry'

(80′)   *saro:jaki huṣa:ru ga: undi*
        Saroja to active   is
        'Saroja is active'

(81′)   *mu:rtiki a:nandam ga: undi*
        Murty to pleasant   is
        'Murty is pleasant'

(82′)   *si:taki sarada: ga: undi*
        Sita to happy   is
        'Sita is happy'

---

[4] The constituent structure of the sentence (79′) implied in Arden's treatment will be of the form:

Ø   *va:ḍiki*   *ko:pamga:*   *undi*
subject   Possessive   Adverbial   Verb
           Phrase   Phrase

contain no verb, but only a Loc.P linked to an adverbial phrase by the verb 'Be' which shows concord to a 'missing' subject noun.

A subjectivization transformation can handle the derivation of the so-called 'subject-less sentences', (79')–(82'), from the same source as that of (79)–(82). This is motivated by the absence of any difference in meaning between the corresponding sentences of these two sets. The following transformation is formulated which is optional when the N of Nom is [+Psychological] and obligatory when it is [−Psychological]:

$$
20) \quad X \quad NP \quad Y \quad \begin{bmatrix} +N \\ +\text{Adjective} \\ +\text{Psychosomatic} \end{bmatrix} \quad Be \quad Z \rightarrow
$$

$$
\quad\quad 1 \quad 2 \quad 3 \quad\quad\quad 4 \quad\quad\quad\quad 5 \quad 6
$$

$$
\rightarrow X \quad NP+LPo.P \quad Y \quad \begin{bmatrix} +W \\ -\text{Adjective} \\ +\text{Psychosomatic} \end{bmatrix} \quad Be \quad Z
$$

$$
\quad\quad 1 \quad 2 \quad +x \quad 3 \quad\quad\quad 4 \quad\quad\quad\quad 5 \quad 6
$$

This transformation adds a Locative Post-position denoting possession to the constituent subject NP and replaces the feature [+Adjective] of the constituent N of the Nom by the feature [−Adjective].

Sentences like (89)–(91) have a constituent Nom marked for the feature [−Psychological].

(89)   *va:ḍiki cali ga: undi*
        him to cold   is
        'He is feeling cold'

(90)   *va:ḍiki ukka ga: undi*
        him to sultry   is
        'He is feeling sultry'

(91)   *va:ḍiki durada ga: undi*
        him to itch   is
        'He is feeling itchy'

The corresponding non-subjectivalized forms of these sentences are unacceptable on surface structure:

(89')   *va:ḍu caliga: unna:ḍu*

(90')   *va:ḍu ukka ga: unna:ḍu*

(91')   *va:ḍu durada ga: unna:ḍu*

This fact gives us the reason for making the optional rule of subjectivization obligatory when the N of the Nom is marked for the feature [+Somatic] (= −Psychological).

The SA element chosen concords with the subject NP, *va:ḍu* 'he' in sentence (79), whereas the corresponding (79') contains an SA element agreeing with the subject *ko:pam* 'anger'.

All those sentences in which a sentence is complemented under the immediate domination of the constituent Nom can also undergo this transformation of subjectivization. Observe the following examples:

(83')   *va:ḍiki ne:nu vacce:nu ani ko:pam ga: undi*
        him to I   came   anger   is
        'He is angry because I came'

(84')   *saro:jaki tanu pari:ṭṣa   pe:sayindi ka:baṭṭi uṣa:ru ga: undi*
        Saroja to she examination passed   hence   active is
        'Saroja is active because she passed her examination'

(85')   *mu:rtiki pillalu ba:ga: caduvutunna:ru ani a:nandam ga: undi*
        Murty to children well   reading   happy   is
        'Murty is happy because his children are studying well'

vii. *Deletion of Be + TE in sentences denoting a 'Universal Fact'.* There is a class of attributive existential constructions in Telugu, where the constituent Be + TE is deleted optionally. However, the sentence as a whole should denote a 'universal fact' or a 'habitual existence'. The denotation of 'universal fact' is attributed to the TE element that follows the Be. Observe the following sets of sentences:

(92)   *a:vu pa:lu telupu*   from (92') *a:vu pa:lu telupu ga: uṇṭa:yi*
        cow milk white   is
        'Cow-milk is white'   'Cow-milk is white'

(93)   *ka:ki mukku nalupu* from (93') *ka:ki mukku nalupa ga:uṇṭundi*
        crow beak black   'The beak of a crow is black'
        'The beak of a crow is black'

(94)   *pancada:ra ti:pi*   from (94') *pancada:ra ti:pi ga: uṇṭundi*
        sugar   sweet   'Sugar is sweet'
        'Sugar is sweet'

E. *Relativization Applied to Existential Constructions*

i. *Formation and Reduction of Relative Clauses.* An existential construction may undergo the various transformations included under pre-nominal modification giving rise to Modifier + N type of NPs on the surface structure. Examine the following sentences:

(95)   *ṭe:bilu mi:da unna pustaka:nni nuvvu ti:sikio:*
        table on   is   book   you   take
        'Take the book which is on the table'

(96) *a-k-kaḍa unna ra:ma:ra:v-ni pilu*
      that at is Ramarao   call
      'Call that Ramarao who is there'

(97) *i-p-puḍu unna pa:ṭham e:miṭi?*
      this at is lesson what
      'What is the lesson now?'

(98) *na:ku unna ḍabbulo: sagam ni:ku ista:nu*
      me to is money in half you to will give
      'I will give you half of the money I have'

(99) *ne:nu poḍugu ga: unna amma:yine: peḷḷa:ḍuta:nu*
      I   tall   is girl only will marry
      'I will marry only that girl who is tall'

(100) *ko:pam ga: unna maniṣito: ja:garta ga: uṇḍu*
      angry   is person with careful   be
      'Be careful with a person who is angry'

The deep-structure of sentence (95) which may illustrate the deep-structure
of sentences (95)–(100) in general is represented in tree-diagram (X).

(X)

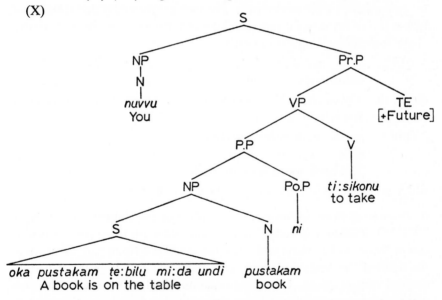

The following sentences are treated as sources for the reduced relative
clauses which function as NPs on the surface structure in sentences (95)–
(100):

(101) *oka pustakam ṭe:bilu mi:da undi*
      one book   table on   is
      'A book is on the table'

(102)   *ra:ma:ra:v a-k-kaḍa unna:ḍu*
         Ramarao that at   is
         'Ramarao is there'

(103)   *oka pa:ṭham i-p-puḍu undi*
         one lesson   this at   is
         'There is a lesson now'

(104)   *konta ḍabbu na:-ku undi*
         some money me to   is
         'I have some money'

(105)   *oka amma:yi poḍugu ga: undi*
         one girl   tall   is
         'A girl is tall'

(106)   *oka maniṣi ko:pam ga: unna:ḍu*
         one person angry   is
         'A person is angry'

The same rules of relative clause formation and reduction are applied to these sentences to obtain the respective reduced relative clauses when embedded in sentences (95)–(100) respectively. For instance the embedded sentence of (95) as shown in the tree diagram will undergo the transformation of relative clause formation giving rise to (101′).

(101′)   *e: pustakam ṭe:bilu mi:da undi o: a: pustakam*
         which book   table   on   is that book

Recall the relative clause reduction transformation which when applied to (101′) gives rise to (101″).

(101″)   *ṭe:bilu mi:da unna pustakam*
         table   on   is   book
         'The book which is on the table'

which is embedded in the matrix sentence as well as in (95).

ii. *Deletion of Relative Participle unna.* Most of the constructions with an NP that dominates the nodes Modifier and Noun on the surface structure can be shown to be matrix sentences, the modifier + Noun part of which is the result of the deletion of the relative participle *unna* from the respective reduced relative clause. This transformation of relative participle deletion which gives rise to Modifier + Noun type of Surface NPs, where the modifier may be an adjective, locative, possessive or a demonstrative, may be formulated as:

21) $X - W + Z_1 + N_1 - Y \rightarrow X - W + N_1 - Y$
       1   2 +3 +4   5   1   2 +4   5

where $Z_1 = unna$, relative participle of *uṇḍu* 'to be'.

iii. *Locative + N type of NPs.* Deletion of the relative participle from the embedded reduced relative clause in sentence (95) gives rise to (95′).

(95′)   *ṭe:bilu mi:da pustaka:nni nuvvu ti:siko:*
          table on   book   you   take
          'Take that book on the table'

(a) Optional deletion of LPo.P and TPo.P. An LPo.P or a TPo.P that follow a DEM may optionally be deleted. By the application of the relative participle *unna* deletion rule we get:

(96′)   *a-k-kaḍa ra:ma:ra:v ni pilu*
          that at   Ramarao   call
          'Call that Ramarao who is there'

(97′)   *i-p-puḍu pa:tham e:miṭi?*
          this at   lesson   what
          'What is the lesson now?'

By deleting LPo.P and TPo.P we get:

(96″)   *a:-ra:ma:ra:v ni pilu*
          That Ramarao   call
          'Call that Ramarao'

(97″)   *i:-pa:tham e:miṭi?*
          this lesson what
          'What is this lesson?'

The rule is formulated as:

$$22)\quad X-DEM+\begin{Bmatrix}LPo.P\\TPo.P\end{Bmatrix}+N-Y \rightarrow X-DEM+N-Y$$

$$1\quad 2\ +\quad 3\quad +4\ \ 5\quad 1\quad 2\ +4\ \ 5$$

Mention may be made of some other occurrences of demonstrative expressions like:

(107)   *a: a:lo:cana*
          'that thought'

(108)   *i: abhipra:yam*
          'this opinion'

However, it will be noticed that we have mainly confined ourselves to spatial and temporal deixis. We believe that other demonstrative expressions are ultimately in the nature of textual cross-references and call for further study.
(b) Obligatory Deletion of LPo.P denoting 'Possession'. The LPo.P denoting possession is obligatorily deleted on the surface structure as a sequel to the relative participle deletion.

23) $X-NP+\begin{bmatrix} LPo.P \\ +Possessive \end{bmatrix} -N-Y \rightarrow X-NP+N-Y$

       1   2   +   3   4 5   1 2 +4 5

This transformation gives rise to sentences like (98'), which is similar to (98).

(98')   *na:-ḍabbu lo: sagam ni:ku ista:nu*
         my money in half you to will give
         'I will give half of my money to you'

iv. *Subject Relativization and Complement Relativization.* It has previously
been mentioned that in the case of transitive sentences the process of relativization may be either subjectival or objectival. A similar pattern is found
in the case of the locative existential sentences. A sentence in which the verb
'Be' is complemented by a Loc.P can be relativized in two ways giving rise
to two types of NPs when embedded in other matrix sentences. In the first
type of the surface NP, the modified N is the subject N of the underlying
sentence and the modifying locative is the complement Loc.P of the underlying form. In the other type the condition is reversed, i.e., the modified N
of the surface NP is derived from the NP that constitutes the Loc.P of the
underlying sentence and the modifying NP from the subject NP of the underlying sentence. The first type of NP we will call the product of subject
relativization and the latter type of NP the product of complement relativization. Observe the sentences (109) and (110):

(109)   *de:muḍu koṇḍa-mi:da unna:ḍu*
         god   hill on   is
         'God is on the hill'
(110)   *mu:rti inṭi-lo: unna:ḍu*
         Murty house in is
         'Murty is in the house'

When embedded in other matrix sentences the sentences (109) and (110) may
undergo subject relativization to give rise to relative clauses (109') and (110')
respectively:

(109')   *koṇḍa-mi:da e: de:muḍu unna:ḍu o: a: de:muḍu*
         hill on   which god   is   that god
(110')   *inṭi-lo: e: mu:rti unna:ḍu o: a: mu:rti*
         house in which Murty is   that Murty

Further reduction and relative participle deletion gives rise to NPs (109")
and (110"):

(109")   *koṇḍa-mi:da de:muḍu*
         'The god on the hill'

(110″)   *inṭi-lo: mu:rti*
          'Murty in the house'

Complement relativization is applicable to (109) and (110) when embedded
in other matrix sentences which results in relative clauses (109a) and (110a)
respectively:

(109a)   *de:muḍu e: koṇḍa-mi:da unna:ḍu o: a: koṇḍa*
          god   which hill on   is   that hill
(110a)   *mu:rti e: inṭi-lo: unna:ḍu o: a: illu*
          Murty which house in is   that house

Further reduction and relative participle deletion gives rise to other types
of NPs like:

(109b)   *de:muḍu koṇḍa*
          'God's hill'
(110b)   *mu:rti illu*[5]
          'Murty's house'

The possibility of undergoing a complement relativization is found in the
case of some possessive sentences. Thus the NPs:

(111)   *oṇṭi kannu maniṣi*
          one eye   person
          'one eyed person'
(112)   *reṇḍu talalapa:mu*
          two   heads snake
          'Two headed snake'

are derived from sentences (111′) and (112′) respectively:

(111′)   *oṇṭi kannu oka maniṣiki undi*
          one eye   one person to is
          'A person has a single eye'
(112′)   *reṇḍu talalu oka pa:muki unna:y*
          two   heads one snake to are
          'A snake has two heads'

Mostly, the modifiers in these derived NPs denote some peculiar or special
feature and that is why NPs like (113) and (114) are rarely found even in
the surface structure:

(113)   **reṇḍu kaḷḷa maniṣi*
          two   eyes man
          'Two eyed person'

---

[5] The compound *mu:rti illu* 'Murty's house' is ambiguous. It may also mean 'the house
that belongs to Murty' when derived from an underlying sentence like *oka illu mu:rtiki
undi* 'Murty has a house'.

(114)   *oṇṭi tala pa:mu
         'One headed snake'

v. *Adjective + Noun type of NPs.* The Adj + N type of NPs on the surface
structure, as mentioned earlier, are derived by application of the relative
participle *unna* deletion from the reduced relative clauses. Observe the
following sentences:

(99')   *ne:nu podugu amma:yine: peḷḷa: ḍuta:nu*
         I   tall   girl only will marry
         'I will marry a tall girl only'
(100')   *ko:pam maniṣito: ja:garta ga: uṇḍu*
         angry   person with careful   be
         'Be careful with an angry man'
(115)   *a: nalla gurram to:ka telupu ga: undi*
         that black horse   tail   white   is
         'The tail of that black horse is white'

As is evident, deletion of the relative participle from the reduced relative
clause of the embedded sentences (99) and (100) gives rise to (99') and (100')
respectively. The deep-structure of sentence (115) is represented in diagram
(XI) to show the possibility of derivation of the Adj + N on to the surface-
structure.

(XI)

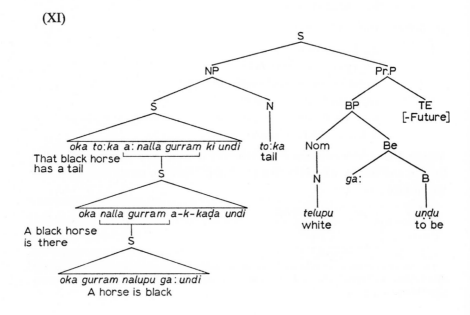

We have observed that in sentences like (61) a gerundival phrase functions as the subject of the attributive construction. A further relativization cannot be applied to these matrix sentences where the subject NP is a gerundival phrase, and so forms like (116) are ill-formed.

(116)   *jo:ru ga: unna saro:ja ka:ru naḍapaḍam

However, a sentence in which the constituent subject NP is a cognate N derived from another underlying sentence may undergo the process of pre-nominal modification. Thus (64') is derived from (64).

(64')   andam ga: unna saro:ja navvu
         'The beautiful smile of Saroja'

Sentences like (117) contain an NP derived from a relativized comparative construction:

(117)   ne:nu na: kaṇṭe poḍugu maniṣini cu:ḷḷe:du
         I   me than tall   person saw not
         'I never saw a person taller than me'

The NP na: kaṇṭe poḍugu maṇiṣi 'a person taller than me' is derived from the sentence:

(118)   oka maniṣi na: kaṇṭe poḍugu ga: unna:ḍu
         one person me than tall   is
         'A person is taller than me'

The deep-structure of (117) is represented in the tree-diagram (XII).

A sentence in which the constituent Nom is complemented by another sentence (as e.g. in (83)) may undergo the process of relativization when embedded in another matrix sentence:

(119)   ne:nu vacce:nu ani ko:pam ga: unna ra:ma:ra:v
         I   came   angry   is   Ramarao
         ne:nu ko:ruṇḍi   ra:le:du ani telisikoni ba:dhapaḍḍa:ḍu
         I   intentionally did not come known   repented
         'Ramarao who was angry because I came, felt sorry after knowing that I did'nt come intentionally'

vi. *Pronominal Compounds.* We have observed in the preceding discussion that a majority of NPs of the form Modifier + Noun on the surface-structure are derived from respective existential constructions at the deep level. Thus, a provision is made to derive an Adjective + N type of NP from a Nom complemented Verb 'Be' construction and a Loc.P + N from a Locative phrase complemented construction.

(XII)

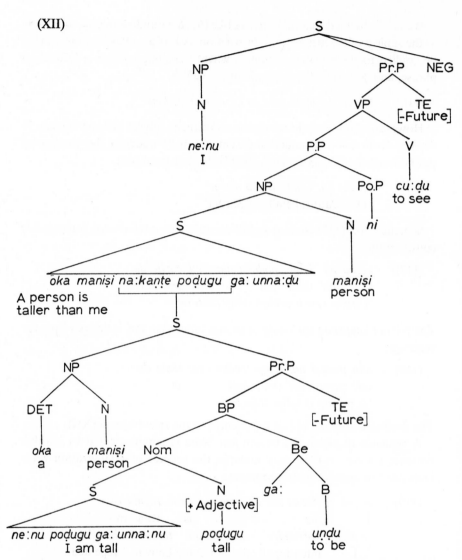

Frequent mention was made by earlier authors[6] of a particular set of NPs which are treated as pronominal compounds in this essay.

In Arden's (1927, p. 217) treatment a 'Composite Noun' may be formed by adding the "Pronominal affixes", *va:ḍu, vaṇḍlu, di, vi* either to adjectives, nouns or pronouns in the genitive or to any of the relative participles.

---

[6] For instance Arden (1927, p. 78): "By affixing *va:ḍu, va:ṇḍlu, di* (or *adi*) and *vi* (for *avi*) to adjectives, and the genitive cases of nouns (and – as will be hereafter shown – to some other parts of speech) a class of words is formed, to which we shall give the distinctive name COMPOSITE NOUNS". [Transliteration mine.]

What Krishnamurti and Sivananda Sarma referred to as "Pronominal Predicates" correspond, in a broader sense, to a subset of the pronominal compounds of the present treatment. From their descriptive view-point Krishnamurti and Sivananda Sarma opine that Telugu does not have the type of constructions in which an adjective can qualify the preceding noun as part of a predicative complement. They describe the formation of the predicative complements as: "... adjectives are pronominalized in Telugu by the addition of *-di* (non-mas singular), or *-wi* (non-human plural) which then occur as predicates of verbless sentences, agreeing with the subject in gender, number and person" (1968, p. 34).

In this essay it will be shown that those forms referred to by Arden as Composite Nouns and by Krishnamurti and Sivananda Sarma as Pronominal Predicates can be derived, transformationally, from underlying existential constructions and some other types of sentences, which are, for lack of a better term, referred to as Pronominal Compounds.

From a descriptive point of view, Arden's derivation of a subset of composite nouns, as mentioned earlier, by affixing a pronominal affix to a relative participle of a verb holds good. But, transformationally, all these forms can be derived from underlying sentences, by application of the relevant rules of pre-nominal modification. The following sentences will illustrate the point:

(120) *mi:ru tiṇṭunna-di e:miṭi?*
        you   eating thing what
        'What is that you are eating?'

(121) *a:yana ceppina-di na:ku bo:dha paḍa le:du*
        he   told thing me to understand   not
        'I did not understand what he told me'

(122) *ne:nu ra:ma:ra:vki iccina-di ba:gu le:du*
        I   Ramarao to gave thing good is not
        'The one which I gave to Ramarao is not good'

The subject NPs of the sentences (120)–(122) contain on the surface structure a relative participle followed by a 'pronominal affix' *-di* (denoting non-human singular), and are derived from sentences (123)–(125) respectively:

(123) *mi:ru okaṭi   tiṇṭunna:ru*
        you   onething eating
        'You are eating something'

(124) *a:yana okaṭi   ceppe:ḍu*
        he   onething told
        'He told something'

(125)   *ne:nu ra:ma:ra:vki okaṭi   icce:nu*
         I   Ramarao to onething gave
         'I gave something to Ramarao'

(123')–(125') are the relative clauses formed from these sentences:

(123')   *mi:ru e:-di   tiṇṭunna:ru o:a-di*
         you   what thing eating   that thing
(124')   *a:yana e:-di   ceppe:ḍu o: a-di*
         he   what thing told   that thing
(125')   *ne:nu ra:ma:ra:vki e:-di   icce:nu o: a-di*
         I   Ramarao to what thing gave   that thing

Further reduction of the relative clauses (123')–(125') gives rise to (123")–
(125") respectively:

(123")   *mi:ru tiṇṭunna-di*
         you   eating thing
         'The thing which you are eating'
(124")   *a:yana ceppina-di*
         he   told thing
         'The thing which he told'
(125")   *ne:nu ra:ma:ra:vki iccina-di*
         I   Ramarao to gave thing
         'The thing which I gave to Ramarao'

which are embedded in (120)–(122) respectively.
   Corresponding to sentences (95)–(100) we have (126)–(130):

(126)   *ṭe:bilu mi:da unna-da:nini nuvvu ti:siko:*
         Table on   is thing   you   take
         'Take the one which is on the table'
(127)   *a-k-kaḍa unna-va:ḍini pilu*
                  is man
         'Call that man who is there'
(128)   *na:ku unn-da:nilo: sagam ni:ku ista:nu*
                  is thing in
         'I will give you half of the thing that I have'
(129)   *ne:nu poḍugu ga: unna-da:nini peḷḷa:ḍuta:nu*
                       is woman
         'I will marry one who is tall'
(130)   *ko:pam ga: unna-va:ḍito: ja:garta ga: uṇḍu*
                   is man
         'Be careful with one who is angry'

The following sentences (131)–(135) are the source for the reduced relative clause found embedded in the sentences (126)–(130).

(131)   *okaṭi ṭe:bilu mi:da undi*
        one thing
        'Something is on the table'

(132)   *okaḍu a-k-kada unna:ḍu*
        one man
        'Some body (man) is there'

(133)   *okaṭi na:-ku undi*
        one thing
        'I have something'

(134)   *okarti poḍugu ga: undi*
        one woman
        'Somebody (woman) is tall'

(135)   *okaḍu ko:pam ga: unna:-ḍu*
        one man
        'Some body (man) is angry'

Deletion of the constituent relative participle *unna* from the reduced relative clauses which are embedded in (126)–(130) brings out the following NPs:

(131') *ṭe:bilu-mi:da-di*
        'The one on the table'

(132') *a-k-kaḍa-va:ḍu*
        'The one (man) over there'

(133') *na:-di*
        'The one of mine'

(134') *poḍugu-di*
        'The tall one (woman)'

(135') *ko:pam-va:ḍu*
        'The angry one (man)'

It may be noted that the NP *na:-di* 'The one of mine' is a result of the obligatory deletion of the LPo.P denoting possession from the corresponding reduced relative clause.

Some more examples of pronominal compounds with an adjective as the modifier are given below:

(136)   *tella-di*   from (136') *okaṭi tella ga: undi*
        'white thing'   'Something is white'

(137)   *sanna-di*   from (137') *okaṭi sannam ga: undi*
        'thin one'   'Something is thin'

(138)   *gaṭṭi-di*   from (138') *okaṭi gaṭṭi ga: undi*
        'hard one'   'Something is hard'

NPs like (139)–(140) have a modifier denoting the role of the modified noun
and are derived from the corresponding sentences (139')–(140'):

(139)   *gumasta:-va:ḍu*   from (139') *okaḍu gumasta: ga: unna: ḍu*
         'A clerk (man)'   'Somebody (man) is a clerk'
(140)   *baṇṭro: tu-va: ḍu*   from (140') *okaḍu baṇṭro: tu ga: unna:ḍu*
         'A peon (man)'   'Somebody (man) is a peon'

The N in the above type of pronominal compounds can optionally be
deleted. This gives rise to (139″) and (140″) respectively:

(139″)   *gumasta:*   'clerk'
(140″)   *baṇṭro: tu*   'peon'

Sentences with an Intensifier + N type of Nom complement may give rise
to corresponding pronominal compounds:

(141)   *ca: la:-tella: di*   from (141') *okaṭi ca: la: tella ga: undi*
         'A very white one'   very
                                             'Something is very white'
(142)   *ba: ga:-pulla-di*   from (142') *okaṭi ba: ga: pulla ga: undi*
         'A very sour one'   very   sour
                                             'Something is very sour'
(143)   *ento:-pedda-va: ḍu*   from (143') *okaḍu ento: pedda ga: unna : ḍu*
         'A very big man'   very big
                                             'Somebody (man) is very big'

We have observed in (131') that a locative may function as the modifier in
a pronominal compound. Some more examples of pronominal compounds
with a locative as the modifier are given below:

(144)   *polam-lo:-di*   from (144') *okaṭi polam lo: undi*
         'The one in the field'   one thing field in is
                                             'Something is in the field'
(145)   *iṇṭi-lo:-va: ḍu*   from (145') *okaḍu iṇṭi-lo: unna:ḍu*
         'The man in the house'   one man house in
                                             'A man is in the house'
(146)   *koṇḍa-mi: da-di*   from (146') *okaṭi koṇḍa mi: da undi*
         'The one on the hill'   hill   on
                                             'Something is on the hill'
(147)   *go: ḍa-venaka-di*   from (147') *okaṭi go: ḍa venaka undi*
         'The one behind the wall'   wall   behind
                                             'Something is behind the wall'

A few more examples of (133') type are given below:

(148)	*cettu-di* 'Something of a tree'	from (148')	*okati cettu-ki undi* tree to 'The tree has something'
(149)	*ma:-va:du* 'Our man/our child'	from (149')	*okadu ma:-ku unna:du* us to 'We have a man/child'
(150)	*ni:-va:llu* 'Your people'	from (150')	*kondaru ni:-ku unna:-ru* some people you to 'You have some people'

(a) 'Demonstrative Pronouns' as Pronominal Compounds. From a descriptive point of view 'third person pronominals' in Telugu are either demonstrative, indefinitive or interrogative. It may be recalled that in the phrase-structure subcomponent of the present analysis no provision is made for the introduction of the so-called 'demonstrative pronouns'. Because of the clearcut similarity between the 'demonstrative pronouns' and other Demonstrative+N types of NP, an attempt was made to find out the transformational history of the demonstrative element and the 'suffix' like part of each 'demonstrative pronoun'. The findings revealed that the so-called 'demonstrative pronouns' should be derived by the same set of transformations as in the case of Demonstrative+N types of NP applied to underlying locative existential constructions, which shows that the 'demonstrative pronouns' are not merely 'pronouns' but surface structure noun phrases.

It may be noted, however, that the anaphoric referential pronoun *va:du* in sentences like *va:du vacce:du* 'he came', which may mean anaphorically, 'The *x* whom we were expecting that *x* came' and so on, is homophonous with the 'IIIrd person human masculine singular remote demonstrative pronoun' *va:du* 'that he'. The process of anaphoric pronominalization is kept out of this discussion. 'Interrogative pronouns' like *evadu* 'which man' also could be treated as transformationally introduced elements. As far as the present analysis is concerned, 'IIIrd person indefinite pronouns' like *okadu* 'a man' and NUM+N types like *okadu* 'one man' are considered as deep structure NPs. The treatment of the socalled 'demonstratives' like *akkada* 'there' as locative phrases in the present analysis by analysing them as consisting of a Demonstrative element *a* 'that' followed by a LPo.P *kada* 'at' facilitated the transformational treatment of the 'demonstrative pronouns'.

Sentence (151) contains a 'demonstrative pronoun' as the object on the surface structure:

(151)   *ne:nu va:-ḍini pilice:nu*
     I   him   called
     'I called him (that man)'

The deep structure of (151) is represented by the tree-diagram (XIII), which shows the source sentence of the 'demonstrative pronoun'.

(XIII)

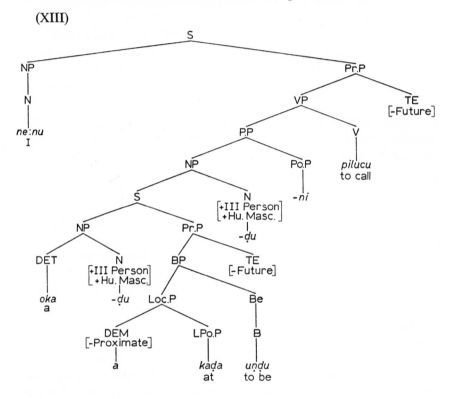

It may be recalled that the embedded sentence in the above sentence is similar to (132). A relative clause formed from this embedded sentence looks like:

(132″)   *eva-ḍu   a-k-kaḍa unna:ḍu o: va:-ḍu*
      which man that at is   that   man

Further reduction of (132″) gives rise to (132a).

(132a)   *a-k-kaḍa unna va:-ḍu*

Recall (127) where we see a reduced relative clause similar to (132a) embedded in the object position. Further deletion of the relative participle *unna* from (132a) gives rise to (132′) *a-k-kaḍa va:-ḍu* 'The one (man) over there'. The deletion of LPo.P applies to (132') to generate the 'demonstrative pronoun'[7] *va:-ḍu* on to the surface structure as seen in (151). Following is a list of other 'demonstrative pronouns' and their respective source sentences:

(152)	*a-di* 'that thing'	from (152')	*okaṭi a-k-kaḍa undi* one thing that at is 'Something is there'
(153)	*i-di* 'this thing'	from (153')	*okaṭi i-k-kaḍa undi* this at 'Something is here'
(154)	*vi:-ḍu* 'this man'	from (154')	*okaḍu i-k-kaḍa unna:ḍu* one man this at 'A man is here'
(155)	*va:-ḷḷu* 'those people'	from (155')	*kondaru a-k-kaḍa unna:ru* some people 'Some people are there'
(156)	*vi:-ḷḷu* 'these people'	from (156')	*kondaru i-k-kaḍa unna:ru* 'Some people are here'
(157)	*a-vi* 'those things'	from (157')	*konni a-k-kaḍa unna:yi* some things 'Some things are there'
(158)	*i-vi* 'these things'	from (158')	*konni i-k-kaḍa unna:yi* 'Some things are here'

2. COPULATIVE PREDICATIONS

Arden in his treatment of "Telugu Equivalent to the Verb to be" deals with the 'translation of the Verb *to be* when it is the copula' by positing a rule (rule 383) that "where in English the verb *to be* is placed between the subject and a noun (or its equivalent), i.e., where the predicate consists of the verb

---

[7] Roughly the following morphophonemic changes take place while the 'demonstrative pronouns' are brought out on to the surface:

$$a + \begin{bmatrix} \text{-ḍu} \\ \text{-ḷḷu} \end{bmatrix} \rightarrow va:\text{-} \begin{bmatrix} \text{ḍu} \\ \text{ḷḷu} \end{bmatrix}$$

$$i + \begin{bmatrix} \text{-ḍu} \\ \text{-ḷḷu} \end{bmatrix} \rightarrow vi:\text{-} \begin{bmatrix} \text{ḍu} \\ \text{ḷḷu} \end{bmatrix}$$

$$\begin{bmatrix} a - \\ i - \end{bmatrix} + di \rightarrow \begin{bmatrix} a \\ i \end{bmatrix}\text{-di}$$

$$\begin{bmatrix} a - \\ i - \end{bmatrix} + vi \rightarrow \begin{bmatrix} a \\ i \end{bmatrix}\text{-vi}$$

Now the status of the 'pronominal suffixes' *-(va:)ḍu, -(va:)ḷḷu -di* and *-vi* is clear. They are nouns but not suffixes and are dominated by the node NP on the surface. A modifier that precedes it may be either an 'adjective' as in *tella-di* 'white thing', a 'locative' in *ṭe:bilu-mi:da-di* 'the one on the table', a 'possessive' in *na:-di* 'the one of mine' or a 'demonstrative' in *a-di* 'that thing'.

to be and a noun (as – *That is a cow. That is not a cow*). In colloquial Telugu in the POSITIVE no verb is used; as – *adi a:vu.* In the NEGATIVE the tense *ka:nu* is added; as *adi a:vu ka:du*". (1927, p. 151) [Transliteration mine.]

Krishnamurti and Sivananda Sarma refer to a distinct set of sentences, viz., 'Simple verbless sentences' which do not contain a verb (1968, p. 3), and which correspond to the set of sentences in positive where 'no verb is used' as in the treatment of Arden. These sentences, in the present analysis, are referred to as equational sentences. In an equational sentence in Telugu the constituent verb is copulative in function and equates the 'subject' with the other constituent NP. As is clear from reading g) of the BP expansion rule the BP is constituted by an NP followed by Be.

The following sentences illustrate the type of predication in question:

(159)   *ra:ma:ra:v poḍugu-va:ḍu*
        Ramarao tall   man
        'Ramarao is a tall man'

(160)   *i:-paṇḍu pulla-di*
        this fruit sour one
        'This fruit is a sour one'

(161)   *a:-pustakam na:-di*
        that book   my one
        'That book is mine'

(162)   *va:-ḍu   ra:ma:ra:v*
        that man Ramarao
        'That man is Ramarao'

Two NPs, in (159) *ra:ma:ra:v* 'Ramarao' and *poḍugu-va:ḍu* 'tall man', are equated by keeping them in apposition. The apparent absence of any verbal element in these sentences of equational type allows them to be described as verbless.

In spite of the complete absence of any verbal element in this type of sentence, a search for a copula at the deep structure was made. The proposal for the presence of a deep-structure copula is motivated by two observations: a) the obligatory presence of a negative copula on the surface structure in the case of negative copulative predications and b) the optional appearance of *avnu* 'is' on the surface in positive copulative constructions. The negative copula is treated as a result of the fusion of Be+NEG. Corresponding to (159)–(162) we have (159')–(162') containing the verbal element *avnu*.

(159') *ra:ma:ra:v poḍugu-va:ḍu avnu*
        Ramarao tall   man   is
        'Ramarao is a tall man'

(160')   *i:-paṇḍu pulla-di   avnu*
           this fruit sour one is
           'This fruit is a sour one'

(161')   *a:-pustakam na:-di   avnu*
           that book   my one is
           'That book is mine'

(162')   *va:-ḍu   ra:ma:ra:v avnu*
           that man Ramarao   is
           'That man is Ramarao'

Sentences (159')–(162') are acceptable but not used frequently compared
with (159)–(162). It should, however, be noted that corresponding sentences
from these two sets are completely similar in meaning. The presence of the
positive copula is observed more frequently when the whole of the sentence
along with its negative counterpart are embedded in another matrix sentence
as in (163):

(163)   *ra:ma:ra:v manci-va:ḍu avna: ka:da: annadi na: presna*
           Ramarao   good man is   is not   my question
           'My question is whether Ramarao is a good man or not?'

When the optional interrogative transformation is applied to positive
copulative constructions the resulting interrogative sentence may contain
an optional copula followed by the interrogative marker *a*:

(164)   *ra:ma:ra:v manci-va:ḍu avn-a:*
           Ramarao   good man   is Q
           'Is Ramarao a good man?'

The other optional form with no copula is:

(164')   *ra:ma:ra:v manci-va:ḍ-a:*
           Ramarao   good man Q
           'Is Ramarao a good man?'

A positive answer to question (164) or (164') may be with or without a
copula as may be observed in (165) and (165').

(165)   *ra:ma:ra:v manci-va:ḍu avnu*[8]

                                   is
           'Ramarao is a good man'

(165')   *ra:ma:ra:v manci-va:ḍu*
           'Ramarao is a good man'

[8] I am thankful to T. D. Francis who made me aware of the possibility of the presence
of a positive copula on the surface structure and its optional deletion. He pointed out a
similar condition of copula in Tamil which he has depicted in his forthcoming thesis on
generative grammar of Tamil.

i. *Be + TE Deletion.* The optional deletion of the copula on the surface structure necessitates the formulation of the following rule:

24)   X   NP   NP   Be+TE   Y   →   X   NP   NP   Y
     1   2   3   4 +5   6   1   2   3   ∅   ∅   6
     where Y ⊉ NEG

The specification Y ⊉ NEG is made in view of the negative copulative predications where the copula is obligatorily present on the surface structure, of course, as fused with the optionally selected NEG. That means when Y includes NEG, the above transformation is not applicable.

ii. *TE Specification.* The Tense element selected in a copulative construction is always marked [−Future]. Future tense can never be denoted in a copulative construction. This restriction throws some more light on the basic difference between equational sentences like (165′) and attributive existential sentences like (166).

(165′)   *ra:ma:ra:v manci-va:ḍu*
         'Ramarao is a good man'

(166)   *ra:ma:ra:v manci ga: unna:ḍu*
         'Ramarao is good'

Arden mentions that "If the sentence has reference to the *innate quality* or *natural condition* of the subject the predicate in Telugu is expressed by a COMPOSITE NOUN; and hence ... what is an *adjective* in English becomes a *noun (composite)* in Telugu ..." (1927, p. 152). He further points out that "This use of the Composite nouns (or rather of the PRONOMINAL AFFIXES) in Telugu closely resembles the use in English of the words *man, woman, people, one, thing, things,* etc., which are frequently added to adjectives expressing *innate quality* or *natural condition*" (1927, p. 153). In his later discussion he specifies that "If the sentence has reference to the *particular state* of the subject *at a particular time,* the predicate in Telugu is expressed both in the positive and negative by the verb *uṇḍu* or the primary verb, preceded by an adverb, i.e., by an adjective (or a noun used as an adjective) with the ADVERBIAL AFFIX *ga:* attached to it. In sentences of this kind in English the adjective is generally used alone, without the addition of any of the words, *man, woman, people* etc." (1927, p. 154).

The above discussion by Arden points to the difference between attributive existential constructions and equational constructions. Taking the set of examples (165′) and (166) into consideration, we find that in (165′) the 'innate quality' or the 'natural disposition' of the subject *ra:ma:ra:v* is denoted whereas in (166) the 'particular state' of the subject *ra:ma:ra:v* 'at a particular time' is mentioned. Thus the difference is between the denotation of a permanent quality of the subject and the temporary quality. To express a temporary quality of the subject the attributive existential construction is engaged whereas to denote the permanent quality of the subject the subject NP is equated with a qualifying NP in a copulative construction.

A distinction of TE into future or non-future is possible in the case of sentences like (166), where the subject is supposed to have the denoted quality for a fixed span of time temporarily. That is why a sentence like (167) as a counterpart of (166) with future tense is possible:

(167)   *ra:ma:ra:v manci ga: unṭa:ḍu*
                              will be
         'Ramarao will be good'

Since an equational sentence like (165') denotes a permanent quality of the subject, it cannot include the future tense. By saying that 'Ramarao is a good man' we mean that 'Ramarao is good' and 'Ramarao was good' but no specification can be made about the future ('Ramarao will be good'). Depending on this motivation the above TE specification is made in the case of equational sentences.[9]

In an equational sentence the subject NP is equated with the complement NP. In view of this phenomenon the subject NP is called the equated NP and the complement NP the equating NP.

The following sentences exemplify the distinction between equating and equated NPs:

(168)   *a-di   na:-manci-pustakam*
         that one my good book
         'That one is my good book'
(169)   *a:-manci- pustakam na:-di*
         that good book   my one
         'That good book is mine'

Sentence (168) is different from (169). The treediagrams (XIV) and (XV) show the difference in their deep-structure.

An equated NP or an equating NP may be derived from underlying sentences other than those containing a BP. Observe the following sentences:

(170)   *ninna   na:to ma:tla:ḍina-va:ḍu ra:ma:ra:v*
         yesterday me with talked   man Ramarao
'The man who talked with me yesterday is Ramarao'

---

[9] Similar is the case with constructions denoting 'identity'. For instance, a sentence like *va:ḍu ra:ma:ra:v* 'He is Ramarao' includes the identification of subject (identified) *va:ḍu* 'that he' with *ra:ma:ra:v* 'Ramarao', the identifying NP. Logically to identify *x* with *y* the knowledge of *y* is presupposed at least at the time of identification. Then, the knowledge that *x* is as identified with *y* may follow. Identifying *x* with *y* can never include any factor of 'future'.

(XIV)

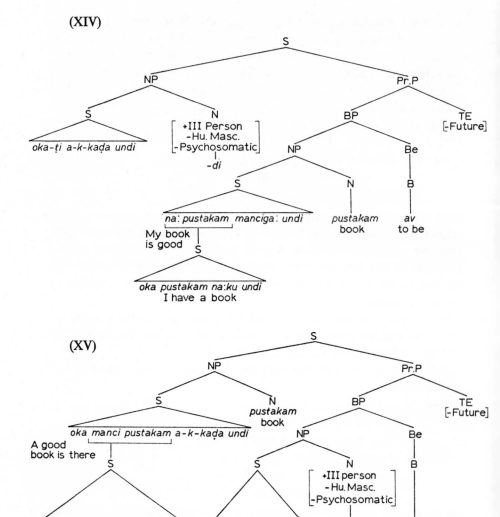

(XV)

(171)   *ne:nu i:-pustaka:nni ra:stunna-va:ḍi-ni*
        I   this book   writing   man
        'I am the person who is writing this book'

---

[10] The verbal root *av-* is usually used to convey the meaning 'to become' like in *ne:nu poḍugu avuta:nu* 'I will become tall'.

(172)   va: ḷḷandarilo: ba: ga: pa: ḍutunna-di   si: ta
        them all in   well   singing woman Sita
        'The one (woman) singing well among them all is Sita'

The equated NP in (170) is derived by prenominal modification from a sentence like:

(173)   okaḍu   ninna   na: to: ma: ṭla: ḍe: ḍu
        one man yesterday me with talked
        'A man talked with me yesterday'

The N of the equating NP and the N of the equated NP should be marked for the same feature of person. That is why sentences like (165') are acceptable whereas (174) is not.

(174)   *ra: ma: ra: v poḍugu-di
        Ramarao   tall   woman

This specification applies to those sentences containing an equated NP with an N marked as [−IIIrd Person] as in (175) and (176).

(175)   ne: nu manci-va: ḍi-ni
        I   good   man
        'I am a good man'
(176)   ne: nu manci-da: ni-ni
                    woman
        'I am a good woman'

In (175) the N ne: nu 'I' of the equated NP is marked $\begin{bmatrix} +\text{I Person} \\ +\text{Masculine} \end{bmatrix}$ and the corresponding feature of the N of the equating NP is found as [+Human Masculine]. So also in the case of (176), the N ne: nu 'I' of the equated NP is marked $\begin{bmatrix} +\text{I Person} \\ -\text{Masculine} \end{bmatrix}$ and the corresponding feature of the N of the equating NP is found as [−Human Masculine].

iii. *SA Introduction.* The SA element is not found in all equational sentences. Only when the Ns of both the NPs of an equational sentence are marked for the feature [−IIIrd Person] then the appropriate SA element marked for the corresponding feature is added. In addition to (175) and (176) observe the following:

(177)   nuvvu manci-va: ḍi-vi[11]
        you   man
        'You are a good man'

---

[11] Sentences denoting identity also follow this selection: ne:nu ra:ma:ra:v-ni 'I am Ramarao', nuvvu ra:ma:ra:v-vi 'You are Ramarao'.

(178)   *nuvvu manci-da:ni-vi*
                woman
        'You are a good woman'
(179)   *mi:ru manci-va:ḷḷu*
        you (pl.)   people
        'You are good people'
(180)   *me:m manci-va:ḷḷ-am*[12]
        we
        'We are good people'

Corresponding to (177)–(180) we have (177′)–(180′) with an overt copula on the surface structure.

(177′)   *nuvvu manci-va:ḍi-vi avnu*
         'You are a good man'
(178′)   *nuvvu manci-da:ni-vi avnu*
         'You are a good woman'
(179′)   *mi:ru manci-vaḷḷu avnu*
         'You are good people'
(180)   *me:m manci-vaḷḷ-am avnu*
         'We are good people'

It may be observed that the presence of an SA element is obligatory when the Ns of both the NPs as in (177)–(180) are marked for the feature [−IIIrd Person]. The following SA introduction rule is obligatorily applied to account for this phenomenon:

$$
25)\ \ X\begin{bmatrix} +N \\ \alpha-\text{IIIrd Person} \end{bmatrix} \ Y\begin{bmatrix} +N \\ \alpha-\text{IIIrd Person} \end{bmatrix} \qquad \text{Be Z}
$$
$$
 1 \quad 2 \qquad\qquad\qquad 3 \quad 4 \qquad\qquad\qquad\qquad 5\ \ 6
$$
$$
X\begin{bmatrix} +N \\ \alpha-\text{IIIrd Person} \end{bmatrix} \ Y\begin{bmatrix} +N \\ \alpha-\text{IIIrd Person} \end{bmatrix} \begin{bmatrix} +SA \\ \alpha-\text{IIIrd Person} \end{bmatrix} \text{Be Z}
$$
$$
1 \quad 2 \qquad\qquad\qquad 3 \quad 4 \qquad\qquad\qquad x \qquad\qquad 5\ \ 6
$$

where Z may optionally include a NEG.

   This rule precedes the Be + TE deletion rule. Optional inclusion of NEG in the cover symbol, Z is explained in the treatment of the negative copulative constructions.

---

[12] Observe the following morphophonemic changes:

manci-va:ḍu + $\begin{bmatrix} \text{ni} \\ \text{vi} \end{bmatrix}$ → manci-va:ḍi- $\begin{bmatrix} \text{ni} \\ \text{vi} \end{bmatrix}$

manci-di + $\begin{bmatrix} \text{ni} \\ \text{vi} \end{bmatrix}$ → manci-da:ni- $\begin{bmatrix} \text{ni} \\ \text{vi} \end{bmatrix}$

manci-va:ḷḷu + $\begin{bmatrix} \text{ḷḷu} \\ \text{am} \end{bmatrix}$ → manci-va:ḷḷ- $\begin{bmatrix} \text{u} \\ \text{am} \end{bmatrix}$

3. NEGATION AND THE VERB 'BE'

An existential or a copulative predication may be negated by undergoing the proper transformations. Following the convention a provision is made for the Negative element, NEG at the base level, by the selection of which the respective transformation is triggered. The negative counterpart of a simple declarative sentence containing a verb other than the verb 'Be' will have the 'negative marker' *le:du* added to the positive infinitive of the verb. Examine the following sentences:

(181)   *ne:nu va:ḍini tiṭṭe:-nu*
           I   him   scolded
           'I scolded him'

(182)   *ne:nu va:ḍini tiṭṭa-le:du*
                          scolded not
           'I did not scold him'

A sentence carrying a verb in durative aspect will have its negative counterpart containing the 'negative marker' *le:du* added to the gerundival form of the verb as seen in (184).

(183)   *ne:nu va:ḍini tiḍutunna:-nu*
                          scolding
           'I am scolding him'

(184)   *ne:nu va:ḍini tiṭṭaḍam-le:du*
                          scolding
           'I am not scolding him'

This introduction to negation in non-verb 'Be' sentences provides a background for the examination of negation triggered by the selection of a NEG following a BP. It is observed that the two-fold distinction in predications, viz., existential and copulative, is strictly maintained even when a NEG is selected by showing an overt difference in selecting the respective 'negative markers' of different phonological shapes for each predication. The following discussion exemplifies the point.

A. *Negative Existential Predications*

Arden (1927, p. 165) pointed out that "Where in the *positive* the verb *uṇḍu* without *ayi* can be used, the tense *le:nu* must be used in *negative*". It is clear that in negativizing an existential construction only *le:* is used as the 'negative verb'.[13] The following examples may be observed:

---

[13] Krishnamurti and Sivananda Sarma (1968:47) mention that "The verbs meaning 'to be' (root *un-*) and 'not to be' (root *lee-*) are among the most basic in Telugu. The peculiarity of the Telugu language is the existence of a separate verb meaning 'not to be'...".

(185)   *de:muḍu le:ḍu*
        God   is not
        'God does not exist'

(186)   *baḍi   iva:ḷa le:du*
        school today is not
        'There is no school today'

(187)   *mo:han iṇṭi-lo: le:-ḍu*
        Mohan home in is not
        'Mohan is not at home'

(188)   *si:ta a-k-kaḍa le:du*
        Sita that at is not
        'Sita is not there'

(189)   *ḍabbu   na:ku le:du*
        money me to is not
        'I have no money'

(190)   *ne:nu poḍugu ga: le:nu*
        I   tall   am not
        'I am not tall'

i. *Be + NEG Fusion.* Sentences (185)–(190) are negative counterparts of the positive existential sentences (27), (30), (33), (37), (39) and (55) in this respective order. On the surface it looks as though the positive existential verb is replaced by the 'negative existential verb' *le:* resulting in (185)–(190). But, transformationally, the negative existential verb *le:* can be treated as a result of the fusion of Be + NEG in non-future tense, as is accounted for by the following rule:

26)   X Be TE NEG Y → X Be + NEG TE   Y
          [−Fut]   [−Fut]
      1   2   3   4   5   1   2 + 4   3   ∅ 5

The entries in the phonological sub-component will contain a realization of the result of the Be + NEG fusion as *le:* 'not to be'. The specification of [−Future] in Tense is made to take into account the fact that the fusion occurs only in non-future tense to result in *le:*, whereas when the TE is marked for [+Future] the fusion never takes place. Instead, a Future negative marker *a* is added to the 'positive infinitive' of *uṇḍu, uṇḍa-*. Observe the difference between (187) and (191):

(191)   *mo:han iṇṭi-lo: uṇḍa-ḍu*
                       will not be
        'Mohan will not be at home'

B. *Negative Copulative Predications*

Corresponding to sentences (159)–(162) we have their negative counterparts (192)–(195) with a negative copula:

(192)   *ra:ma:ra:v poḍuga-va:ḍu ka:du*
                                      is not
        'Ramarao is not a tall man'

(193)   *i:-paṇḍu pulla-di ka:du*
                           is not
        'This fruit is not a sour one'

(194)   *a:-pustakam na:-di ka:du*
                                is not
        'That book is not mine'

(195)   *va:-ḍu ra:ma:ra:v ka:du*
                             is not
        'That man is not Ramarao'

The obligatory transformation that is formulated for the Be+NEG fusion in the case of negation of existential constructions may be recalled; it will apply to the optionally chosen NEG and the copula. Hence, the copula negation is accounted for by the rule:

26)   X Be TE NEG Y →   X Be+NEG TE   Y
             [−Fut]   [−Fut]

       1   2   3   4   5   1   2 + 4   3 Ø 5

The specification of TE as [−Future] holds good here also since in equational sentences TE is always [−Future].

As is observed in the above sentences the fused product of Be+NEG is phonologically represented on the surface as *ka:*, the so called negative copula.

A negative copula can optionally carry an SA element. Compare (192′) with (192):

(192′)   *ra:ma:ra:v poḍugu-va:ḍu ka:-ḍu*
         'Ramarao is not a tall man'

and (195′) with (195):

(195′)   *va:-ḍu ra:ma:ra:v ka:-ḍu*
         'That man is not Ramarao'

i. *SA Introduction.* An optional SA element introduction rule is posited to account for this optional occurrence of SA element:

27) $X \begin{bmatrix} +N \\ \alpha III \ Person \end{bmatrix} Y \begin{bmatrix} +N \\ \alpha IIIrd \ Person \end{bmatrix} Be+NEG \ Z \ \rightarrow$

　　　1　　2　　　　　3　　4　　　　　　5+6　　7

$X \begin{bmatrix} +N \\ \alpha III \ Person \end{bmatrix} Y \begin{bmatrix} +N \\ \alpha IIIrd \ Person \end{bmatrix} Be+NEG+ \begin{bmatrix} +SA \\ \alpha IIIrd \ Person \end{bmatrix} Z$

　　1　　2　　　　　3　　4　　　　　　5+6　+　x　　　　　7

Whenever the optional SA is not selected an enunciative marker -*du* is added to the Be+NEG fused form *le:*. Rule 27) follows 25). By applying 25) followed by the application of 27) we get sentences like (196)–(199):

(196)　*nuvvu manci-va:ḍi-vi ka:-vu*
　　　　you　good　man　　are not
　　　　'You are not a good man'

(197)　*nuvvu manci-da:ni-vi ka:-vu*
　　　　　　　　　woman
　　　　'You are not a good woman'

(198)　*mi:ru manci-va:ḷḷu ka:-ru*
　　　　　　　　　people
　　　　'You are not good people'

(199)　*me:m manci-vaḷḷ-am ka:-m*
　　　　'We are not good people'

When the above optional transformation is not applied we get (196′)–(199′) corresponding to (196)–(199) with no difference in meaning.

(196′)　*nuvvu manci-va:ḍi-vi ka:du*
　　　　'You are not a good man'

(197′)　*nuvvu manci-da:ni-vi ka:du*
　　　　'You are not a good woman'

(198′)　*mi:ru manci-va:ḷḷu ka:du*
　　　　'You are not good people'

(199′)　*me:m manci-vaḷḷ-am ka:du*
　　　　'We are not good people'

IV. SUMMARY AND CONCLUSION

To sum up, the following are some of the important findings in this essay:

i. The existential *to be* and the copulative *to be* are quite different both phonologically and semantically. The difference of existential and copulative functions of *to be* is more prominently expressed by the difference in the phonological realization of the respective Be+NEG fused products.

ii. What are apparently verbless sentences do really have a copula at the deep structure which may optionally show up on the surface.

iii. Four main types of 'existence' are marked by the four construction types of existential predication, viz., absolutive, temporal, locative and attributive. Possession is considered to be a sub-variety of location. In Telugu x 'exists with' (more precisely 'exists to') y where y is the 'possessor' and x is the 'possessed'. Spatial demonstratives are found to be another sub-variety of locatives. In Telugu 'there' means 'at that place' and 'here' 'at this place'. Consequently 'that x' is derived from 'the x at that place' and 'this x' from 'the x at this place'. All these construction types of existential predication can undergo the same set of transformations showing a homogeneity. The derivation of the so-called subjectless sentences from a subset of attributive existential sentences clarifies the existing irregularity.

In conclusion it may be mentioned that other related topics like the syntax of Telugu equivalents of the verb 'to be' as verbal operators, the syntax of Telugu equivalents of the verb 'to become' and the absolute necessity of the verb 'to be' at the base level are worth exploring.

Centre of Advanced Study in Linguistics,
University of Poona, India

BIBLIOGRAPHY

Arden, A. H.: 1927, *A Progressive Grammar of the Telugu Language*, Madras.
Asher, R. E.: 1968, 'Existential, Possessive, Locative and Copulative Sentences in Malayalam', in Verhaar, John W. M. (ed.) (1968).
Bach, E.: 1967, '*Have* and *Be* in English Syntax', *Lg.* **43**, 462–86.
Chomsky, N.: 1965, *Aspects of the Theory of Syntax*, M.I.T. Press, Cambridge, Mass.
Graham, A. C.: 1965, '"Being" in Linguistics and Philosophy', *FL*, **1**, 223–31.
Graham, A. C.: 1967, '"Being" in Classical Chinese', in Verhaar, John W. M. (ed.) (1967).
Kachru, Y.: 1968, 'The Copula in Hindi', in Verhaar, John W. M. (ed.) (1968).
Krishnamurthi, Bh.: 1961, *Telugu Verbal Bases*, Berkeley.
Krishnamurthi, Bh.: 1964, 'Compound Verbs in Telugu', *Winter Seminar of Linguistics*, Deccan College, Poona.
Krishnamurti, Bh. and Sivananda Sarma, P.: 1968, *A Basic Course in Modern Telugu*, Hyderabad.
Langendoen, T. D.: 1967, 'Mundari Verb Conjugation', *Linguistics* **32**, 39–57.
Langendoen, T. D.: 1967a, 'The Copula in Mundari', in Verhaar, John W. M. (ed.) (1967).
Lisker, L.: 1963, *An Introduction to Spoken Telugu*, New York.
Postal, P. M.: 1969, 'On the So-called Pronouns in English', in D. A. Reibel and S. A. Schane, pp. 201–24.
Reibel, D. A. and Schane, S. A.: 1969, *Modern Studies in English*, New York.
Rosenbaum, P. S.: 1967, *The Grammar of English Predicate Complement Constructions*, M.I.T., Cambridge, Mass.
Ross, J.: 1967, *Constraints on Variables in Syntax*, Ph.D. Diss. (Reproduced by the Linguistic Club of Indiana University, Fall, 1968.)
Sivaramamurthi, N.: 1968, *Telugu Grammar*, Ph.D. Diss. University of Poona.
Staal, J. F.: 1965, 'Reification, Quotation and Nominalization', in Tymieniecka and Parsons (eds.), 151–87.

Tymieniecka, A.-T. and Parsons, C.: 1965, *Contributions to Logic and Methodology in Honor of J. M. Bocheński*, Amsterdam.

Verhaar, John W. M. (ed.): 1967, *The Verb 'Be' and its Synonyms*, Part 1 (Foundations of Language Supplementary Series, Vol. 1), Dordrecht-Holland.

Verhaar, John W. M. (ed.): 1968, *The Verb 'Be' and its Synonyms*, Part 2 (Foundations of Language Supplementary Series, Vol. 6), Dordrecht-Holland.

Vesper, D. R.: 1968, 'A Generative Grammar of Kurukh Copula', in Verhaar, John W. M. (ed.) (1968).

ILSE LEHISTE

'BEING' AND 'HAVING' IN ESTONIAN*†

I. INTRODUCTION

The problem to be considered in this paper is the expression of the notions of 'being' and 'having' in Estonian. The theoretical framework for the paper is provided by Charles J. Fillmore's 'Case Grammar', especially as elaborated in his recent paper, 'Lexical Entries for Verbs'.[1] In this paper, Fillmore proposes to treat verbs as predicates (in a sense partially similar to that used in the so-called 'predicate calculus' of symbolic logic), and to classify them according to the type and number of arguments they can take. I shall claim that the distinction between 'being' and 'having' in Estonian is one of different arguments taken, under special conditions, by the same verb. I shall propose further that all Estonian verbs, including 'be', can best be classified according to the number and types of arguments they can take, and that there is no need in Estonian for a special copula.

II. ARGUMENTS OF THE VERB 'BE' EXPRESSING 'BEING' AND 'HAVING'

2.1. Dative, Locative, and Objective

The problems connected with the expression of the notions of 'having' and 'being' become obvious, when one considers the surface identity of certain locative and possessive constructions in Estonian. There is no surface verb corresponding to the English verb 'have'. Possession is expressed by using a

* Sponsored in part by the National Science Foundation through Grant GN 5341, from the Office of Science Information Service to the Computer and Information Science Research Center, The Ohio State University.
† This paper appeared originally in *Foundations of Language* 5 (1969) pp. 324–341, and is here reprinted by permission of the author. (Ed.)
1 Charles J. Fillmore, 'Case for Case', *Universals in Linguistic Theory* (ed. by Emmon Bach and Robert T. Harms), New York, 1968, pp. 1–88; Charles J. Fillmore, 'Lexical Entries for Verbs', in *Foundations of Language* 4 (1968) 373–93. I have discussed the ideas expressed in this paper with my colleagues at The Ohio State University, especially C. J. Fillmore, D. T. Langendoen, and S. S. Annear, and have received written comments from Huno Rätsep and Haldur Õim of the University of Tartu, Estonia. I, and I trust also the paper, have benefited greatly from their suggestions; however, since the suggestions were sometimes divergent and since I have not followed all of them, the responsibility for the final shape of the paper rests with me.

construction like

(1a)   ISAL ON RAAMAT
        'Father has (a) book'

where *isal* is the noun 'father' in the adessive case,[2] *on* is 3. sg. pres. of the verb 'be', and *raamat* is the noun 'book' in the nom. sg. case.

Sentence (2a) has the same surface structure:

(2a)   LAUAL ON RAAMAT
        'On the table is (a) book'

where *laual* is the noun 'table' in the adessive case, and the other two words are identical in form and meaning with the corresponding words in the preceding sentence.

In the first sentence, we can consider the verb 'be' as a predicate with two arguments, of which one indicates the possessor and the other the object possessed. (In the following, these two arguments will be referred to as DATIVE and OBJECTIVE.[3]) In the second sentence, 'be' likewise has two arguments, the first indicating location (henceforth called LOCATIVE[4]), the second the object located (OBJECTIVE). If we consider sentence (3a), we see that DATIVE and LOCATIVE may be simultaneously present:

(3a)   EMAL ON TOIT LAUAL
        'Mother has food on the table'

where *emal* is the noun 'mother' in the adessive case, *toit* is the noun 'food' in the nominative case, and *laual* the noun 'table' in the adessive case.

Let us consider the surface cases in which these three arguments may appear, leaving aside for the moment the question of additional arguments (i.e., the possibility that 'be' may have more than three arguments, as well as the possibility that there may be arguments standing in relationships to 'be' that are different from OBJECTIVE, DATIVE, and LOCATIVE).

DATIVE appears on the surface in the adessive case. LOCATIVE may appear

---

[2] The fourteen cases of Estonian will be referred to by traditional names, printed in lower-case letters. Deep structure cases, in the sense of Case Grammar, will be printed in small capital letters.

[3] The arguments are labeled according to suggestions made and definitions given by Fillmore in 'Case for Case' (p. 24). DATIVE is Fillmore's label for "the case of the animate being affected by the state or action identified by the verb," and OBJECTIVE is "the semantically most neutral case, the case of anything representable by a noun whose role in the action or state identified by the verb is identified by the semantic interpretation of the verb itself". It will be shown later that DATIVE is not restricted to animate beings in Estonian.

[4] Fillmore, 'Case for Case': "Locative, the case which identifies the location or spatial orientation of the state or action identified by the verb" (p. 25).

in several other cases in addition to the adessive:

(4a)   MEES ON MAALT
        'The man is from the country' (ablative)

(5a)   MEES ON LINNAST
        'The man is from town' (elative)

(6a)   MEES ON LINNAS
        'The man is in (the) town' (inessive)

It appears to me that these three, plus the adessive, are the only surface cases that may manifest the LOCATIVE with the verb 'be'. The distinction between internal and external local cases is in some instances automatic; e.g., a place name may 'require' internal or external local cases. This is true, for example, for the names of the two Estonian towns Tapa and Tartu, the first of which 'requires' external local cases, the second internal ones. In other instances the selection of an internal or external local case carries a semantic difference. The problem will not be considered any further in the present paper.[5]

The allative and illative cases, although properly local cases, seem to me to fulfill different functions with the verb 'be'; consider, for example, sentences (7a) and (8a):

(7a)   KIRI ON ISALE
        'The letter is for the father'

where *isale* is the noun 'father' in the allative case, and the argument expresses the function Fillmore has called BENEFACTIVE.[6]

(8a)   LAPS ON ISASSE
        'The child is like (takes after) the father'

where *isasse* is the noun 'father' in the illative case. I do not believe this

---

[5] The fact that there are semantic differences associated with the surface local cases that manifest the deep structure case LOCATIVE presents serious problems in determining the relationship between the cases of Case Grammar and semantics. If I understand Case Grammar correctly, the cases constitute semantic relationships, and there is no semantic layer 'below' that of cases. However, the generalization involved in using LOCATIVE makes this case into an intermediate stage between what the speaker wants to say and the surface case form in which the argument in LOCATIVE finally emerges. It is questionable whether such a many-to-one-to-many mapping is justified. The alternative would be to recognize as many deep structure cases as there are surface cases. The same problem arises in connection with other deep structure cases where the choice of the surface case reflects a semantic difference, e.g., the ESSIVE.

[6] The term is introduced by Fillmore in 'Case for Case' (p. 32), to express the being for whose benefit the action of the verb takes place. The term is not defined as precisely as the other deep structure cases.

construction to be productive in the same sense as the other constructions (LOCATIVE and BENEFACTIVE) discussed in this context, and prefer to treat it as an idiom, as far as the relationship with 'be' is concerned.

The argument OBJECTIVE may be in the nominative or partitive case. All nouns may appear in the nominative singular. Mass nouns may also appear in the partitive singular. If OBJECTIVE is in the plural, all nouns may appear in nominative plural (mass nouns only in special instances), and count nouns may also be in the partitive plural. There is a semantic difference associated with the selection of partitive or nominative: the partitive expresses the notion that only a part of the noun in OBJECTIVE role is under consideration. Some examples:

(1b)   ISAL ON RAAMATUD
        'Father has (the) books'

(2b)   LAUAL ON RAAMATUD
        'On the table are (the) books'

(3b)   EMAL ON TOIDUD LAUAL
        'Mother has the food (here: separate dishes, different kinds of food) on the table'

(4b)   MEHED ON MAALT
        'The men are from the country'

(5b)   MEHED ON LINNAST
        'The men are from the town'

(6b)   MEHED ON LINNAS
        'The men are in the town'

(7b)   KIRJAD ON ISALE
        'The letters are for the father'

(8b)   LAPSED ON ISASSE
        'The children take after the father'

(1c)   ISAL ON RAAMATUID
        'The father has (some) books'

(2c)   LAUAL ON RAAMATUID
        'On the table are (some) books'

(3c)   EMAL ON TOITU LAUAL
        'Mother has (some) food on the table'

(4c)   EMAL ON TOITE LAUAL
        'Mother has (some) dishes (some kinds of food) on the table'

(5c)   MEHI ON MAALT
            '(Some) men are from the country'

(6c)   MEHI ON LINNAST
            '(Some) men are from the town'

(7c)   MEHI ON LINNAS
            '(Some) men are in the town'

(8c)   ISALE ON KIRJU
            'There are some letters for the father'

The idiomatic nature of sentence (8a) seems to preclude a surface partitive.

2.2. *Topicalization*

I inverted the word order in (8c), because KIRJU ON ISALE seemed to me less natural. The rules for word order have not been conclusively formulated for Estonian, and they may resist formulation for some time; however, they seem to play a certain part in deciding whether a given adessive case fulfills the function of LOCATIVE or DATIVE. Let us consider the following sentences:

(9a)   LAUAL ON NELI JALGA

(10a)   NELI JALGA ON LAUAL

Both sentences contain the same words: the noun *laud* 'table' in the adessive, the verb *on* 'be' 3. sg. pres., and the phrase *neli jalga* 'four legs' (*neli* is the numeral 4 in the nominative, *jalga* is the noun *jalg* 'leg' or 'foot' in partitive singular, the surface case being governed by the numeral). Realized with neutral intonation, sentence (9a) would mean 'The table has four legs', and (10a) would be glossed as 'Four legs (or feet) are on the table'; in other words, *laual* functions as DATIVE in (9a) and as LOCATIVE in (10a). Sentence (9a) would answer the question 'What does the table have?', whereas (10a) would answer the question 'Where are the four legs?'

Let us reconsider sentence (2a): LAUAL ON RAAMAT 'On the table is a book'. This sentence would answer the question 'What is on the table?' Another permutation of (2),

(2d)   RAAMAT ON LAUAL
            'The book is on the table'

would answer the question 'Where is the book?'

The word *laual* 'on the table' functions as LOCATIVE in both sentences, although formally sentence (2a), LAUAL ON RAAMAT, might also mean 'The table has a book', in the same way as (9a) means 'The table has four legs'.

Sentences (2a) and (9a) have identical surface structures; yet in (2a), *laual* is clearly LOCATIVE and in (9a) clearly DATIVE. Obviously semantic considerations enter into the picture here; we know that a table may 'possess' four legs, but may not 'possess' a book except in some metaphoric, poetic sense.[7]

However, there is a difference in focus (topicalization) between RAAMAT ON LAUAL and LAUAL ON RAAMAT. The order OBJECTIVE-'be'-LOCATIVE seems to be neutral; the order LOCATIVE-'be'-OBJECTIVE seems to indicate that OBJECTIVE is 'in focus'. As was indicated above, sentence (2d) would answer the question 'Where is the book?', while sentence (2a) would answer the question 'What is on the table?' Topicalization produced by changing the position of arguments may be overridden by emphasis manifested by phonological means. While RAAMAT ON LAUAL normally answers the question 'Where is the book?', *RAAMAT* ON LAUAL answers the question '*What* is on the table?'

These relationships between neutral word order (OBJECTIVE-'be'-LOCATIVE) and topicalization of OBJECTIVE (LOCATIVE-'be'-OBJECTIVE) apply when the two arguments, OBJECTIVE and LOCATIVE, are simultaneously present. Let us now consider the constructions where 'be' has the arguments DATIVE and OBJECTIVE.

Sentence (1a) ISAL ON RAAMAT, answers the question 'What does the father have?' and the sentence is neutral, if no emphasis appears on any word. I see no way of topicalizing the possessor by inverting the word order:

(1d)   *RAAMAT ON ISAL
          ?'The book is on the father'?

seems to me unnatural and unacceptable.[8] However, topicalization by emphasis is possible: *ISAL* ON RAAMAT would answer the question '*Who* has a book?'

In this sentence, I see no way of treating *isal* as LOCATIVE; however, the reasons for this seem to be semantic in nature. Let us therefore consider again sentences (9a) and (10a), where *laual* can be both DATIVE and LOCATIVE.

In (9a), the normal word order is DATIVE-'be'-OBJECTIVE. The inversion given as sentence (10a) does not change the topic, but changes the roles: *laual* now appears as LOCATIVE rather than DATIVE. Change of topic in (9a) can, however, be produced by emphasis (as was the case with sentences

---

[7] It is clear that if the label DATIVE is to be used for the argument of 'be' that indicates the possessor, the noun in DATIVE need not be animate.

[8] However, if OBJECTIVE is topicalized by the use of a demonstrative pronoun or some other means, the word order OBJECTIVE-'be'-DATIVE is possible. Thus the following sentence (suggested by Huno Rätsep) is perfectly all right: SEE RAAMAT ON PROFESSOR A'L 'Professor A. has this book'.

(1) and (2) discussed above):

(9b)   *LAUAL* ON NELI JALGA

would answer the question '*What* has four legs?' rather than 'What does the table have?' The DATIVE role of *laual* does not change.

In (10a), OBJECTIVE-'be'-LOCATIVE, OBJECTIVE can be topicalized only by emphasis, not by inversion; as in the case of (9a), the inversion would result in a change of roles. Emphasis retains the function of the arguments as before:

(10b)   *NELI JALGA* ON LAUAL

would answer the question '*What* is on the table?' Inversion (i.e., changing (10a) to (9a)) would produce the same kind of change of roles as was noted above when (9a) was converted to (10a).

It seems that if no emphasis is present, the arguments have to appear in a given order: DATIVE precedes OBJECTIVE, and OBJECTIVE precedes LOCATIVE. If no semantic ambiguity threatens (i.e., if LOCATIVE does not involve a noun that may also function as DATIVE), the OBJECTIVE-LOCATIVE order may be inverted for a change in topicalization. This inversion is not normally possible for DATIVE-OBJECTIVE sequences; here a change in topicalization has to be shown by emphasis on DATIVE. Emphasis may also be used in OBJECTIVE-LOCATIVE sentences to change topicalization without change in position.

Let us now consider the role of word order in sentences where the predicate 'be' is accompanied by all three arguments simultaneously (OBJECTIVE, DATIVE, LOCATIVE). Consider again sentence (3a):

(3a)   EMAL ON TOIT LAUAL
         'Mother has food on the table'

where *emal* is DATIVE, *toit* is OBJECTIVE, and *laual* is LOCATIVE. This word order appears to me normal or neutral (unmarked): DATIVE-'be'-OBJECTIVE-LOCATIVE. The four elements allow for 24 possible orderings. I would reject 12 of these immediately as nongrammatical: those in which 'be' appears in either initial or final position, as, for example, in *ON EMAL TOIT LAUAL and *EMAL TOIT LAUAL ON. Of the remaining 12, some are immediately acceptable, although with subtle focus differences; others are less acceptable, and still others have to be rejected. Of the six possible sentences beginning with DATIVE, I would accept two:

(3a)   EMAL ON TOIT LAUAL   D-'be'-O-L

(3e)   EMAL ON LAUAL TOIT   D-'be'-L-O

The difference between (3a) and (3e) is in topicalization: (3a) is neutral, whereas in (3e) *toit* is the topic.

Of the six possible sentences beginning with OBJECTIVE, I would accept one, provided that it is pronounced with emphasis on OBJECTIVE:

(3f)   TOIT ON EMAL LAUAL   O-'be'-D-L

Of the six possible sentences beginning with LOCATIVE, I would accept one:

(3g)   LAUAL ON EMAL TOIT   L-'be'-D-O

In (3g), *laual* would have to be produced with emphasis in order that the sentence be acceptable.

Thus four sentences are fully acceptable. Of the remaining 8 (excluding the twelve with 'be' in initial and final position) some are more acceptable than others: (3h) and (3i) seem more natural to me than (3j)–(3o), which represent various degrees of relative ungrammaticality.

(3h)   TOIT EMAL ON LAUAL   O-D-'be'-L

(3i)   LAUAL EMAL ON TOIT   L-D-'be'-O

(3j)   *LAUAL ON TOIT EMAL

(3k)   *EMAL LAUAL ON TOIT

(3l)   *EMAL TOIT ON LAUAL

(3m)   *TOIT ON LAUAL EMAL

(3n)   *TOIT LAUAL ON EMAL

(3o)   *LAUAL TOIT ON EMAL

It appears that LOCATIVE and OBJECTIVE may change positions for purposes of topicalization: acceptable pairs are (3a) and (3e), (3f) and (3g), and (although less natural) (3h) and (3i). On the other hand, LOCATIVE and DATIVE may change places only if emphasis is added; inversion without emphasis would produce a change in role. (3e) can be changed to (3g) only with added emphasis on LOCATIVE, if the roles of the arguments are to be maintained.

It seems to me that (3h) and (3i) are acceptable only if both OBJECTIVE and LOCATIVE are produced with emphasis. The unmarked order thus seems to be

D-'be'-O-L (3a)

OBJECTIVE may become topic by inversion with LOCATIVE:

D-'be'-L-O (3e)

DATIVE may become topic by emphasis, keeping the unmarked order.

OBJECTIVE may be emphasized by inversion with DATIVE and added emphasis on OBJECTIVE:

$$\text{O-'be'-D-L (3f)}$$

LOCATIVE may be emphasized by inversion with DATIVE and added emphasis on LOCATIVE:

$$\text{L-'be'-D-O (3g)}$$

It appears that (3a) and (3h) are, furthermore, in a similar relationship to each other as (3e) and (3i). In both (3h) and (3i), there seems to be an intonation break (a 'juncture') after the first word, i.e., after *toit* in (3h) and *laual* in (3i). The change from (3a) to (3h) and (3e) to (3i) seems to involve a more complicated phonological process than is present in either changes of topic or changes of emphasis. For the time being I shall call this 'double emphasis', since both OBJECTIVE and LOCATIVE appear to be stressed in (3h) and (3i). The difference between (3h) and (3i), on the other hand, appears to be one of topicalization or focus, as was the difference between (3a) and (3e), which also involved inversion of OBJECTIVE and LOCATIVE.

III. OTHER POSSIBLE ARGUMENTS OF THE VERB 'BE'

3.1. *Benefactive*

I would like to come back now to the possible arguments of the predicate 'be' other than OBJECTIVE, LOCATIVE, and DATIVE. Consider again sentence (7a):

(7a)   KIRI ON ISALE
         'The letter is for the father'

where *kiri* is OBJECTIVE and *isale*, in the surface allative case, would correspond in function to the BENEFACTIVE of Fillmore's Case Grammar. An inversion is possible, with concomitant change in focus:

(7b)   ISALE ON KIRI
         'There is a letter for father'

One of the possible arguments of 'be' thus is BENEFACTIVE.[9]

3.2. *Essive*

Another possible argument is ESSIVE, which may appear in several surface cases, sometimes with semantic distinctions between them, as was the case with the argument labeled LOCATIVE. I shall group under ESSIVE the arguments

---

[9] Neither DATIVE nor BENEFACTIVE correspond directly to an indirect object in the ordinary sense of the term.

appearing in nominative, (surface) essive and translative cases:

(11)   NN ON MEIE SAADIK LONDONIS
        'NN is our ambassador in London'

(12)   NN ON MEIE SAADIKUNA LONDONIS
        'NN is our ambassador in London'

(13)   NN ON MEIE SAADIKUKS LONDONIS
        'NN is our ambassador in London'

In all three sentences, NN is OBJECTIVE, *meie saadik* 'our ambassador' is
ESSIVE, and *Londonis* is LOCATIVE (in the surface inessive case). ESSIVE is
manifested as surface nominative in (11), surface essive in (12), and surface
translative in (13). The semantic differences involved are subtle, but clear:
(11) implies that being ambassador is a permanent (inalienable) characteristic
of NN, (12) implies that NN is (temporarily) in London in his capacity as
ambassador (he need not be the permanent or regular ambassador to
London, or he may be in London occasionally in other capacities), and (13)
implies that NN is fulfilling the role of ambassador (in an official capacity,
but it is not a permanent characteristic of NN).

ESSIVE may also appear in the surface partitive case, with partitive meaning,
as was the case with OBJECTIVE. The surface partitive seems to require
plurality, even when OBJECTIVE (i.e., the surface subject of the sentence with
'be' as predicate) is in the singular. Compare (14) and (15):

(14)   NN ON PARIM ÕPILANE KLASSIS
        'NN is the best student in the class'

where NN is OBJECTIVE, *parim õpilane* 'best student' is ESSIVE in the nominative singular case, and *klassis* 'in the class' is LOCATIVE in the inessive
singular.

(15)   NN ON PARIMAID ÕPILASI KLASSIS
        'NN is one of the best students in the class'

where *parimaid õpilasi* is ESSIVE in partitive plural.

One might ask now what constitutes the difference between the arguments
OBJECTIVE and ESSIVE, especially since both may appear in the same surface
cases (the arguments have surface nominative and partitive in common as
possible cases). I shall opt for Fillmore's solution[10] and claim that only one
element can fulfill a particular role at any one time. OBJECTIVE takes prece-

---

[10] Cf. 'Lexical Entries for Verbs'. Fillmore has recently modified this statement, recognizing that at least as far as LOCATIVE is concerned, more than one argument of the same type
may be simultaneously present. This holds for Estonian as well as English; cf. below
under Subsection 3.3.

dence over ESSIVE.[11] If only one argument that might fulfill either role is present, it becomes OBJECTIVE. If an OBJECTIVE is already present, the other element assumes the role of ESSIVE.[12]

3.3. Terminative

Of the 14 surface cases of Estonian, 'be' thus has been shown to take arguments in nominative, partitive, the six local cases, essive and translative. If indeed 'be' may have arguments in all 14 cases (which need not be true), terminative, abessive, comitative, and genitive must be accounted for.

Consider a sentence like (16):

(16)   VESI ON KAELANI
         'The water is (i.e., reaches) up to the neck'

In this sentence, *vesi* is the noun 'water' in nominative singular, appearing in the role of OBJECTIVE. *Kaelani* is the noun *kael* 'neck' in the surface terminative case. The terminative case expresses limitation in space and/or time; the class of words that may appear in this function is rather large. Consider the following additional examples:

(17)   AIATÖÖD OLI LUMENI
         'There was gardening (work) until snowfall'

(18)   OLIME HOMMIKUNI
         'We were (stayed) until morning'

(19)   OLGE LÕPUNI
         'Remain (stay) until the end'

The arguments appearing in the terminative case could perhaps be grouped with the external and internal local cases under LOCATIVE. The fact that the terminative is frequently used with expressions of time should not argue against it, considering that other local cases are likewise used in time

[11] Here and in many instances, there is a hierarchy among the arguments which might be compared with valence in chemistry: in combining with each other, certain elements require a given proportion, and some elements take precedence over other elements in entering a compound. It will be shown below that some arguments may appear only when another argument is already present.

[12] The addition of ESSIVE to Case Grammar is an innovation. Fillmore, according to oral communication, would treat 'be' with arguments I have labeled ESSIVE as complex predicates. I see no essential difference between the arguments in ESSIVE and other arguments of 'be'; if 'be' constitutes a complex predicate with an argument in ESSIVE, its occurrences with other arguments should likewise be treated as complex predicates. As will be shown below, 'be' shares all of its arguments with other verbs, even those in ESSIVE; and I cannot accept the necessary conclusion that the same word, in the same surface case and the same function (that is, in the same deep structure case), is part of a complex predicate when the verb is 'be', and an argument of a predicate when the verb is something else.

expressions. A more serious objection would be the claim, expressed by Fillmore in 'Lexical Entries for Verbs', that in Case Grammar only one argument may be present in a given function, and LOCATIVE would be pre-empted in sentences like (20):

(20)   NN ON KAELANI VEES
         'NN is in the water up to (his) neck'

where *vees* is the noun *vesi* 'water' in the inessive case, obviously manifesting the argument LOCATIVE. Sentence (20) could be considered a counter-argument for the claim that only one argument may be present in a given case; however, the claim cannot be upheld anyway, considering that multiple locatives abound in Estonian (as well as in other languages). If words in the terminative case are treated as manifestations of LOCATIVE (even when used in a temporal sense), sentence (20) would simply contain two LOCATIVES, one in inessive, the other in terminative.

3.4. *Associative*

The abessive and comitative cases seem to reflect the positive and negative aspects of the same relationship. In the case of 'be', only the associative meaning is present; with other verbs, the functions of instrument and accompaniment (association) seem to have merged and are expressed by the same surface cases. I shall call the argument ASSOCIATIVE.[13] With the verb 'be' as predicate, ASSOCIATIVE is usually not the only argument, but some other argument (such as LOCATIVE) is also present:

(21a)   NN ON SÕPRADETA
         'NN is without friends'

where *sõpradeta* is abessive plural of the noun *sõber* 'friend', and the sentence implies a more or less permanent state of friendlessness;

(22a)   NN ON SÕPRADEGA
         'NN is with friends'

where *sõpradega* is the same noun in comitative plural, and the sentence seems somewhat incomplete (one expects a LOCATIVE to be present also: NN is *somewhere* with friends).

---

[13] My ASSOCIATIVE includes Fillmore's INSTRUMENTAL. Cf. 'Case for Case' (p. 24). It might be argued that the comitative and instrumental represent different functions and therefore should be kept separate. I am not sure that the distinction is a necessary one, at least from the point of view of Estonian; it appears to me that the problem might be handled at the level of the lexicon. The unity of the ASSOCIATIVE is also reflected in the fact that the surface abessive case is used to negate both positive aspects of ASSOCIATIVE, comitative as well as instrumental.

Both sentences seem more acceptable with other arguments present, e.g.:

(21b)   NN ON SÕPRADETA LINNAS
        'NN is in town without friends'

(22b)   NN ON SÕPRADEGA LINNAS
        'NN is in town with friends'

The arguments DATIVE and ASSOCIATIVE seem to exclude each other; if DATIVE has been chosen, ASSOCIATIVE may not appear. This explains the relationship between (23) and (24), which are paraphrases of each other:

(23)   NOORMEHEL ON UHKE HOIAK
        'The young man has a proud bearing'

(24)   NOORMEES ON UHKE HOIAKUGA
        'The young man is with a proud bearing'

In sentence (23), 'be' has the arguments DATIVE (*noormehel* 'the young man' in the adessive case) and OBJECTIVE (*uhke hoiak* 'proud bearing' in the nominative singular). In sentence (24), 'be' has the arguments OBJECTIVE (*noormees* 'the young man' in nominative singular) and ASSOCIATIVE (*uhke hoiakuga* 'proud bearing' in comitative singular).

It was stated above that with 'be', OBJECTIVE takes precedence over ESSIVE. It now appears that DATIVE and OBJECTIVE both take precedence over ASSOCIATIVE. The hierarchy of arguments a verb may take constitutes another part of the information that has to be included in the lexical entries for verbs.

3.5. *Dative again*

The last surface case to be considered is the genitive. Consider again sentence (1):

(1a)   ISAL ON RAAMAT
        'Father has a book'

where *isal* is DATIVE in the adessive case. It was pointed out above that the inversion of this sentence is not acceptable: (1d) *RAAMAT ON ISAL is not a topicalization of DATIVE, but a change of the role of *isal* from DATIVE to LOCATIVE which is unacceptable on semantic grounds. It is now possible to suggest a reason for the unacceptability of (1d): if DATIVE is topicalized (i.e., placed after 'be'), it changes from the surface adessive to genitive, and often is reinforced by the particle *oma* 'own'. Thus (1e) is a perfectly acceptable topicalization of the DATIVE and genitive is another possible surface case of the DATIVE:

(1e) RAAMAT ON ISA (OMA)
      'The book is father's'

IV. ARGUMENTS OF 'BE' SHARED BY OTHER VERBS

4.1. Dative

In the Introduction, I advanced the claim that all Estonian verbs can be best classified according to the number and types of arguments they take, and that there is no need to assume that 'be' has a special copula function that sets it off from other verbs. I shall now briefly support this claim by showing that other verbs exist that share the same arguments with 'be'.[14] (Verbs should be grouped in the same class, if they take exactly the same kinds of arguments; but the classes will have extensive overlaps among themselves.)

The order in which the arguments are presented is the same as was followed above, although it is not necessarily the most logical one.

Consider the following examples:

(25) AEDNIKUL ON MITMESUGUSEID LILLI
      'The gardener has many kinds of flowers'

(26) AEDNIKUL ÕITSEB MITMESUGUSEID LILLI
      'The gardener has many kinds of flowers in bloom'

The difference between the two sentences is in the verbs appearing as Predicate: in (25) *on* is 'be' in 3 sg. pres., and in (26) *õitseb* is 'bloom' in the

---

[14] Haldur Õim has raised the question whether the very fact that 'be' can have so many different arguments is not suspicious and indicative of some kind of syncretism. In my analysis, 'be' can have six arguments: DATIVE, LOCATIVE, OBJECTIVE, BENEFACTIVE, ESSIVE, and ASSOCIATIVE. I do not consider six arguments excessive; there are numerous verbs that take at least as many arguments as 'be'. Consider, for example, the verb *võtma* 'to take', which takes five of the six arguments of 'be', and a few additional ones: AGENTIVE, FACTITIVE, and INSTRUMENTAL (if the latter is to be considered distinct from ASSOCIATIVE). Examples: EMA VÕTAB LASTEGA HOMMIKUEINET 'Mother takes breakfast with the children' (*Ema* – AGENTIVE, *lastega* – ASSOCIATIVE, *hommikueinet* – FACTITIVE); MEES VÕTTIS ROOBIGA TULEST SÜSI 'The man took coals from the fire with a poker' (*tulest* – LOCATIVE, *roobiga* – INSTRUMENTAL, if this is to be considered different from ASSOCIATIVE); VEND VÕTTIS LAPSEPÕLVE SÕBRATARI NAISEKS '(The) brother took (his) childhood sweetheart as wife' (i.e., married her) (*naiseks* – ESSIVE in translative); TA VÕTTIS SEDA NALJANA 'He took it as a joke' (*naljana* – ESSIVE in (surface) essive); TA VÕTTIS SELLE OMALE PÄRISEKS 'He took it for himself as permanent possession' (omale – BENEFACTIVE); TA VÕTTIS MUL SÕNAD SUUST 'He took the words out of my mouth' (*mul* – DATIVE). LOCATIVE may appear in all local cases as well as in the terminative case. The only real case-structure difference between 'be' and 'take' is the presence of OBJECTIVE with 'be' and AGENTIVE and FACTITIVE with 'take'. This difference is shared by many other verb pairs.

same form. In both sentences, *mitmesuguseid lilli* is OBJECTIVE in partitive
plural, and *aednikul* is DATIVE in the adessive case. The class of verbs which
may appear in this Predicate includes also *kasvab* 'grows', *juurdub* 'takes
root', *närtsib* 'wilts', *edeneb* 'makes progress', *lõhnab* 'gives off fragrance',
etc. Examples could be multiplied; I shall limit myself in the future to one
apiece.

4.2. *Objective*

Since I have chosen to call the surface subject of a sentence OBJECTIVE,[15] 'be'
shares this argument with practically all verbs in the language, excepting,
of course, instances in which the verb appears in the impersonal voice.
These verb forms preclude the presence of a surface subject, but admit a
surface object (in the nominative and partitive); I would classify the surface
object as FACTITIVE in Case Grammar.[16] Sentences (25) and (26) may serve
also to illustrate that 'be' and 'blossom' share the argument OBJECTIVE, here
mitmesuguseid lilli 'many kinds of flowers' in partitive plural.

4.3. *Locative*

Most verbs can have a LOCATIVE argument; however, verbs differ among
themselves which of the six local cases may appear as this argument. The
verb 'come' shares four manifestations of LOCATIVE with 'be':

(27)   (cf. 4) MEES TULEB MAALT
         'The man comes from the country'

(28)   (cf. 5) MEES TULEB LINNAST
         'The man comes from town'

(29)   (cf. 7) ISALE TULI KIRI
         'A letter came for the father'

(30)   (cf. 7) MEES TULEB MAALE
         'The man comes to the country'

(31)   (cf. 8) MEES TULEB LINNA
         'The man comes to town'

Semantic reasons seem to exclude the surface cases inessive and adessive
from appearing with 'come',[17] but other verbs, such as 'work', may have

---

[15] Except where it is clearly AGENTIVE. Cf. 'Case for Case' (p. 24).
[16] Cf. 'Case for Case' (p. 25).
[17] Adessive and inessive are possible, provided another LOCATIVE argument is present.
Huno Rätsep has suggested sentences like MEES TULEB TÄNAVANURGAL AUTOSSE 'The man
comes into the car (i.e., enters the car) at the streetcorner', where *tänavanurgal* is LOCATIVE
in the adessive case and *autosse* is LOCATIVE in the illative case.

them:

(32)   (cf. 6) MEES TÖÖTAB LINNAS
        'The man works in the city'

(33)   (cf. 2) MEES TÖÖTAB MAAL
        'The man works in the country'

Note that (30) has a purely locative sense, whereas in (7), the allative served to manifest an underlying BENEFACTIVE. This is one difference between the verbs 'come' and 'be' that has to be entered in the dictionary when the two verbs are lexically specified.

4.4. *Benefactive*

As was mentioned above, a surface allative may serve as LOCATIVE (although not with 'be') and as BENEFACTIVE. A great number of predicates may take this argument; its scope is much wider than that of the traditional indirect object, although indirect objects are encompassed under BENEFACTIVE. Consider an example:

(34)   (cf. 7) ISALE TULI KIRI
        'A letter came for the father'

4.5. *Essive*

A much smaller group of verbs can take an ESSIVE argument. The group that may take ESSIVE arguments in essive or translative cases includes 'to work' and 'to appoint'. Consider (35) and (36):

(35)   (cf. 12) NN TÖÖTAB MEIE SAADIKUNA LONDONIS
        'NN works in London as our ambassador'

(36)   (cf. 13) NN MÄÄRATI MEIE SAADIKUKS LONDONI(S)
        'NN was appointed our ambassador in London'

The list of verbs that can take an ESSIVE argument in nominative and/or partitive is very small, and the group seems semantically definable: these verbs signify seeming, appearing, being taken for etc. The examples I can think of at the moment have adjectives rather than nouns in ESSIVE (but since there is a very fluid boundary between nouns and adjectives, this need not be a significant restriction):

(37a)   RASKUS ON ÜLETAMATU
        'The difficulty is insurmountable'

(37b)   RASKUS NÄIB ÜLETAMATU
        'The difficulty seems insurmountable'

4.6. Terminative

Many verbs can have arguments in the terminative case, which is considered
a possible surface case of LOCATIVE. Examples include (38) and (39):

(38)   (cf. 16) VESI ULATUB KAELANI
        'The water reaches up to the neck'

(39)   (cf. 18) TÖÖTASIME HOMMIKUNI
        'We worked until morning'

4.7. Associative

As was mentioned above, the argument ASSOCIATIVE has the function of
accompaniment rather than instrument with the verb 'be'. Other verbs may
have arguments in the surface comitative (and abessive) cases in both
functions:

(40)   ISA KÕNELEB LASTEGA
        'Father speaks with the children'

(41)   ISA LOEB PRILLIDEGA
        'Father reads with spectacles'

(42)   ISA SÖÖB KAHVLIGA
        'Father eats with a fork'

(43)   ISA SÖÖB KAHVLITA
        'Father eats without a fork'

4.8. Other Arguments

There are some arguments suggested by Case Grammar that do not appear
with 'be' in Estonian. In particular, the arguments AGENTIVE and FACTITIVE
appeared unnecessary for the development of the description. I believe that
their absence is significant as regards the semantics of 'be'; in other words,
it is one of the characteristics of 'be' (which it shares with a large number of
other verbs) that it takes neither a FACTITIVE nor an AGENTIVE argument.

It has been shown that so far as its relationship to arguments is concerned,
'be' in Estonian functions just like any other verb and that it is not necessary
to postulate a 'copula'.[18] There is a further bit of evidence that 'be' is a

---

[18] It may be relevant in this connection that verbless sentences (so-called nominal sentences) exist in present-day Estonian and in related languages, and are reconstructed for the protolanguage. In such sentences the relationships between elements are expressed simply by cases. Very similar observations have been made regarding early stages of Indo-European. W. Lehmann has stated (in the Collitz lecture delivered at the summer 1968 meeting of the Linguistic Society of America at Urbana, Illinois) that a copula need not be reconstructed for Proto-Indo-European. Incidentally, the similarity extends to the construction used in Estonian to express 'having'. According to Lehmann, Proto-Indo-European went through a stage in which the verb 'have' had not yet evolved (cf., for example, Latin *mihi est liber* = 'I have a book', literally 'to me there is a book').

regular enough verb: it may be modified by a manner adverb like the majority of verbs.[19] Compare sentences (44) and (45):

(44)   ASJAD ON HALVAD
'Things are bad'

(45)   ASJAD ON HALVASTI
'Things are badly' (i.e., are going badly, are in a bad state)

In (45) *halvasti* is an adverb, derived from the adjective *halb* 'bad' by the productive adverbial suffix *-sti*. Adverbs of this kind can be formed from most adjectives, and they modify most (if not all) verbs.

The ideas expressed above are very tentative, and the 'testing for fit' between Case Grammar and Estonian syntax has only just begun. The situation looks, however, promising. It seems to me that it is possible to explain Estonian grammatical facts more naturally and intuitively more acceptably within the framework of Case Grammar than within any other grammatical framework, and I hope that more serious work in this direction will be undertaken soon.

The Ohio State University

---

[19] I am leaving unanswered at the moment the question of how adverbs should be treated in a Case Grammar description of Estonian.

A. C. GRAHAM

'BEING' IN LINGUISTICS AND PHILOSOPHY:
A PRELIMINARY INQUIRY*

The concept of Being is a good test for the thesis of Benjamin Whorf[1] that the grammatical structure of language guides the formation of philosophical concepts. Consider these three facts:

(1) A verb 'to be' which serves both as copula ('X is Y') and as indicator of existence ('X is', 'There is X') is almost confined to Indo-European languages.[2]

(2) A concept of Being combining essence (what X is *per se*) and existence is confined to philosophies developed in languages of the Indo-European family. In the two major philosophical traditions which developed outside this family, Arabic *wujūd* and Chinese *yu* are not 'being' but 'existence'.[3]

(3) Although the first language of Western philosophy was Greek, its main stream passed through Semitic languages (Syriac, Arabic, Hebrew) before returning to Indo-European languages (scholastic Latin, French, English, German). It was in Arabic, which sharply separates the existential and copulative functions, that the distinction between existence and essence emerged.[4]

An adequate account of the development of theWestern concept of Being in its linguistic context would require the co-operation of specialists in many disciplines. But it may be useful to offer a preliminary sketch, as a focus for future criticism and inquiry. I shall therefore cover much ground in a little space, and intrude into several fields within which I am not an authority.

---

* This paper appeared originally in *Foundations of Language* **1** (1965) pp. 223–231, and is here reprinted by permission of the author. The author has communicated to the editor that, as it was composed before the specialist papers on some of the languages touched upon appeared in the present series, it should be judged in the light of those later publications. (Ed.)

[1] *Language, Thought and Reality*, New York 1956.

[2] Cf. Ernst Locker, 'Être et Avoir. Leurs expressions dans les langues', *Anthropos* **49** (1954) 481–510.

[3] For *wujūd* cf. page 226 below. For *yu* cf. A. C. Graham, 'Being in Western Philosophy compared with shih/fei and yu/wu in Chinese Philosophy', *Asia Major* (NS) **7** (1959) 79–112.

[4] Cf. E. Gilson, *Le Thomisme*, Paris 1948, p. 55; M.-D. Roland-Gosselin, *Le 'De ente et essentia' de S. Thomas d'Aquin*, Paris 1948, pp. xix, xx, 150–56; Soheil M. Afnan, *Avicenna*, London 1958, pp. 115–21.

Verhaar (ed.), The Verb 'Be' and its Synonyms **5**, 225–233. *All Rights Reserved.*
Copyright © *1972 by D. Reidel Publishing Company, Dordrecht-Holland*

It is well known that Greek philosophy hardly ever distinguishes between the existential and copulative functions of *einai* 'to be'. Thus Plato argues that since everything is double or big or heavy in relation to some things and half or small or light compared with others, we have an equal right to say that it is (exists) or that it is not (does not exist).[5] Aristotle ignores the distinction when he analyses the senses of *einai* in *Metaphysics* V.vii, although he carefully separates being *per se* and *per accidens*, being as 'truth', and potential and actual being, and differentiates being *per se* according to the categories. The great exception is the second book of *Posterior Analytics*, where the question 'whether it is' (*ei esti*) is contrasted with the question 'what it is' (*ti esti*). By 'whether it is' Aristotle means 'whether it exists', but it is interesting to notice that it costs him some trouble to make this plain: "I mean the question whether or not it is absolutely, not whether it is white or not" (το δ' εἰ ἔστιν ἢ μὴ ἁπλῶς λέγω, ἀλλ' οὐκ εἰ λευκὸς ἢ μή).[6] He has no verb corresponding to 'exist' and except for *ousia* (which embraces the concepts later distinguished by *essentia* and *substantia*) he has no noun corresponding to 'essence' to replace his *ti esti* ('what *X* is') and *ti ēn einai* ('what it is to be *X*'). Confined to constructions with *einai*, he can distinguish between existential and copulative functions only by such expressions as: "the substance being not this or that but absolutely, or not absolutely but something *per se* or *per accidens*" (... τοῦ εἶναι μὴ τοδὶ ἢ τοδὶ ἀλλ' ἁπλῶς τὴν οὐσίαν, ἢ τοῦ μὴ ἁπλῶς ἀλλά τι τῶν καθ' αὐτὸ ἢ κατὰ συμβεβηκός), and "whether it absolutely is, not is one of its attributes, or whether it is one of its attributes" (... ἢ ἁπλῶς καὶ μὴ τῶν ὑπαρχόντων τι, ἢ τῶν ὑπαρχόντων).[7]

Whenever Aristotle dispenses with such constructions we are left doubtful whether or not he has lost sight of the distinction, although in many contexts the impossibility of replacing *einai* by the less flexible English 'to be' forces translators to prejudge the issue by resorting to 'to exist'. Thus when Aristotle observes that definition shows what a thing is (*ti esti*) but not 'that it is' (*hoti esti*), which is known not by definition but by demonstration, it is convenient and sometimes hardly avoidable to translate *hoti esti* as 'existence', although it certainly embraces not only the existence of *X* but its being in fact what it is defined as being:

ut sup. 92b20–25 φανερὸν δὲ καὶ κατὰ τοὺς νῦν τρόπους τῶν ὅρων ὡς οὐ δεικνύουσιν οἱ ὁριζόμενοι ὅτι ἔστιν. εἰ γὰρ καὶ ἔστιν ἐκ τοῦ μέσου τι ἴσον, ἀλλὰ διὰ τί ἔστι τὸ ὁρισθέν; καὶ διὰ τί τοῦτ' ἔστι κύκλος; εἴη γὰρ ἂν καὶ ὀρειχάλχου φάναι εἶναι αὐτόν. οὔτε γὰρ ὅτι δυνατὸν εἶναι τὸ λεγόμενον

---

[5] *Republic*, Book 5, 479.

[6] *Posterior Analytics* 89b 33.

[7] *Ut supra* 90a 10–2, 33.

προσδηλοῦσιν οἱ ὅροι οὔτε ὅτι ἐκεῖνο οὗ φασὶν εἶναι ὁρισμοί, ἀλλ' ἀεὶ ἔξεστι λέγειν το διὰ τί. "It is evident also from the methods of defining now in use that those who define do not prove *the existence of the definiendum* (*hoti esti*, 'that *X* is'). Even supposing that there is something equidistant from the centre, why *does* the object so defined *exist* (*esti*)? and why is it a circle? One might equally well assert that it is the definition of mountain-copper. Definitions do not include evidence that it is possible for what they describe *to exist* (*einai*), nor that it is identical with that which they claim to define. It is always possible to ask *why*" (Tredennick).[8]

Although Tredennick translates *hoti esti* as 'existence' (no doubt because in the second underlined instance it is grammatically impossible to replace *esti* by 'is'), the phrase implies both that something described as equidistant from a centre exists and that it is in fact a circle.

ἔτι ἕτερον τὸ τί ἐστι καὶ ὅτι ἔστι δεῖξαι. ὁ μὲν οὖν ὁρισμὸς τί ἐστι δηλοῖ, ἡ δὲ ἀπόδειξις ὅτι ἔστι τόδε κατὰ τοῦδε ἢ οὐκ ἔστιν. "To reveal the essence of a thing is not the same as to prove a proposition about it; now definition exhibits the essence, but demonstration proves that an attribute is, or is not, predicated of a subject."[9] (Literally: "Moreover to show what it is is different from showing that it is; now definition shows what it is, demonstration on the other hand that with regard to this this is or is not.")

Here the *einai* of *hoti esti* 'that it is' is primarily the copula between subject and predicate; unable to use 'exist', Tredennick is driven in a different direction, and a reader of the English would hardly guess that in both passages Aristotle is discussing the same topic in the same terminology.

While in Greek it is much more difficult than in English to distinguish existential and copulative 'to be', in Arabic there is no convenient word which combines both functions. Arabic has an existential verb *kāna* 'be, become'; but for "*A* is *B*" it uses the sentence pattern "*A* (nominative) *B* (nominative)", or, interposing the third-person pronoun *huwa* (feminine *hiya*), "*A* (nominative) *huwa B* (nominative)", or, with the particle *inna*, "*Inna A* (accusative) *B* (nominative)". The contrast is not quite absolute, for there is also a copulative pattern with *kāna*: "*Kāna A* (nominative) *B* (accusative)". But the Arabic translators did not in fact exploit any possibility there may have been of regularly reproducing *einai* by *kāna*, an unsuitable equivalent in any case because of its suggestion of 'becoming'.[10] The version of Aristotle's *Categories* made by Isḥaq ibn Ḥunayn (died AD 910/911), which

---

[8] Hugh Tredennick, *Posterior Analytics* (Loeb Classical Library), London and Cambridge, Mass. 1960, pp. 197, 199.

[9] *Ut supra*, p. 185.

[10] Cf. A.-M. Goichon, *La distinction de l'essence et de l'existence d'après Ibn Sīnā*, Paris 1937, p. 29, note 4.

Khalil Georr has studied in detail[11], deals with *einai* by the following devices:

(1) Existential *einai* in ordinary contexts is represented by *kāna*, when used technically by the passive of *WaJaDa* 'find', in a usage not unlike that of English "Lions are found in Africa". For *to einai* it uses the infinitive *WuJūD*, for *to on* the passive participle *maWJūD* 'what is found/what exists'.

(2) For "*A is B*" it occasionally uses "*Kāna A B*", but generally "*A B*" or "*A huwa B*". In conjunction with *mā* 'what', the usual formula for '*ti esti...*' 'what is...?' is '*mā huwa...*' (feminine '*mā hiya...*'). The coinage *māhiyyah* 'quiddity', an abstract noun probably formed from *mā hiya*[12], appears several times in the phrase *māhiyyatu-hu*, "its quiddity', translating *hoper esti*, "just what it is". This became a key term in Arabic philosophy, as did *dhāt*, feminine of *dhū* 'possessor' (used in ordinary Arabic in such phrases as *dhū 'ilmin* "possessor of learning/learned man"), that to which accidents belong. This appears regularly in the phrase *bi dhāti-hi*, 'in its *dbāt*', translating *kath' hauto* (*per se*). The versions of other writings of Aristotle introduce other technical terms; thus in the crucial passage on the different senses of 'Being' in *Metaphysics* V.vii *einai* is represented by *huwiyyah*, an abstract noun formed from the interposed pronoun in "*A huwa B*".[13] It may be noticed that the Arabic 'essence'-words are independent of Greek *ousia* (in imitation of which the Latin *essentia* was formed). The Arabic equivalent of *ousia* is *jawhar* 'substance', believed to be a Pahlawi loan-word.[14]

The Arabic versions of Aristotle are very literal, yet because of the structure of the language they transform him at one stroke into a philosopher who talks sometimes about existence, sometimes about quiddity, *never about being*. In place of the single verb *einai* the Arabs found in Aristotle a set of abstract nouns, each rooted in either the existential verb or the copulative sentence patterns. This deformation often obscured Aristotle's meaning, a fact which some of the Arabs discerned.[15] But it also gave Arabic ontology a fresh start, free from the confusion from which Greek philosophy was barely beginning to find the way out. It is a misplaced compliment to credit.

---

[11] *Les catégories d'Aristote dans leurs versions syro-arabes*, Beyrouth 1948. For the Arabic ontological vocabulary cf. Goichon *ut supra*, pp. 15–7, 29–49; and *Lexique de la langue philosophique d'Ibn Sīna*, Paris 1939; *Vocabulaires comparés d'Aristote et d'Ibn Sīna*, Paris 1939; Soheil M. Afnan, *Philosophical Terminology in Arabic and Persian*, Leyden 1964, pp. 29f, 94–7, 99–102, 117–24. My data are from these authorities (who, of course, bear no responsibility for the conclusions drawn from them), and from my own comparisons, made with a very limited knowledge of Arabic, of the Greek and Arabic texts of samples of Aristotle and the Arabic and Latin texts of samples of Avicenna and Averroes.

[12] Cf. Afnan, *loc. cit.*, pp. 117–120

[13] Averroes, *Tafsīr mā ba'd aṭ-ṭabi'āt* (ed. by M. Bouyges), Beyrouth 1942, pp. 552–63.

[14] Afnan, *loc. cit.*, p. 99.

[15] Afnan, *loc. cit.*, p. 29; Averroes, *Compendio de metafisica* (edited with Spanish translation by Carlos Quiros Rodriguez), Madrid 1919, Book 1/21. (Of doubtful authenticity, cf. Bouyges ut sup. LIII–LIV.)

Al-Fārābī (died 950) and Ibn Sīnā (Avicenna, 980–1037) with the discovery of the ontological difference between essence and existence; it was impossible for an Arab to confuse them, although he might, as did Ibn Rushd (Averroes, 1126–1193), choose for reasons of his own to identify them. The general assumption of Arab philosophers other than Averroes is that existence cannot belong to the quiddity of anything which does not exist necessarily, from which Avicenna concludes that the existence of things is added to their quiddities by the single necessary existent, God.

The Latin translators of Avicenna and Averroes inherited an ontological vocabulary formed in Roman times by translation from Greek. Standard Latin *esse* cannot reproduce *einai* through the whole range of its forms, since it has no participle and gerund, and there is no Latin article with which to establish the case of *esse* treated as an undeclinable noun. (Contrast Greek *to einai* 'being', *tou einai* 'of being'.) Philosophical Latin filled most gaps by supplying an artificial participle (*ens*) and gerund (*essendum*), and by such constructions as *hoc esse* ('this being') *huius esse* ('of this being'). But since it used *ens* only for the nominal *to on*, it was never able to cope with all uses of the Greek participle, and Latin translators were forced on occasion to use either the indicative or *existens* for *ōn, ousa, on*:

Aristotle, *Categories* 2b, 5, 6: μὴ οὐσῶν οὖν τῶν πρώτων οὐσιῶν ἀδύνατον τῶν ἄλλων τι εἶναι.

Aristoteles latinus 1/1–5 (ed. by L. Minio-Paluello, Oxford 1961) p. 8 (Boethius, c. AD 510): Si ergo primae substantiae non sunt, impossibile est aliquid esse ceterorum. p. 49 (Editio composita, before AD 822): Non existentibus ergo primis substantiis, impossibile est esse aliquid aliorum. "Therefore were there no primary substances it would be impossible for any of the others to be."

The word *essentia* was coined not later than the first century as Latin equivalent for *ousia*[16], for which however Boethius in his translations preferred *substantia*. For Boethius, who remained the primary authority for the use of the word throughout the early Middle Ages, *essentia* still coincided in meaning with *ousia* and had not contracted to the later sense of 'essence' (what *X* is *per se*, what is presented by its definition):

Contra Eutychen III 29–35[17]: Atque uti Graeca utar oratione in rebus quae a Graecis agitata Latina interpretatione translata sunt: αἱ οὐσίαι ἐν μὲν τοῖς καθόλου εἶναι δύνανται. ἐν δὲ τοῖς ἀτόμοις καὶ κατὰ μέρος μόνοις ὑφίστανται, id est: essentiae in universalibus quidem esse possunt, in solis vero individuis et particularibus substant.

---

[16] Roland-Gosselin, *loc. cit.*, p. 9.
[17] H. F. Stewart and E. K. Rand, *Boethius: The Theological Tractates.* (Loeb Classical Library), London and Cambridge, Mass. 1962, p. 86.

"And, if I may use Greek for matters which raised by the Greeks have been translated into Latin, ... that is: *essentiae* indeed have potential being in universals, but are substantial in individuals and particulars alone."

In the 12th and 13th centuries translations from Arabic and Hebrew, of the Arabic and Jewish philosophers and of previously unknown writings of Aristotle, contributed to the revival of Aristotelianism in Latin Europe. The translations use the following equivalents (The earlier Greek-Arabic and Greek-Latin equivalents are added in brackets):

> *wujūd* 'existence' (*einai*)... *esse* (*einai*), occasionally *existere* (*einai*)
> *mawjūd* 'existent' (*to on*)　　*ens* (*to on*)
> *dhāt* 'possessor' (—)　　　　　*essentia* (*ousia*)
> *māhiyyah* 'quiddity' (—)　　　*quidditas* (—), *essentia* (*ousia*)
> *jawhar* 'substance' (*ousia*)　*substantia* (*ousia*).

This word-list invites two comments. In the first place it contains the new word *quidditas* apparently directly modelled on *māhiyyah* (this suggestion is of course vulnerable to a single example of *quidditas* earlier than the 12th century) and the old word *essentia* finally detached from its historical connexion with *ousia* and sharply separated from *substantia*. Mediaeval philosophers, for better or for worse, are now like the Arabs equipped to speak of the essence or quiddity of a thing, not merely of what it is (*ti esti*) and what it is to be it (*to ti ēn einai*). In the second place the sharp Arabic distinction between existence and quiddity is partially obscured; *wujūd* 'existence' is replaced by the more general *esse*, and *dhāt* 'possessor' (etymologically independent of *wujūd*) by *essentia* (etymologically derived from *esse*). We can see the effect of this in the *De ente et essentia* of Aquinas, who follows Avicenna closely yet is radically unlike him in the very starting-point of the inquiry ("Ex significatione entis ad significationem essentie procedendum est"[18], "One should proceed from the meaning of 'being' to the meaning of 'essence'". Cf. the later "Essentia autem est secundum quam res esse dicitur"[19], "But essence is that according to which a thing is said to be"). The Arabic and Greco-Latin ontologies have in fact already been spliced in the process of translation; the Mediaeval absorption of essence within the concept of Being is already implicit in the Latin Avicenna and Averroes, just as the Arabic refusal to embrace existence on the one hand and quiddity on the other within any common concept is already implicit in the Arabic Aristotle. We may illustrate this by comparing a passage of Averroes with its 13th century Latin version and with a passage of Aquinas which refers to it:

---

[18] Roland-Gosselin, *loc. cit.*, p. 2, ll. 6–7.
[19] *Ibidem,* p. 10, ll 4–5.

Averroes, *Tafsīr mā ba'd aṭ-ṭabī'at* (edited by Maurice Bouyges, Beyrouth vol. 2 (1942) 561): "But you should know in short that the name *huwiyyah* (abstract noun formed from the copula) which indicates the *dhāt* of the thing is other than the name *huwiyyah* which indicates the true, and likewise the name *mawjūd* ('existent') which indicates the *dhāt* of the thing is other than the *mawjūd* which indicates the true".

Aristotelis stagiritae Metaphysicorum libri XIV cum Averrois Cordubensis in eosdem commentariis (Venice 1552), Book 5, f 55v, left column, ll. 56–58: Sed debes scire universaliter quod hoc nomen ens, quod significat essentiam rei, est aliud ab ente, quod significat verum. (The copulative and existential words are both replaced by *ens*, and the two sentences reduced to one; *dhāt* is replaced by *essentia*).

Aquinas, *De ente et essentia* (edited by M.-D. Roland-Gosselin, Paris 1948) 3, ll. 7–12: Nomen igitur essentie non sumitur ab ente secundo modo dicto... sed sumitur essentia ab ente primo modo dicto; unde Commentator in eodem loco dicit quod ens primo modo dictum est quod significat essentiam rei.

"Therefore the name 'essence' is not taken from 'being' (*ens*) used in the second sense... but 'essence' is taken from 'being' used in the first sense; whence the Commentator (Averroes) says in the same place that 'being' used in the first sense is what signifies the essence of a thing." (The novelty here is that essence is assumed to *take its name* from the etymologically cognate *ens*).

When philosophers began to write in French and English they treated *être* and 'to be' as synonymous with *einai* and *esse*. But this verb, which is characteristic of the Indo-European family, is unstable even within the Indo-European family. In Sanskrit and in Russian it is nearly as definitely existential as the Arabic *kāna*; in Greek it is primarily existential and not obligatory as copula; in English and French on the other hand it is almost exclusively the copula, existence being indicated by the formulae 'there is' and *il y a* and by the verbs 'to exist', *exister*, which have entered ordinary language from scholastic Latin. The Latin *exsistere*, *existere*, ('step out from') settled into its present meaning very gradually. For Alexander of Hales (c. 1175–1245) it was still *ex alio sistere* 'to stand out from the other'[20]; Aquinas (c. 1225–1274) still discusses existence and essence in the terminology of the title of his work. *De ente et essentia*; but by the next century Ockham (c. 1280–c. 1349), for example, is discussing the distinction as between *esse existere* or *existere* and *essentia* or *entitas*.[21] The word 'exist' is perhaps the most valuable legacy of the ontological vocabulary of scho-

[20] Gilson, *loc. cit.*, p. 73.
[21] Ockham, *Philosophical Writings*, a selection edited and translated by Philotheus Boehner, London 1957, 92–5.

lasticism, since it illuminates the distinction at the level of the verb, while *essentia* and *quidditas* are nouns which illuminate it only as a metaphysical distinction between concepts.

The extent of the change is very visible in modern translations from Greek. Although '*X* is' is still intelligible as an archaism, however willing the translator may be to archaise he finds the verb 'to be' grammatically much less flexible than *einai*. We cannot replace "Is there *X*?" and "Does *X* exist?" by "Is *X*?", nor "There is life on Mars" and "Life exists on Mars" by "Life is on Mars" (in which 'is' would be understood as copula). It is therefore not only inconvenient but grammatically impossible to translate *einai* consistently by 'to be', as can be seen in the examples quoted earlier in this article from the *Posterior Analytics*. Forced to substitute 'exist' for *einai*, and for other reasons 'essence' for *to ti ēn einai*, we re-interpret Aristotle in a terminology with fifteen hundred years of further development behind it.

Such formulae as 'There is', *il y a*, *es gibt*, did not really attract the attention of philosophers until recently, because these formulae cannot be turned into abstract nouns. But philosophers use them and are influenced by them whether they notice them or not; and these formulae, since they cannot without artificiality be grammatically analysed into subject and predicate, undermine the assumption that existence is a logical predicate. (Attacking this assumption, Kant took the example *Gott ist allmächtig* 'God is almighty', cut it down to *Gott ist* 'God is', and immediately added *oder es ist ein Gott* 'or "There is a God"'. [22]) Similarly the contraction of the scope of 'to be' to its copulative function has shifted emphasis away from the existential function; Kant, as we have just noticed, starts his discussion of existence from 'God is almighty'; Hegel actually defines 'Being' in copulative terms, "'Being' may be defined as '*I* = *I*, as absolute indifference, or identity, and so on" ("Sein kann bestimmt werden, als Ich = Ich, als die absolute Indifferenz oder Identität u.s.f.". [23]) If we could wipe out the memory of all past philosophy from a man's mind, and start him thinking afresh in contemporary English, would it not be natural for him to conceive 'Being' as purely copulative, as clearly detached from existence as Arabic *dhāt* and *māhiyyah* from *wujūd*? But in practice of course the continuity of the philosophical tradition makes a final divorce of the two concepts impossible. Kant still supposes that when he replaces "God is almighty" by "God is" he is using 'is' in the same sense as before, philosophers still discuss "I think, therefore I am" without rephrasing it in contemporary English, and the abstract noun 'being' with its plural 'beings' remains primarily existential even in common speech.

[22] *Kritik der reinen Vernunft*, Elementarlehre, Part 2, Division 2, Book 2, Chapter 3, Section 4.
[23] *Logik*, 96.

A philosopher therefore cannot adapt his use of 'Being' to the functions of 'to be' in English grammar; he must either stick bravely to the conviction that there is a single concept of Being behind the different functions of *einai*, which is hidden by the grammars of non-Indo-European languages, and which even among the languages of Western philosophy is perfectly displayed only in Greek and Latin, or he must discard the verbal noun 'being' as incurably ambiguous. However difficult he may find it to choose the second alternative while he is thinking in the living language with its deep roots in the past, the artificial language of symbolic logic enables him to make the choice without even noticing what he is doing. In symbolic logic the verb 'to be' dissolves into the sign of existence ($\exists$), which is not a predicate but a quantifier, and three separate copulae, the signs of identity ($=$), class membership ($\in$) and class inclusion ($\subset$).

School of Oriental and African Studies, University of London

FOUNDATIONS OF LANGUAGE

SUPPLEMENTARY SERIES

Edited by Morris Halle, Peter Hartmann,
K. Kunjunni Raja, Benson Mates, J. F. Staal,
Pieter A. Verburg, and John W. M. Verhaar

1. John W. M. Verhaar (ed.), *The Verb 'Be' and its Synonyms. Philosophical and Grammatical Studies*. Part I: *Classical Chinese. Athapaskan. Mundari*. 1967, VIII +100 pp.
Dfl. 23,—

2. Nicholas Rescher, *Temporal Modalities in Arabic Logic*. 1967, IX +50 pp. Dfl. 16,—

3. Tullio de Mauro, *Ludwig Wittgenstein. His Place in the Development of Semantics*. 1967, VIII +62 pp. Dfl. 19,—

4. Karl-Otto Apel, *Analytic Philosophy of Language and the Geisteswissenschaften*. 1967, X +63 pp. Dfl. 16,—

5. J. F. Staal, *Word Order in Sanskrit and Universal Grammar*. 1967, XI +98 pp.
Paper Dfl. 32,—

6. John W. M. Verhaar (ed.), *The Verb 'Be' and its Synonyms. Philosophical and Grammatical Studies*. Part II: *Eskimo Hindi. Zuni. Modern Greek. Malayalam. Kurukh*. 1968, IX +148 pp. Dfl. 30,—

7. Hugo Brandt Corstius (ed.), *Grammars for Number Names*. 1968, VII +123 pp.
Dfl. 32,—

8. John W. M. Verhaar (ed.), *The Verb 'Be' and its Synonyms. Philosophical and Grammatical Studies*. Part III: *Japanese. Kashmiri. Armenian. Hungarian. Sumerian. Shona*. 1968, VIII +125 pp. Dfl. 28,—

9. John W. M. Verhaar (ed.), *The Verb 'Be' and its Synonyms. Philosophical and Grammatical Studies*. Part IV: *Twi. Modern Chinese. Arabic*. 1969, VIII +125 pp. Dfl. 28,—

10. F. Kiefer (ed.), *Studies in Syntax and Semantics*, 1969, IX +242 pp. Dfl. 50,—

11. A. C. Senape McDermott, *An Eleventh-Century Buddhist Logic of 'Exists'*. 1969, X +88 pp. Dfl. 25,—

12. Karl Aschenbrenner, *The Concepts of Value. Foundations of Value Theory* 1971, XVII +462 pp. Dfl. 100,—

In Preparation:

13. F. Kiefer and N. Ruwet (eds.), *Generative Grammar in Europe*.

15. H. J. Verkuyl, *On the Compositional Nature of the Aspects*.

16. Charles H. Kahn, *The Verb 'Be' in Ancient Greek*.

17. W. G. Klooster, *The Structure Underlying Measure Phrase Sentences*.